Issa and the Meaning of Animals:
A Buddhist Poet's Perspective

for Adam,

David G. Lanoue

David G. Lanoue

ISBN-10: 0991284038
ISBN-13: 978-0-99-12840-3-0

The cover art shows two original sketches by Issa.

Issa and the Meaning of Animals:
A Buddhist Poet's Perspective

FOR OSCAR (1993-1995)

TABLE OF CONTENTS

ACKNOWLEDGEMENTS

I would like to thank Shinji Ogawa, Sakuo Nakamura, Keizo Kuramoto, Hiroshi Kobori, Toru Kiuchi, and Shokan Tadashi Kondo—as well as the many visitors to my *Haiku of Kobayashi Issa* website who, over the years, have shared their insights on various haiku. In addition, I am grateful to my writing group at Xavier University of Louisiana for feedback as this book slowly grew to become what it is: Violet Harrington Bryan, Kathleen E. Davis, Liz Edgecomb, Bart Everson, Nicole Pepinster Greene, Oliver Hennessey, Lourdes Rincon, Robin Runia, Jay Todd, Jeremy Tuman, and Cocoa Williams. I also thank my mentor, Paul A. Olson, for invaluable editorial advice, and Jason Berntsen, who reviewed the manuscript with a philosopher's eye. Finally, I make a deep bow (Japanese-style) to my students in World Literature and Global Haiku Seminar at Xavier University; their interpretations of Issa are always fresh and, often, amazing.

INTRODUCTION: What Issa Brings to the Table

In *Animals and Ethics* (2009), Angus Taylor notes that "philosophers sympathetic to the project of fundamentally rethinking our traditional view of animals were concerned in the beginning to show that the case for animal liberation could be made on strictly rational grounds, untainted by appeals to sentiment" (176). The notion that sentiment "taints" this debate—that only a purely rational approach to the question of animal rights deserves serious attention—has been a guiding principle in the West, though challenged in recent years by feminist ethicists who have insisted that "feminine" values such as compassion, empathy, and sympathy must also play a role in how we understand and interact with members of other species (Garner 39). In their landmark study, *Animal Rights and Human Obligations* (1976), Tom Regan and Peter Singer sought to answer, by strictly rational means without any "tainting" appeals to emotion, the two questions implicit in the volume's title: Do animals have rights? And, do human beings have obligations to nonhuman (so-called "lower") animals? Early in their book Regan and Singer cite three giants of Western philosophical tradition—Aristotle, René Descartes, and Immanuel Kant—all of whom answer both questions emphatically in the negative. In Aristotle's view, we can have no duties toward animals, since we can have duties only to fellow beings capable of reason, in other words, to *human* beings. Descartes saw animals as automata lacking consciousness, the power of thought, and (according to many of his interpreters[1]) the feeling of pain, making animal rights ludicrous and animal cruelty an impossibility. And Kant claimed that only human beings have intrinsically worthwhile existences because, in his words, only "man is an end in himself."[2] Regan and Singer go on to offer essays and excerpts from more animal-friendly scholars, such as Charles Darwin, in whose evolutionary perspective "the difference in mind between man and the higher animals, great as it is, certainly is one of degree and not of kind" (80); Arthur Schopenhauer, who maintained that "the essential or principal thing in the animal and man is the same," the distinguishing factor between them being simply "the degree of the cognitive faculty" (127); and Albert Schweitzer, for whom a reverence for life—for *all* life, including that of animals—formed the very basis of human ethics (133-38).

Japanese haiku poet Kobayashi Issa (1763-1828)[3] has much to contribute to the contemporary dialogue over the treatment of animals. Whereas scholarly books on the topic, such as that of Regan and Singer, focus exclusively on the rational arguments of Western thinkers, Issa in his poetry promotes a non-Western head-*and*-heart under-standing of human relations with animals. Born Kobayashi Yatarō, Issa (this being his penname) was a prolific writer who lived during Japan's early modern period in the years before that country's opening to the West. A farmer's son from a poor, mountainous province who migrated to Edo (today's Tokyo) at an early age, Issa was recognized in his own time as a master of the one-breath poetry of haiku, and regarded by posterity as one of the four greatest of the genre, joining the ranks of Matsuo Bashō, Yosa Buson, and Masaoka Shiki. Though he wrote as a poet, not a philosopher, Issa's journals and over twenty-thousand poems are filled with heartfelt insights that can be instructive for those who struggle today with the ethical, scientific, religious, economic, and political implications of how animals are treated, and mistreated, by human beings. Issa portrays his fellow creatures with compassion and warmth, describing them at times as his "cousins"—a moniker that in light of evolutionary theory is perhaps not merely metaphorical. Issa, of course, lived in a time before Darwin devised a theory of evolution that envisions all life forms as related descendants with common ancestors. Issa's sense of family connection with nonhuman creatures derived largely from a Buddhist understanding of all beings as fellow travelers on the karmic road toward enlightenment. This religious concept, supplemented by a lifetime of personal encounters and interactions with animals that he faithfully recorded and thoughtfully reflected on in haiku, accounts for Issa's poetic vision of living beings, plants and animals alike, as family.

A haiku is not a philosophical argument. It is an elliptical, succinct, imagistic poem that invites readers to complete with their imaginations what is only suggested or hinted at on the page. For this reason, a haiku can be a powerful inducement to personal discovery and, accordingly, make a deep impression on one's thinking and life. In the hands of a master poet such as Issa, a haiku engages the reader's brain and heart simultaneously, pointing toward revelations that depend upon one's creative participation. This verse by Issa illustrates how this works.

山鳩が泣事をいふしぐれ哉[4]
yama-bato ga nakigoto wo iu shigure kana

the mountain pigeon
grumbles . . .
winter rain

Issa is popular with Japanese children but often dismissed by his adult readers for being childishly anthropomorphic in the attribution of human moods and emotions to animals—a practice that one mid-twentieth-century Japanese critic labeled, *gijinhō* 擬人法: "personification" (Fujimoto 415). Indeed, one might infer that Issa is merely projecting in this haiku his own displeasure at the winter rain onto the pigeon. Even so, his comic poem leaves space for readers to question whether or not the bird may in fact have its own consciousness, feelings, and point of view. Perhaps humans are not the only creatures who can feel annoyed under a cold winter downpour.

Issa's method is not to make overt claims regarding animals and how they should be treated. Instead, his haiku poetry, as in the above example, nudges readers toward a rethinking of their relationship with their fellow creatures. Issa leads them to wonder if a pigeon might have feelings, and, if so, to try to imagine what those feelings might be on a day of winter rain. A scientist might gather empirical evidence that animals feel, remember, and think; but Issa plays a different role: not to prove but to provoke. And yet, even though he was no scientist, he was a keen, patient observer, basing most of his haiku portraits on personal experience. For this reason, it might not be surprising that scientific research has confirmed many of his insights about animals, as will be shown in this book. His core insight, in fact, radically extends to all animals Darwin's idea that "higher animals" like chimpanzees and gorillas are different from people only by degree. Although Issa never denies that human beings have some abilities that set them apart from other animals (indeed, as we shall see, he reflects on what it means to be human in many passages); he chooses to emphasize the often overlooked or unnoticed similarities that make human life and, for example, the life of a pigeon, qualitatively the same thing. Life, for Issa, is life.

A darker example of how the unspoken in a haiku can invite deep introspection into the question of how to relate to and treat animals is the following.

花さくや目を縫れたる鳥の鳴 (1808; *IZ* 1.210)
hanasaku ya me wo nuwaretaru tori no naku

cherry blossoms –
birds with eyes stitched shut
singing

Although Jean Cholley believes that the haiku depicts a poultry market in the Muromachi district of Edo, where birds' eyes have been sewn shut to keep them immobile while being fattened in their cages (237), Tamaki Tsukasa envisions hunters stitching shut the eyes of decoy birds, thereby causing them to cry out more, luring other birds (254). Either way, the image is stark. Composed over 160 years before Singer and Mason published *Animal Factories*—a hard-to-read exposé of mass-produced animals and the large-scale barbarism of the food industry—Issa's haiku is just as effective in provoking sympathy as are that book's disturbing depictions of confused, harried, "de-beaked" hens imprisoned in factory cages. In fact, Issa's poem, because it is a haiku that requires reader participation to complete it, does more than simply arouse sympathy for the mutilated creatures. Readers may discover in the juxtaposition of blooming cherry blossoms and sightless birds powerfully evocative symbolism. The blinded birds cannot, and will never again, see the cherry blossoms, which might be understood to stand for the fragile, ephemeral beauty of this world. Ironically, the people who have done this to the birds—and others in Japanese society who aid and abet the cruelty by their silent acquiescence—might be perceived by readers as the ones who are truly blind, for they have closed their eyes to the connectedness of living things. Failing to recognize the birds as fellow travelers on the road to Amida Buddha's Pure Land (as Issa, a Pure Land Buddhist, believed that they were), these people have lost sight of the meaning and value of their fellow creatures, and in the process, in a sense, have lost themselves. The poem strives (ironically) to open the eyes of such individuals among Issa's readership, nudging them to reconsider how they think of, and treat, nonhuman beings. This skillfully crafted haiku is not a philosophical argument, yet it can motivate readers profoundly to re-imagine their relationship with animals.

Issa's Buddhism raises two important questions. One is the question of relevance to readers of different (or without) religious backgrounds: How pertinent are Issa's thoughts about animals and their treatment to non-Buddhist readers? I would answer: *very* pertinent. One need not literally believe that one can be reborn into a Western Paradise to appreciate the underlying wisdom of Buddhist metaphors such as the image of all creatures as travelers on the same road. A Buddhist might sincerely believe, or at least hope, that the road of existence leads to a Pure Land and ultimate enlightenment; a non-Buddhist might have no such notion and yet still come to accept the idea that, wherever the path of life leads, all creatures walk it together, and this idea of sameness and connection has ethical implications.

A second question concerning Buddhism is this: Didn't Issa, as a Buddhist, have an uncomplicated idea of animals and how humans should relate to them, given that he was only following Gautama Buddha's first precept to refrain from taking life? As such, the value of a book that investigates his poetry in relation to the treatment of animals might have questionable value. Other scholars have already explored the life-respecting ethics of Eastern religious traditions in relation to animal rights. Mary Evelyn Tucker and Duncan Ryuken Williams have published a splendid collection of essays, *Buddhism and Ecology: The Interconnection of Dharma and Deeds*; David Landis Barnhill employs, in a brilliant essay, Chinese Huayan Buddhist thought to argue for the need to transform our stance toward nature from one of exploitation to one that recognizes the relational connections in the web of life. And Angus Taylor, in the book cited at the beginning of this Introduction, invokes *ahimsa*—the doctrine of non-injury to living beings espoused by Hinduism, Jainism, and Buddhism—to answer the question of how people should treat animals (35). These writers and editors have sought to correct the omission of non-Western sources in early animal advocacy arguments, and so if Issa is doing nothing more than echoing a simple Buddhist rule against killing, the present book can add little to the debate.

Issa is not a poet who merely repeats the "do no harm" edict of Buddhism. In the first place, the faith that he practiced throughout his life proposes a rather complicated position vis-à-vis animals. Issa belonged to the Jōdoshinshū ("True Teaching Pure Land") sect founded by Shinran, the most widely popular of Buddhist sects in Japan in Issa's time and still today. Shinran's followers believe that not only animals but, in Issa's words, "even trees and plants . . . will acquire Buddha-nature" (*IZ* 6.137). While this belief might instill in the faithful a deep respect for animals and plants, since all living beings find themselves on the same path to enlightenment, Shinran also taught that rebirth in Amida's Pure Land, the only possible means to enlightenment in our depraved age of *mappō* 末法, cannot be earned by the Self Power (*jiriki* 自力) of following Buddha's five precepts. Even hunters and butchers, he insisted, can be reborn in the Pure Land if they rely on Amida's Other Power (*tariki* 他力). This surprising tenet of

Shinran's Pure Land sect vastly complicates the stance of his followers in relation to animals and animal killing. On one hand, they know that taking the life of a fellow traveler to nirvana is forbidden. On the other hand, they realize that whether or not they kill, in the final analysis, is irrelevant to their personal karmic future. All that truly matters is the depth and sincerity of their reliance on Amida's Other Power. This is why, when Issa describes himself in one of his journals as a sinner "sowing the seeds of a future life in hell, catching the flies that swarm on my lap and condemning, one by one, the mosquitoes that rove over my table," his tone is playfully self-ironic (*IZ* 6.148). Deeply devout Pure Land Buddhists (as Issa certainly was) know that fly- and mosquito-killing does not assure one's condemnation to a next life in hell. Issa regrets, possibly sincerely, that he isn't a good enough Buddhist to spare the lives of the pesky insects, yet he knows—and articulates this knowledge elsewhere in the same journal, *Oraga haru* おらが春 ("My Spring")—that although he is "covered with the dust of worldliness," he will ultimately trust in the saving power of Amida Buddha (*IZ* 6.135-36). Issa's Buddhism does not lead him to simple answers regarding animals and the question of human obligations to them, and this makes his poetry especially useful for readers who have not yet solidified their opinions on the question of how animal deserve to be treated: readers who are willing to open their minds and, just as importantly, their hearts in the search for answers. Issa's own struggle to find meaning in his relationship with animals through a lifetime of haiku proves to be complex, nuanced, personal, and, for all these reasons, of enormous value to readers today.

In my online archive that features ten thousand of Issa's haiku in Japanese with English translations, a number approaching half his total work, animals appear in thousands of verses, his top ten favorites being cuckoos

(251), butterflies (250), cats and kittens (225), nightingales (207), geese (202), frogs (200), dogs and puppies (191), sparrows (178), fireflies (157) and mosquitoes (146). The pages of his journals are populated by these and many other creatures, including, but not limited to, ants, bats, bees, boars, caterpillars, chickens, cormorants, cows, crabs, cranes, crickets, crows, deer, dragonflies, ducks, fish, fleas, flies, foxes, hawks, herons, hornets, horses, horseflies, larks, leeches, lice, katydids, mice, monkeys, moths, pigeons, pigs, plovers, snakes, snails, spiders, swallows, thrushes, toads, turtles, wolves, worms, and wrens.

Issa's habit of treating animals in human terms—"Sir Horse," "Mr. Toad," "Lord Monkey," and "Mr. and Mrs. Goose"—is, as any child knows, fun and humorous, but there is a deeper level to these poems. Describing animals as persons, he acknowledges and draws our attention to a thing that many humans overlook: animals also have souls, or to state the case another way, they, like people, *are* souls. Issa de-emphasizes the differences between human and nonhuman animals, because, as we have seen, he believed that all living beings might one day find themselves sitting together in the Pure Land of the West, becoming Buddhas.

Many readers and critics in Japan and elsewhere fail to perceive the serious, underlying messages encoded in Issa's child-friendly verses. Some regard the poet's haiku—especially his haiku in which he addresses or interacts with animals—as primarily children's literature, while others, fixating on his many personal tragedies, view his work as subjective and merely biographical. The Japanese critic Ōshiki Zuike, adopting the latter approach, titled his study of Issa, *Jinsei no hiai* 人生の悲哀: "The Sorrow of Life." Still others, like the writers of *The Princeton Companion to Classical Japanese Literature*, have dismissed Issa as a poet of "sentimentality" (Miner 94).

15

While it is true that children can delight in many of Issa's poems and that these poems often do include biographical references and deep, personal feeling; it is wrong to think of his work in exclusively these terms. Issa was a serious artist of words who set for himself a serious creative agenda, and one of his most emphasized projects in that agenda was to seek to mend the rift between the human and animal worlds: to depict people and animals sharing common space and a common destiny. Animals play many supposed "human" roles in his haiku: as poets, lovers, guides, roommates, town criers, dancers, singers, family members, blossom-viewers, moon-gazers, workers, bosses, holy men, and even Buddhists. While there is often humor on the surface of these seemingly anthropomorphic portraits, if we examine them closely we find the poet challenging his readers' assumption that animals and people differ in their essence. While he occasionally uses animals to make a satirical point about human behavior (a "boss" frog croaking self-importantly on the "seat of honor" by a pond) or to hint at a better way for people to live (when lightning flashes, "only the puppy's face is innocent"), Issa more often approaches birds, reptiles, amphibians, insects, arachnids, mollusks, crustaceans, invertebrates, fish, and his fellow mammals as peers and fellow travelers. His haiku about animals can motivate readers to change their thinking so that they might connect or, in some cases, reconnect with fellow members of the extended family of earthly existence. Long before the ecological movement, Issa was a green poet. This is not to say that he didn't swat at flies and mosquitoes, drown his lice, or cook and eat fish and snails. But even when the pond snails were simmering in his kettle, he remained cognizant of their little cries of pain, and made readers aware of this, too, in his poetry. He may have eaten the snails, but he never denied their intrinsic value—or their suffering.[5] Issa understood from his Buddhism that to live is to sin, one particularly onerous sin being that of arrogantly denying that the life of an animal that one kills, even for a good reason, has no worth.

Issa's nature poetry is perhaps even more pertinent today than it was two centuries ago when he first wrote it, in that it calls for a realignment with nature and nature's creatures at a critical moment in human history. Richard Louv, in *Last Child in the Woods*, warns that young people in today's wired society suffer from "Nature-Deficit Disorder" caused by the growing divide between them and the natural world. "For a new generation," he warns, "nature is more abstraction than reality" (2). A direct experience of nature, in Louv's opinion, is both necessary and psychologically healing. Issa's poetry offers a timely prescription for contemporary readers who find themselves alienated from the natural world; in thousands of poems he chronicles personal encounters with plants and animals, subliminally inviting his readers to adopt a posture of accepting openness toward nature's inter-related and interdependent citizens. Issa's haiku underscore relationships and connections; a frog, for example, is never an objectified "it" for Issa but rather a comrade and a peer, a he or a she. In this respect his poetry prefigured the contemporary "dark green religion" movement which, according to Bron Taylor, constitutes a spirituality that flows "from a deep sense of belonging to and connectedness in nature, while perceiving the earth and its living systems to be sacred and interconnected" (13). Issa, to use Taylor's term, is consistently biocentric, relating to the world's nonhuman life forms in a way that calls to mind primatologist Jane Goodall's intimate eye-to-eye communications with the chimpanzee David Graybeard, using "a language far more ancient than words" (qtd. in Taylor 25). As a poet, he employs words as his medium of expression, and yet as a poet of a genre that purposefully leaves much unsaid, he creates in his animal verses deep, nonverbal resonance; they speak in the language of the heart to evoke perspective-changing insights on the urgent topic of animal treatment.

Arne Næss coined the term "deep ecology" in an article published in 1973, defining it as a "rejection of the man-in-environment image in favour of *the relational, total-field image*" (Naess and Rothenberg 28). As if anticipating the deep ecology movement, Issa's depictions of myriad "conversations" and encounters with nonhuman animals highlight mutual relationship and connection. Næss once noted, astutely, that "without the relation, A and B are no longer the same thing" (28). In this book I hope to show that Issa conveys the same point through his poetry. When he stares at a frog, for example, he recognizes and celebrates the fact that the frog, unintimidated, is staring back at him.

おれとして白眼くらする蛙かな (1819; *IZ* 1.162)
ore to shite niramikura suru kawazu kana

locked in a staring contest
me . . .
and a frog

In his journal, *Hachiban nikki* 八番日記 ("Eighth Diary"), Issa prefaces this well-known haiku with the phrase, "Sitting alone" (*hitori za* 独座). The astonishing discovery in the moment, however, is that he is *not* alone; a frog stares at him while he stares at the frog. To use Næss's terms, A and B not only perceive but require one another. Issa recognizes that the frog has autonomy and consciousness, and he hints that, without the frog in the scene looking back at him, he would be truly, sadly, "Sitting alone"; in fact, he would no longer be Issa, because he crafted for himself in his writing the persona of gentle companion to the world's frogs, sparrows, birds, fleas, and flies. And the world's frogs, sparrows, birds, fleas, and flies—one might conclude from a haiku such as this one—need Issa to be what *they* are. His is a poetic art of dynamic, interconnected relationship. Without knowing or needing to know the term, Issa is the consummate poet of deep ecology, as Laurence Stacey has so perceptively suggested.[6]

A traditional haiku in Japanese, called *haikai* 俳諧 in Issa's time, consists of seventeen sound units arranged in a five-seven-five pattern. Though written in three phrases, it normally exhibits a two-part structure divided by a "cutting word" or *kireji* 切れ字, a sort of verbal punctuation mark that splits the verse into two sections, creating a juxtaposition of images. Another usual requirement is the inclusion of a seasonal reference. As mentioned earlier, a haiku poet purposefully leaves much to the reader's imagination. In fact, one of the earliest Western commentators on the genre, Lafcadio Hearn, noted in 1899,

> The term *ittakkiri*—meaning 'all gone,' or 'entirely vanished,' in the sense of 'all told,'—is contemptuously applied to verses in which the verse-maker has uttered his whole thought;—praise being reserved for compositions that leave in the mind the thrilling of a something unsaid (155).

A haiku, to repeat, requires readers to fill in its unspoken gaps with their own images, feelings, and ideas. Each little poem, according to Bulgarian critic and poet Ludmila Balabanova, isn't entirely the record of the author's perception but rather "an invitation to the reader to achieve his own enlightenment."[7] A haiku is a prompt for private meditation and therefore allows for enormous freedom of interpretation, as every reader's vision is, in theory, as legitimate as anyone else's. However, all interpretations are not equally useful, especially when they address the work of a poet such as Issa, who left behind him not only many thousands of haiku but also *haibun* 俳文 (prose works with haiku included), *renku* 連句 ("linked verses"), *haiga* 俳画 ("haiku paintings"), some *waka* 和歌 (the five-phrase poetry popularized in medieval Japan), and many instructive prose introductions to his verses. While it may be true that the reader of a haiku enjoys a nearly absolute freedom in filling in its undefined spaces—imagining what else might be in the scene, its tone and deeper possibilities of meaning—the interpretations of Issa's poetry in this book will be informed by (1) a study of Japanese language of the Edo period; (2) knowledge of Issa's biography and historical context; (3) a consideration of introductory notes and other prose comments in his travelogues and journals; (4) a study of literary, folkloric, and other cultural precedents in China and Japan; and (5) a contextual appreciation of the poems: a rigorous attempt to understand the feeling and sense of any particular haiku in light of the feeling and sense of others in the canon. If Issa had written only one haiku in his life, readers would be free to interpret that poem any way they saw fit. The fortunate reality is different. Because he wrote so prolifically, our understanding of individual haiku can and should be shaped by our perceptions of everything else that the poet wrote, all the stars in a poetic galaxy exerting gravitational pull on one another.

Following the above approach, we will learn that Issa's poetry can be read as impassioned advocacy for the humane, respectful, and appreciative treatment of nonhuman animals. This is not to say that Issa considered himself to be an advocate or that he set out consciously to champion the welfare of animals. His aim, as a poet, was strictly to respond with sensitivity to, and create art from, the universe that surrounded and included him. In fulfilling this artistic mission, animal-human sameness emerged as an important, richly explored theme from which readers today can distill valuable insights pertinent to the question of how to treat animals. Issa wrote poetry, not manifestos or arguments. At times his intent may seem plain as day; at other times his intent seems unfathomable, but the important thing to focus on (the focus of this book) is not authorial intent but rather the questions and implied answers that Issa's words on the page, two centuries later, can still provoke. Though Issa offered no cogent, overt argument about the ethical treatment of animals, I intend to piece together such an argument in the course of this book. Whether the feeling that he expresses toward animals in his poetry are genuine (as I choose to believe) or merely invented for literary effect has no bearing on the eloquent argument about the treatment of animals derivable from his words.

While I do not pretend to offer in this book a complete disclosure of all that Issa has to contribute to the debate over the treatment of animals, I do propose to provide some stepping stones toward further contemplation and investigation. Viewed as a whole, his haiku about animals invite readers to question what it means to be human and to re-think their relationship to other life on the planet—in the process confirming Arne Næss's dictum that humans are participants in the ecosystem, not the privileged rulers of it. This book will show that Issa (that is, Issa as he presents himself in his writing, not the unknowable, actual person) viewed animals not as vastly inferior creatures occupying a low position in a hierarchy of being. Animals in Issa's haiku portraits are more like peers who employ their own languages, express and appreciate beauty, raise families, work and play, cohabitate with people in shared spaces, benefit from the blessings of Shinto, participate in the rituals of Buddhism, reincarnate and follow the law of karma, and, in some cases, are shown to be possibly superior, in a spiritual sense, to human beings. Issa's poetry about animals, presented and pondered in this book, may ultimately contribute to their enlightened and ethical treatment.

Chapter 1. TALKING TO ANIMALS

I. Issa's masks

Although Kobayashi Issa's interactions with non-human creatures as dramatized in his haiku might be interpreted (I would argue, *mis*interpreted) as exercises in whimsy crafted with the primary intent of delighting children, beneath the gentle humor of his dealings with "boss frogs" and "lover cats" he skillfully plants seeds of a life-transforming change of perspective. To borrow the terminology of Israeli philosopher Martin Buber, many people—even nominally Buddhist Japanese—conceive of their dealings with animals as an "I – it" connection: animals are objects to be exploited (raised, hunted, killed, butchered) rather than fellow travelers with their own perspectives, desires, and needs. Issa's poetry redefines the meaning of animals, replacing objectivity with subjectivity. In this way, he establishes, or, in the long view of the history of *homo sapiens*, *reestablishes* with animals what Buber describes as an "I – Thou" relationship: a mutual subjectivity that promises important consequences for humans and animals alike. The insight that animals are the poet's peers and fellow travelers emerged early in his work.

In Third Month of 1791, the young poet left Edo (today's Tokyo) on his first haiku-writing journey recorded in his first travel journal, *Kansei san nen kikō* 寛政三年紀行 ("Third Year of Kansei Era Diary"). It contains this tender image.

青梅に手をかけて寝る蛙哉 (1791; *IZ* 1.157)
aoume ni te wo kakete neru kawazu kana

resting his hands
on the green plum, asleep. . .
a frog

The scene presages a haiku that he will write twenty-eight years later, in 1819.

初瓜を引とらまへて寝た子哉 (1819; *IZ* 1.414)
hatsu uri wo hittoramaete neta ko kana

first melon of the season
in her grasp . . .
sleeping child

This portrait of the poet's second child, his baby daughter, Sato, echoes the decades-earlier frog poem. In the later haiku a human child clutches summer's first ripe melon: a precious treasure that will not be surrendered even in sleep. In the earlier one, a frog clings to the prize of a green plum while dozing. In Issa's imagination and heart[8], there is no great gulf between human and frog. In both poems there is tenderness in his tone, suggesting in one the love of a father for his baby girl, and in the other a genuine affection for a very small, though not human, individual.

The image that Issa created for himself as a man whose tender heart opens as readily for a sleeping frog as for a sleeping child relates to three authorial masks that he invented and chose to wear throughout his long and productive literary career, all of which, we shall see, contributed to his relationship with animals. He put himself forth as "Shinano Province's Chief Beggar," as "Stepchild Issa," and as "Priest Issa of Haikai Temple."[9]

Donning the masks of beggar, step-child, and priest, he infused aspects of his own life into his poetry and, consequently, into our understanding of that poetry, more so than can be said of any other master of Japanese haiku tradition. It must be understood, however, that these masks, though grounded in the poet's real life, are literary constructs. It would be dangerous to attempt to draw equal signs between Issa's biography and the self-portraiture in his work. Almost everything that we know about his life comes to us through his journals and poems and, as such, has been shaped to serve various poetic and personal ends. On the other hand, Issa's invention of himself as a beggar, a stepchild, and a priest—along with all of the details of his real life that he chooses to weave into his writing—practically compels us to read and interpret his haiku in these contexts. Issa becomes part of his poetry, often explicitly announcing his presence in scenes with the pronouns "I" or "me," and other times implying an unspoken but understood consciousness that interacts with people, animals, and plants. In Chapter 4 we will consider how "priest" Issa's Buddhism influenced his understanding and treatment of animals. For now, let us examine how his masks of beggar and stepchild affected his relationship with animals in his poetry.

In his guise as a poor man—a hermit living in a "trashy hut" or *kuzu-ya* 屑屋, the son of a farmer who wanders the roads of Japan: Shinano Province's Chief Beggar—Issa felt particularly drawn to sparrows. If the nightingale (*uguisu* 鶯) is considered royalty among Japanese birds, sparrows are commoners. Issa the Beggar feels a natural kinship with plebeian sparrows.

鶯にだまつて居らぬ雀かな (1808; *IZ* 1.132)
uguisu ni damatte oranu suzume kana

not hushing up
for the nightingale . . .
sparrows

The common sparrows will not stifle their own songs so that those of the princely nightingale might be heard, making for a moment of humor as well as social commentary. The reader senses Issa's presence in the scene: noticing, approving, and identifying with the plucky sparrows.

鶯や雀は竹にまけぬ声 (1824; *IZ* 1.138)
uguisu ya suzume wa take ni makenu koe

nightingale –
in bamboo the sparrow sings
not conceding

In this example, once again the nightingale's song may be lovely, but the humble sparrow, not to be outdone, chirps on. By admiring the sparrow in this competition with a nightingale, Issa hints that his own poetry is like sparrow song: undaunted, non-aristocratic, and, to use Abraham Lincoln's phrase, "of the people."

Issa identifies with sparrows as fellow peasants, fellow beggars, and, often, fellow orphans, which brings us to the second of his literary masks. He sees his own childhood in the plight of abandoned baby sparrows, and so as a consequence such birds appear to him in his haiku as peers and playmates rather than as lesser beings.

雀子や人のこぶしに鳴初る (1809; *IZ* 1.127)
suzumego ya hito no kobushi ni naki someru

baby sparrow
inside a person's fist
its first cry

A human hand (Issa's hand?) provides a cradle for an orphan bird that has fallen from its nest. Inside this protective hand, the little bird utters its first cheep. In a later haiku, Issa suggests the emotion that an abandoned baby sparrow evokes.

慈悲すれば糞をする也雀の子 (1824; *IZ* 1.130)
jihi sureba hako wo suru nari suzume no ko

when you hold him kindly
he poops on you . . .
baby sparrow

The Japanese expression, *jihi suru* 慈悲する, signifies the act of showing mercy, benevolence, or compassion to another being, usually a person. We can imagine that the bird's gift has not at all lessened this feeling. *Jihi* does not describe a condescending attitude in this haiku moment: the magnanimity of a supposedly superior being for a smaller, weaker, and less intelligent creature. Instead, it describes the poet's heartfelt response to a sparrow that, like himself at a young age, has become motherless.

On the seventh day of Eighth Month in 1765, at the age of three, Issa (known then by his given name, Yatarō) lost his mother.[10] The memory of this trauma still stung at age fifty-two, when he wrote the following haiku.

我と来てあそぶや親のない雀 (1814; *IZ* 1.129)
ware to kite asobu ya oya no nai suzume

coming to play
with me . . .
orphan sparrow

In a later revision, he changes the verb to a command,
directly addressing the sparrow. This is the more popular
version of the poem in Japan today.

我と来て遊べや親のない雀 (1819; *IZ* 1.129)
ware to kite asobe ya oya no nai suzume

come and play
with me . . .
orphan sparrow

This revised version appears in the poetic diary of 1819,
Oraga haru. He prefaces it with a description of himself as
a lonely, sad child at age six, cruelly taunted by village
children for being motherless. He would spend long days
by himself, crouched in the shade of the piled-up wood
and reeds behind his home's garden. His life then, he
wrote, was all "grief and sorrow" (*IZ* 6.147). In a
different text, he supplies more details: "A parentless
sparrow made himself known by singing pitifully, alone.
In a little shack in the back yard, I cared for it all day" (*IZ*
1.129). This is one of Issa's most famous examples of a
haiku in which he addresses an animal as a friend and a
peer, memorized by generations of school children in
Japan. He feels not only sympathy for the motherless
bird; he sees the bird as himself.

After his father remarried when the future poet was
eight, his new stepmother, Satsu, was cruel and abusive,
according Issa. However, as Huey and Bolitho both point
out, we should take his damning depiction of Satsu with a
grain of salt; since, when he wrote about her in his
journals the two of them were embroiled in a bitter

inheritance dispute (Huey 29, Bolitho 63). Regardless of the exact biographical details of the case, Issa's childhood following the death of his mother was without doubt an unhappy one. "Stepchild Issa" saw himself in motherless sparrows, and so when he portrays them in haiku he is portraying, in the same breath, Yatarō: the little, wounded boy inside the man.

鳴よ鳴よ親なし雀おとなしき (1810; *IZ* 1.127)
nake yo nake yo oya nashi suzume otonashiki

sing, sing!
orphan sparrow . . .
so quiet

夕暮とや雀のまま子松に鳴 (1811; *IZ* 1.128)
yūgure to ya suzume no mamako matsu ni naku

evening falls –
a stepchild sparrow
cries in the pine

Issa talks to animals in his haiku not only in an effort to be comical—though readers, especially young readers, certainly appreciate this aspect. He speaks to them because he recognizes that they are like him. In the case of sparrows, as we have seen, this recognition of sameness becomes especially evident when he portrays these fellow creatures, Issa-like, as commoners or motherless children. At times the sparrows in Issa's haiku appear morally superior to human beings, as in the following poem in which he draws on Japanese folklore to emphasize their innocent decency.

梅守に舌切らるるなむら雀 (1803; *IZ* 1.192)
ume mori ni shita kiraruru na mura suzume

don't let the plum blossom guard
cut your tongues . . .
sparrows!

In the story of "The Tongue-Cut Sparrow,"[11] a kind old
man, whose wife has not borne children and has
refused to allow him to adopt one, keeps a sparrow as a
sort of surrogate child that he treats with paternal
kindness (Griffis 30). At one point his wife, a mean old
woman, cuts the sparrow's tongue with scissors just
because he has pecked at some of her starch (31). She
then tosses him into the air, and the poor, bleeding
sparrow flies away. Her husband later happens upon
the home of this same sparrow, where he is welcomed
and treated with politeness by the entire sparrow family
for several days, eating wonderful food and (in one
charming version of the story) playing games of *go*, a
strategy board game, with the sparrows' daughter (33).
The sparrows even offer him a going-away present,
allowing him to choose between two baskets: a light
one and a heavy one. He politely picks the light basket,
which turns out to be filled with money and gems
(Cavallaro 49). The old woman, greedy for her own
gift, goes to visit the sparrows' house and demands to
have one. Presented the same choice as her husband,
she picks the heavy basket, thinking that it surely
contains even more wealth than he received, but when
she opens it, "a horrible cuttlefish rushe[s] at her, a
skeleton poke[s] his bony fingers in her face, and finally
a long, hairy serpent, with a big head and lolling
tongue, [springs] out and coil[s] around her, cracking
her bones, and squeezing out her breath, till she die[s]"
(Griffis 36). According to Dani Cavallaro, the story
shows an "unbending devotion to dramatic justice"
while, at the same time, a Japanese "passion for the

sudden eruption of grotesque and monstrous forms" (49). In the story's happy ending the long-suffering husband, free at last, adopts a son.

In Issa's haiku the person guarding plum blossoms is cast in the role of the wicked old woman of the tale. The tone is comic, sure to raise smiles among his Japanese readers, but by referring to a story in which a family of sparrows live in a house and follow all the conventions of Japanese etiquette, he also hints at an essential sameness between human and bird. In fact, compared to the avaricious old woman, these polite and generous sparrows appear *better* than people, or at least better than this particular individual. When he humorously warns the sparrows to beware the tongue-cutting blossom guard, Issa hints that the guard is a mean old grouch more likely to harm than to feed them. The sparrows, by implication, are friends worthy of such a warning.

Issa's self-identification as a beggar led him to view small and downtrodden animals as his comrades. His self-identification as a stepchild led him to see motherless animals as mirror reflections of himself. Both of these literary masks contributed to his habit of perceiving and underscoring deep resemblances between himself and animals.

あのやうに我も老しか秋のてふ (1804; *IZ* 1.539)
ano yō ni ware mo oishi ka aki no chō

will I grow old
like you?
autumn butterfly

Issa, age forty-two at the time of the poem's composition, was growing older, but growing *old* was not guaranteed. Butterflies are associated with springtime in Japan, so the autumn butterfly is, in the poet's imagination, quite ancient. His question to the butterfly can be understood in at least two ways. Perhaps he is wondering if he, too, will live to a ripe old age. Or, perhaps, he wonders if one day he will be old like the autumn butterfly is old: frail, trembling, and helpless. The facts of aging and death make human and butterfly existence essentially the same. Of course, a butterfly is born, grows old, and dies within a year, making its life a sort of high-speed movie when compared to a human one. Issa's sympathy for the butterfly grows out of his recognition that he and it share the same existential situation. Its brief, flitting sojourn on planet Earth inspires the human poet to gain perspective on his own: autumn and winter will come for all; there is no escaping death.

Another point of similarity between people and animals noted by Issa is that both (though some readers, following Descartes, might vehemently object to this claim) have feelings.

籠の鳥蝶をうらやむ目つき哉 (1823; *IZ* 1.174)
kago no tori chō wo urayamu metsuki kana

caged bird –
watching the butterfly
with envy

The caged bird of the poem might be a nightingale (*uguisu* 鶯), in light of an earlier haiku:

鶯やあきらめのよい籠の声 (1821; *IZ* 1.137)
uguisu ya akirame no yoi kago no koe

the nightingale
resigned to his fate . . .
voice in a cage

Whatever the species, Issa perceives sadness in the bird's demeanor or song in the first example; he yearns to fly free, like the butterfly. In the second example, paying close attention to the tone of the caged bird's voice, the poet concludes that the cuckoo has resigned himself to his fate. Now, he sings (Issa imagines), accepting the fact that no female will respond to his call. Issa would have been baffled by the Cartesian argument that animals are soulless machines that lack consciousness and feeling. To his ears and mind, a nightingale can pour forth sorrow, joy, or melancholic resignation in his warbling, depending on the situation. Viewing the matter through a more scientific lens, one might ask: When a male bird confined to a cage sings for a mate that can never come, might it be possible that such a bird experiences, somewhere in his tiny brain, a feeling that humans would describe as disappointment or frustration? How can we, who are not birds, be certain that he doesn't? The question recalls a famous conversation (that Issa certainly knew) between the ancient Chinese Taoist sage Chuang-tzu and his companion, Hui. After making an offhand comment on the "joy of fishes," Chuang-tzu is instantly challenged by Hui: "Since you are not a fish, how do you know what makes fishes happy?"—to which Chuang-tzu replies, "Since you are not I, how can you possibly know that I do not know what makes fishes happy" (97)?

II. Animal interlocutors

Since animals resemble people in so many ways, Issa takes the next logical step in his poetic depictions: he speaks to them. In this next haiku, for example, he alerts a frog of a wonder to behold.

小便の滝を見せうぞ鳴蛙 (1812; *IZ* 1.159)
shōben no taki wo mishō zo naku kawazu

get ready to see
my piss waterfall!
croaking frog

This is a haiku of two perspectives: Issa's perspective, looking down at the frog as a sort of Gulliver among Lilliputians, and the frog's perspective, from which Issa appears as a giant and his bodily function a roaring cascade. Both points of view are legitimate. Through his playful imagination, Issa invites us to consider how the world looks through the eyes of another of the world's citizens, a frog.

He presents the same double perspective in a haiku addressed to sparrows.

雀来よ炬燵弁慶是に有 (1813; *IZ* 1.702)
suzume ko yo kotatsu-benkei kore ni ari

come, sparrows!
get warm at my brazier
I'm a great hero!

Here, he refers to himself Benkei: a gigantic twelfth-century warrior-monk who, according to Japanese folklore, possessed the strength of a Hercules. This self-portrait of Issa as a swaggering, muscled hero drips with irony. The Japanese expression, *kotatsu-Benkei* 炬燵弁慶 ("a Brazier Benkei"), refers to someone in a house who is putting on airs.[12] The poet obviously pokes fun at himself, on one level of interpretation, calling to the reader's attention how unalike he is to the legendary Benkei; he is, indeed, a blustering Benkei of the brazier, not the real item. Nevertheless, to sparrows on a cold winter's day, he might indeed appear a benevolent giant, offering them the warmth of his fire. Again, Issa invites readers to imagine and appreciate an animals' perspective.

The final phrase of the above haiku, *kore ni ari* 是に有, literally means, "Here I am." Three years later, in 1816, he uses the same phrase to cap another haiku in which he addresses an animal, a verse that has become one of his most famous, as widely memorized among Japanese children as his "Come and play with me . . . orphan sparrow."

痩蛙まけるな一茶是に有り (1816; *IZ* 1.161)
yasegaeru makeru na issa kore ni ari

scrawny frog, hang tough!
Issa
is here

In his journal Issa explains, "I stooped to watch a frog scuffle on the 20th day of Fourth Month" (*IZ* 3.81). The haiku originated in a real moment and should be understood, first and foremost, as a depiction of that real moment. Beyond that, it also can be read as a symbolic representation of the human social order, wherein the bigger, bully frog might stand for the well-fed warlords of Tokugawa Japan, his scrawny, hungry-looking opponent representing the downtrodden peasants. "Beggar" Issa, of course, feels special kinship with the latter and is eager to cheer him on. In my first translation of the haiku, I presented Issa as the skinny frog's would-be ally in the turf war: "scrawny frog, fight on!/ Issa/ to the rescue." A Japanese visitor to the website, Keizo Kuramoto, objected to this interpretation, arguing that we should not imagine Issa jumping into the pond to help the frog with which he plainly identified. The frog, Keizo wrote, must ultimately fight his own battles. The poem's conclusion,

"Issa is here," conveys the message, Keizo believes, that "Life is tough. Don't give up! I feel for you." Whether one chooses to imagine the poet physically intervening or merely encouraging the frog to be strong, at least this much is clear: he speaks to the frog as a conscious, feeling being with whom he compassionately identifies.

While he often talks to animals while attempting to imagine their perspective, at times Issa invites them to see what he sees and to feel what he feels. In one haiku of this type, he calls to sparrows, welcoming them to share a scene of melting snow and, he suggests, his joy of the season.

雀来よ四角にとけし門の雪 (1813; IZ 1.95)
suzume ko yo yosumi ni tokeshi kado no yuki

come, sparrows
in all four corners the gate's
snow is melting!

In another example, when he notices moss blooming, sparrows come to listen to the happy announcement.

苔咲くや自慢を聞に来る雀 (1814; IZ 1.409)
koke saku ya jiman wo kiki ni kuru suzume

moss is blooming!
sparrows come
to hear me brag

One Japanese reader of this poem, Shinji Ogawa[13], comments, "Issa's reasoning for the sparrows' visit is so egocentric, and that makes the haiku humorous." The haiku is indeed funny, but there is at least one serious thread of thought running through it and the previous example. Springtime belongs to and profoundly affects all creatures—people and sparrows alike. Issa's personal pride in the blooming of *his* moss seems merely silly only if we assume an absolute separation of him and the tiny plants. On the other hand, if we believe that nature joins all life forms in a unified web, then the moss and its blossoms are indeed part of Issa, as he is part of them. The springtime joy that he feels, inspired by the miniscule beauty of blossoming moss, might also be felt, on some level, by the sparrows too—or so the haiku implies.

Issa's agenda is slightly different in a poem addressed to a cat. In it, he playfully echoes the sound of a cat's meowing with the words, *mi yo mi yo*見よ見よ ("look! look!").

のら猫よ見よ見よ蝶のおとなしき (1813; *IZ* 1.169)
nora neko yo mi yo mi yo chō no otonashiki

stray cat
look! the butterfly's
well-behaved

On the surface Issa is attempting to exert peer pressure: "See how gently the butterfly behaves; why can't *you* be like that?" Deeper, he presents the well-behaved butterfly as a role model not only for the stray cat but also for himself and for readers of his poem. Very few people (or cats) ever achieve a butterfly-like state of quiet gentleness, but such a state *is* attainable, Issa suggests. He chides the cat and his readers in a single breath.

A bird singing in the darkness moves the poet to lodge a sly complaint in the form of two haiku.

この闇に鼻つままれなほととぎす (1820; *IZ* 1.344)
kono yami ni hana tsumamare na hototogisu

in this darkness
don't get your nose picked!
cuckoo

山人に鼻つままれなほととぎす (1821; *IZ* 1.345)
yamaudo ni hana tsumamarena hototogisu

don't get your nose picked
by the mountain hermit!
cuckoo

In these poems Issa plays with the humorous idiom, *hana tsumamare temo wakaranai hodo kurai* 鼻撮まれても解らないほど暗い: "It's so dark you can't tell who's picking your nose." In the first haiku he warns the cuckoo to be careful in the blackness of night. In the second one, he identifies a possible nose picker in the darkness: *yamaudo* 山人, literally, a "mountain person" but figuratively a hermit. Issa could possibly be speaking specifically about himself in the third person, or issuing a more generalized warning. Given the night's darkness, we can assume that he doesn't see the bird but is aware of its presence because of his singing. His advice to the cuckoo humorously implies that the bird has no business singing in the darkness, keeping hermits (like Issa) awake.

Issa offers other helpful suggestions to animals in his haiku. In the following two poems he solicitously provides advice about digestion.

来い来いと腹こなさする雀の子 (1814; *IZ* 1.128)
koi koi to hara konasasuru suzume no ko

come! come here!
digest your food
baby sparrow

うの花に食傷するな時鳥 (1816; *IZ* 1.342)
u no hana ni shokushō suru na hototogisu

> don't get indigestion
> from the tofu dregs!
> cuckoo

In the first haiku, he calls the baby sparrow over to him for an after-meal rest, as if speaking to a human child. One can picture Issa scattering seeds or crumbs that the young sparrow has been devouring, perhaps too quickly for intestinal health, in the poet's opinion. In the second haiku, a cuckoo has also been gorging himself, in this case with the lees by-product of tofu-making, called *u no hana* うの花, literally, "deutzia blossom"—so named because the whiteness of the tofu by-product is similar to that of the early summer deutzia flower. Issa warns the bird to not get sick by eating too much of the tofu dregs that he has scattered, an act of generosity that he describes further in a haiku composed earlier that same month and year (Fifth Month 1816).

うの花も馳走にちりぬほととぎす (1816; *IZ* 1.342)
u no hana mo chisō ni chirinu hototogisu

> I scatter tofu dregs too
> for his feast . . .
> cuckoo

These interactions are typical of Issa, his compassion for the hungry birds expressed in a parental tone suggesting sincere concern and deep connection.

Sometimes his spoken advice to animals sounds philosophical.

烏等も恋をせよとてやく野哉 (1814; *IZ* 1.115)
karasura mo koi wo seyo tote yaku no kana

make love, crows
while you can!
burning fields

Lewis Mackenzie points out that Issa wrote this haiku the month before he married his first wife, Kiku, in Third Month 1814, and so it might have biographical meaning. Issa was fifty-two when he married Kiku, who was then twenty-eight. He had finally settled the inheritance dispute with his stepmother and had returned to live in his side of the divided family home in Kashiwabara. Issa wanted to have children as quickly as possible, as if to make up for years of lost time, so his *carpe diem* advice to the crows can be read as self-advice. The burning fields present an eloquent image of time running out for lovers—crows and humans alike. Death is a fast-approaching, raging fire, but for now, in his advice to the crows Issa hints at his own resolution to seize the present moment and make love.

When he offers advice to animals, Issa indicates the great degree to which he sympathizes with their perspectives. He coaches a swallow from below in the following haiku.

蚊柱をよけよけ這入乙鳥哉 (1813; *IZ* 1.368)
ka-bashira wo yoke-yoke hairu tsubame kana

into the mosquito swarm
take care! take care!
swallow

The mosquitoes are swarming in a column (*ka-bashira* 蚊柱). Issa encourages the mosquito-eating bird to enter it skillfully, perhaps so that it might better feast, or perhaps (he implies with tongue in cheek) to avoid getting bitten. In a similar example of sympathetic expression, he cajoles a tardy bat.

かはほりよ行々京の飯時分 (1808; *IZ* 1.335)
kawahori yo yuke-yuke kyō no meshi jibun

get a move on, bat!
it's dinnertime
in Kyoto

It is dusk in the emperor's city, which means, from a bat's perspective, the air has become a living smorgasbord of flying insects. Issa encourages the bat to hurry up and claim his share. The phrase, "dinner time in Kyoto" (*kyō no meshi* 京の飯) suggests a communal vision in which bats and people dine in the same city at the same time, underscoring their essential sameness. It is worth noting that in both of the above poems he expresses no sympathy for the insects that will be eaten. While it is true that in other haiku Issa shows concern for the welfare for insects, spiders, and creeping, crawling creatures covered by the general Japanese term, *mushi* 虫, the fact that he cheers on the *mushi*-gobbling birds and bats in the present example indicates an acceptance of their natures. His respect for animals does not lead Issa to the radical position of a Jain sweeping the path before his feet for fear of stepping on an insect; he does not condemn the swallows and bats for being carnivores. An ecologist might describe their aerial predation as playing a necessary role in the checks and balances of the biome; the poet Issa insightfully depicts their feasting in the air as perfectly mirroring the actions of the humans who dine below.

In some cases, Issa's advice to animals in his poetry seems to cloak ironic commentary on the human world.

鶯や男法度の奥の院 (1819; *IZ* 1.136)
uguisu ya otoko hatto no oku no in

hey nightingale –
no men allowed
in the harem!

In Buddhist temples and Shinto shrines, the "inner sanctuary" (*oku no in* 奥の院) is a sacred place where the main image or divine spirit is enshrined. In this context, however, Issa is more likely referring to the women's quarters of the shogun's palace, where the supreme military commander's wife and concubines lived. No men, other than the shogun himself, were allowed inside. Beatrice M. Bodart-Baily notes that the women of the shogun's *oku* were, "in modern terms, the production team for an elaborate show that could be called upon to perform at any time" (26). Issa humorously warns the male songbird to avoid this forbidden, erotic holy of holies in which feminine beauty and talent were reserved for the gaze and the enjoyment of the shogun alone. Of course, the intrepid bird does not care about such a restriction, a life-or-death matter for human beings. Issa's warning to the nightingale, tinged with envy, suggests, on a deeper level, a complaint about social inequality. Birds are free to fly where they will; human beings, subject to the authority of their superiors, must read and obey signs that say, "Keep Out!"

Issa offers a bit of friendly advice to a cuckoo in this next poem.

そっと鳴け隣は武士ぞ時鳥 (undated; IZ 1.347)
sotto nake tonari wa bushi zo hototogisu

sing soft!
a samurai lives next door
cuckoo

In the military-controlled society in which Issa lived, samurai, bristling with weapons, enforced harsh laws imposed by the shogun in Edo or by local warlords, the daimyo. Since commoners were forbidden to bear arms— other than the short *wakizashi* sword when traveling— they found themselves powerless against the samurai's armory of long swords, truncheons, staffs, spears, and arresting ropes (Cunningham 22). Issa is joking about no joking matter. His warning to a loudly singing cuckoo reminds us of his admonition to the nightingale in the previous example. Both haiku express mock-concern for the birds while calling to mind real dangers for humans. Without saying anything directly critical of the military authority in Japan, from the shogun down to samurai, Issa hints of tyranny and mortal danger in these "innocent" verses addressed to birds. In both of these satirical haiku, human beings with their violent, possessive ways do not compare favorably with the nightingales and cuckoos.

The next example recalls the 1812 haiku in which Issa advised a frog to prepare to see his "piss waterfall." In this case, a katydid is the recipient of the poet's direct address. A katydid (*kirigirisu* きりぎりす) is a green or light brown insect, a cousin of crickets and grasshoppers. The males possess special organs on the wings with which they produce shrill calls. Although "katydid" is the closest English equivalent, many translators (such as R. H. Blyth) use the more familiar "grasshopper" and "cricket" when translating this word (*Haiku* 4.1068-69).

小便をするぞ退け退けきりぎりす (1821; *IZ* 1.550)
shōben wo suru zo noke noke kirigirisu

I'm taking a leak
look out! look out!
katydid

Issa, of course, is smiling as he writes this, and he invites his readers to smile too. At the same time, his warning to the katydid shows concern for the tiny creature and his perspective. As he does so often in his poetry, he folds into his humor a deeper message of understanding, sympathy, and sensitivity to an animal's point of view.

In another haiku that shows sympathy for an animal's situation, Issa alludes to a sparrow's need for clean air.

参詣のたばこにむせな雀の子 (1814; *IZ* 1.128)
sankei no tabako ni musena suzume no ko

temple visit –
don't choke on the pipe smoke
baby sparrow!

Issa enjoyed smoking tobacco, but he worries here that the baby bird might suffocate from the noxious clouds that he and his fellow pilgrims are spewing. His tone may seem flippant because, after all, what is a baby sparrow supposed to do with this information? How does telling it not to choke help it? The haiku is indeed an example of joking banter, yet Issa weaves into it more than situational humor. The setting, a Buddhist temple, is significant. As we will explore more deeply in Chapter 4, Issa believed that Pure Land Buddhism with its promise of rebirth in Amida's Western Paradise must apply equally to humans, animals, and even to plants. All are essentially the same: life manifesting in different bodies with different abilities (to fly, to breathe underwater, to write a haiku). A baby sparrow might be a future human being or, in time, a future Buddha. For this reason, we owe it respect and consideration. Once again, there is a serious subtext to Issa's levity. The sparrow in the smoky temple precincts, a fellow traveler toward enlightenment, deserves our compassion.

In the next poem, Issa admonishes a cat, and the cat, he asks us to believe, hears and understands.

浮かれ猫いけんを聞いて居たりけり (1815; *IZ* 1.121)
ukare neko iken wo kiite itari keri

the love-crazed cat
listens
to my scolding

Shinji Ogawa notes that *iken* いけん means, in this context, "remonstrance." Issa is telling the cat, "We've got to talk about your recent behavior," and, to his (and our) amusement, the cat appears to be listening. As in earlier examples, the joke once again has deeper implications. Of course, a tomcat carousing from partner to partner is only following his instinct and for this reason is exempt from human morality and the concomitant sense of shame that Issa is humorously attempting to trigger. His scolding of the cat reminds us, even as we smile, of the cat's sexual freedom and human beings' comparative lack thereof. Issa might even be suggesting that his readers have cause to envy the sexually uninhibited cat, just as they might envy the nightingale of the earlier-cited poem that can fly freely to and from the shogun's harem quarters.

Sometimes Issa depicts himself as the one being scolded by his animal peers.

時鳥のらくら者を叱るかや (1813; *IZ* 1.340)
hototogisu norakura mono wo shikaru ka ya

hey cuckoo –
are you scolding
the loafer?

The loafer in this haiku is almost definitely the poet—
who often appears in comic self-portraits as a "lazybones"
who lies around while others work. Here, Issa imagines
that the cuckoo, industriously going about the business of
trying to attract a mate to continue the species, is
critiquing his own sloth, perhaps his sloth in a general
sense or, more specifically, his sexual indolence. In 1813
he was fifty-one years old by Japanese reckoning and still
a bachelor. The cuckoo might be telling him to get a
move on. A year later, he seemingly followed the
cuckoo's advice when he married Kiku. During that year
of his first marriage, he wrote a haiku about a Himalayan
cuckoo (*kankodori* かんこ鳥) that possibly sheds light on
this earlier poem. He compares the bird's warbling to
haiku writing, suggesting an equivalence between a bird's
singing and a poet's art.

俳諧を囀るやうなかんこ鳥 (1814; *IZ* 1.349)
haikai wo saezuru yōna kankodori

like warbling pure haiku
mountain
cuckoo

Issa's loafing in the previous example might, therefore,
have two implications: he isn't looking for a wife, though
he should be, and/or he isn't writing haiku, though,
again, he should be. If we infer the latter, the poet has a

bit of fun writing a haiku in which he is scolded for not writing one.

III. Interrogating animals, investigating sameness

Issa often poses direct questions to animals—a playful way to imagine their perspectives while hinting at deep, experiential connections between human and nonhuman creatures.

足元へいつ来りしよかたつぶり (1801; *IZ* 1.385)
ashi moto e itsu kitarishi yo katatsuburi

at my feet
when did you get here?
snail

Issa wrote the above haiku on the fifth day of Fifth Month, 1801, as part of his *Journal of My Father's Last Days* (*Chichi no shūen nikki* 父の終焉日記), an account of his father's final illness and death. In the prose passage that precedes the poem, Issa describes how he was watching his father sleeping, checking his pulse and fanning the fire to keep him warm. Seeing that his father's color was good, he dared to start to believe that he might yet recover. This, however, he soon laments, turned out to be just "empty hope" (*IZ* 5.74). This prose preface adds poignancy to the haiku. A wandering son has returned to his native village after long absence to find his father dying. He nurses him as best he can and becomes so absorbed in his father's life signs that, when he finally notices a snail at his feet, he has no idea when it arrived. Of course, the haiku also works well without the reader's knowledge of its death room setting. A snail moves

47

slowly but can surprise human beings too preoccupied with their own worlds to notice the tiny life around them and underfoot. Through his question, Issa challenges us to imagine the snail's perspective: When did it arrive? Where is it going? What is it thinking? Fast-paced humans for the most part have no idea about a snail's destination or motives, unless they find themselves confined to a room for months with a nearby snail to observe in its bedside habitat, as did Elizabeth Tova Bailey, who chronicled the experience in her marvelous book, *The Sound of a Wild Snail Eating*. Issa's father is dying, but life goes on, even if unnoticed and unappreciated. The poet subtly chides himself and his readers for being so often oblivious to the small, quiet creatures with whom we share the world.

In another haiku addressed to a snail, he wonders about the mollusk's feelings.

朝やけがよろこばしいかかたつぶり (1805; *IZ* 1.385)
asayake ga yorokobashii ka katatsuburi

does the red dawn
delight you
snail?

By forming the question Issa strongly implies that he feels a sense of delight at the dawn colors. He wonders if that feeling is mutual. A scientifically minded reader might view the poem as simply humorous; how could the sky's color possibly be important to—or for that matter noticed by—a color-blind snail? The poem seems, at first glance, an anthropomorphic fantasy aimed purely to amuse. However, Issa's question deserves deeper consideration. Might a snail possibly feel stirred, at some level, by the start of a new day of life? Might some basic instinct, some primordial excitement, be sending it forth on its morning hunt for nourishment, shade, or sex? Might this be the equivalent, in a snail's consciousness—however rudimentary—to what humans call "delight?" Issa is doing much more in this haiku than merely amusing his readers. He invites them to consider the possibility that even a snail, at the start of the day, has identity, sentience, perspective, purpose, and feelings.

Snails, like most human beings, must work for a living, though their slow pace makes their business unknowable to most human observers—the aforementioned Elizabeth Tova Bailey being a notable exception.

かたつむり何をかせぐぞ秋の暮 (1808; *IZ* 1.441)
katasumuri nani wo kasegu zo aki no kure

O snail
how do you make your living?
autumn dusk

The seasonal reference, "autumn dusk" (*aki no kure* 秋の暮), carries two meanings in Japanese: the dusk of any day in autumn and the end of the autumn season, its metaphorical "dusk." These combined notions of end of day (night approaching) and end of autumn (winter approaching) evoke an elegiac feeling. As in the earlier-cited haiku about the autumn butterfly, Issa and the snail find themselves sharing the same existential situation: neither can escape the death that will follow life's "dusk." Issa's question implies an essential sameness of human and snail, just as his earlier query to the aging butterfly did. At the end of life's autumn, how does a snail make its living? How does a poet? By raising the first question and implying the second—and providing no answers—Issa leaves his readers to muse on the reality of death and how this reality might lead them to re-imagine their relationship with animals, replacing the common objectification of animals with a conception of them as fellow beings that face similar struggles, experience similar joys, and finish life, sooner or later, in the same way.

When Issa questions a cuckoo in the next haiku, he reminds us once again that animals and humans share common life experiences.

日光の祭りはどうだ時鳥 (1815; *IZ* 1. 341)
nikkō no matsuri wa dō da hototogisu

how was the festival
up at Nikko . . .
cuckoo?

Nikko is a famously scenic city in modern-day Tochigi Prefecture. The festival that the cuckoo has attended (in Issa's imagination) is the *shunki reitaisai* 春季例大祭: the Grand Festival of Spring held at Nikko Toshogu Shrine. Dedicated to the first shogun Tokugawa Ieyasu (1542-1616), the festival includes a procession of one thousand men dressed as samurai, re-enacting the transference of his grave from Shizuoka Prefecture to Nikko, which occurred in 1617 in accordance with Ieyasu's will. Issa, we have noted, set off on his first poetic journey in 1791 and, thereafter, traveled often, imitating earlier itinerant Japanese poets such as Saigyō Hōshi and Matsuo Bashō. In the travel diary that he kept for that first trek, he described himself as a restless "madman" (*kyōjin* 狂人): "Rambling to the west, wandering to the east, there is a madman who never stays in one place. In the morning, he eats breakfast in Kazusa; by evening, he finds lodging in Musashi. Helpless as a white wave, apt to vanish like a bubble in froth—he is named Priest Issa."[15] When he asks the cuckoo about the festival in Nikko, he does so as one traveler addressing another. As usual, his playful question has far deeper resonance, for it subtly underscores an important similarity between cuckoo and poet.

In other moments, Issa inquires into animal behavior that on the surface would seem to have no direct relation to human experience.

どれ程に面白いのか火とり虫 (1820; *IZ* 1. 365)
dore hodo ni omoshiroi no ka hitorimushi

why is playing
with fire such fun . . .
tiger moth?

Issa not only puns on the moth's Japanese name, *hitorimushi* 火とり虫 ("flame-loving bug"), he wonders why the tiger moth finds the flame so attractive—a fascination both dangerous and self-destructive. His question to the moth has also been asked, and thus far not conclusively answered, by entomologists, who theorize that artificial light may disrupt a moth's internal navigation system, or that male moths may perceive in fire the same light frequency as that produced by female moths' sex pheromones. The wording of Issa's inquiry contains a hint of his own admittedly unscientific answer to the mystery: Is it, perhaps, "fun" (*omoshiroi* 面白い)? Whatever the answer may be, he implies that it lies in the consciousness of the tiger moth and nowhere else. While the question is perhaps unanswerable, by asking it in the way that he does Issa reminds his readers, yet again, that animals have their own reasons for their actions, their own awareness, and their own perspectives.

我天窓草と思ふかきりぎりす (1813; *IZ* 1.548)
waga atama kusa to omou ka kirigirisu

do you think my head's
grass?
katydid

The fact that he attempts to imagine a katydid's experience as well as its mental processing of that experience is in itself a lesson in empathy. Issa absolutely assumes that the katydid, like the tiger moth, enjoys a unique, particular perspective. By attempting to imaginatively reconstruct that perspective, he coaxes his readers toward a deeper awareness of, and respect for, animal consciousness.

When he questions a bird in the next haiku, his language resonates with historical significance.

我汝を待こと久し時鳥 (1810; *IZ* 1. 338)
ware nanji wo matsu koto hisashi hototogisu

I've waited long
for thee
O cuckoo!

This poem was originally composed in Fourth Month, 1810. Later, Issa recopied it twice again with these explanatory head notes: "A painting of an old man sitting on a rock handing over a scroll" and "In a picture an old man sitting on a rock, handing over a scroll."[15] According to Chinese legend, Huang Shigong (Kōsekikō in Japanese), a third century master of strategy known as the Yellow Stone Elder, met Zhang Liang (Chōryō in Japanese), former governor of Han, at Yishui Bridge, where the former conferred upon the latter a scroll containing his tactics of war. Chōryō arrived late, and was greeted by the old man with the words, "I've waited long for thee!" Issa humorously applies this famous quote to describe his own long wait to hear the song of the summer cuckoo. By addressing the ancient Chinese governor's feathered stand-in as "thee" (*nanji* 汝), Issa defines his relationship with the bird in "I – Thou" terms, the schema that, as we have noted, Martin Buber favored over the more common and demeaning "I – it" approach for dealing with animals. Issa perceives the cuckoo as a welcome, long-overdue companion. Furthermore, because the bird is particularly noticed and praised for his song, we might draw an equal sign between his singing and the poet's haiku writing (recall the mountain cuckoo, described elsewhere by Issa, "warbling pure haiku"). In addition, the fact that the cuckoo's annual summer arrival is an occasion eagerly anticipated by haiku poets throughout Japan, the connection between bird and Issa becomes even stronger: the former is necessary for the latter's identiy and artistic mission. Without the seasonally encoded natural events that a haiku poet celebrates—such as, in this case, the singing of a cuckoo in summertime—haiku poetry, hence haiku poets, could not exist. Issa appreciates the cuckoo not only as a friend and fellow poet but also as a *necessary* part of his own life. Without the bird, he would be less of a poet, less of a man, and he realizes this. Fortunately, for one more year, the long-overdue cuckoo has nevertheless returned, bringing song and, for the haiku poet, motivation and purpose.

Issa imagines that insects and birds will continue to sing their songs after his own death, over his grave.

此次は我身の上かなく烏 (1809; *IZ* 1.745)
kono tsugi wa waga mi no ue ka naku karasu

will I be the next one
you caw over?
crows

我死なば墓守となれきりぎりす (undated; *IZ* 1.546)
ware shinaba haka mori to nare kirigirisu

when I die
guard my grave
katydid!

The first haiku has a head note, "Elegy for Master Kōshun." Kōshun 耕舜 was Issa's friend (Cholley 237). At his grave, the poet asks the crows if he might be next to die and to be cawed over. The second haiku, though not exactly dated, was composed in the 1790s when Issa was just beginning his travels and his poetry. Among all of the over twenty thousand haiku that he would eventually write, this early poem is on the short list as a candidate for his death verse. He asks the little insect to guard his grave and, we presume, to continue his poetic legacy by singing over it.

IV. The animals talk back

Issa deems animals of all species, large and small, worthy enough of his recognition of their consciousness and agency that he addresses his thoughts to them in the form of speech. In many haiku, animals return the favor and speak back to him, providing his critics with even more reason to accuse him of succumbing to the "pathetic fallacy" of anthropomorphism. Only human beings can use language, according to experts who define language in strictly human terms: as a system comprised of a set of finite rules of grammar and a finite lexicon that, together, can produce infinite possibilities of utterances—from baby talk to Shakespeare. Animals of other species than human have, unsurprisingly, not proven that they can meet this lofty standard. The game, of course, is fixed. One could, in parallel fashion, claim that people are incapable of jumping, if the minimum height for a jump is to be set by kangaroos. Leaving the fraught phrase, "animal language," aside for others to argue, in this book we will admit that many animals, like people, at least communicate. Recent studies by animal behavior scientists have explored the purring of domestic cats, the social calls of fruit bats, the responses of lemurs to the alarm calls of birds, the "flash communication" of Asian fireflies, the courtship signals of European tortoises, the threat vocalization by the great black-backed gull . . . and the list goes on.[16] The notion that animals are able to communicate in their own fashion is neither childish nor fanciful but scientific fact.

Issa asserts the notion that animals can express thoughts, desires, and moods early in his poetry, in his first travel journal, *Kansei san nen kikō*. In spring of 1791, the twenty-nine-year-old poet took a journey to visit fellow writers of haiku in Shimōsa Province. He left Edo on the 26th day of Third Month, thrilled to be following the example of earlier itinerant "poet-priests" of Japanese tradition, most notably (as we have mentioned before) Saigyō and Bashō. In this first presentation of Issa's road poetry, he *seems to* describe the warble of a cuckoo as an act of communication.

時鳥我身ばかりに降雨か (1791; *IZ* 1.336)
hototogisu waga mi bakari ni furu ame ka

cuckoo –
is this rain falling
only on me?

I use the words, "seems to," because readers must decide for themselves how to picture the scene. Is the poet listening to a singing cuckoo and then adding his own complaint about the rain? Or, might the cuckoo be the one complaining in his own way, which Issa somehow deciphers and understands? One of my Japanese advisors, Hiroshi Kobori, believes that both interpretations are not only possible but desirable. By keeping his meaning ambiguous, Issa invites readers to perceive the haiku as the ironic complaint of poet and bird in unison. Even though his implication that the bird might be communicating annoyance does not arise from scientific observation or experimentation, scientists would certainly agree with Issa that the calls of the male *hototogisu* carry meaning—especially to other members of his species. Issa playfully projects his own thought as to what that meaning might be in this moment of pouring rain.

The ambiguity of "Who's talking?" in this and similar poems allows Issa to suggest that his thoughts and an animal's thoughts, his experience and an animal's experience, overlap and merge. When spring arrives, in the next example, he or some other person might be voicing this exciting fact, or else a crow is doing so.

さあ春が来たと一番烏哉 (1814; *IZ* 1.53)
saa haru ga kita to ichiban karasu kana

"Well, spring has come!"
the year's first
crow

The first crow of the year is cawing (I picture, in a misty morning field). Its cry seems to be announcing, loudly and publicly, "Spring has come!" A scientist might doubt this transcript of the crow's vocalizations. Alarm calls, assembly calls, distress calls, and many other signals have been identified by bird researchers—but certainly not "Spring has come!" This statement would seem to flow directly from the mind of the crow's listener and interpreter: a season-obsessed haiku poet for whom the beginning of spring was a momentous occasion. However, by attributing this thought to a crow, Issa hints at another level of signification: perhaps a crow, too, senses the change of season with its promise of mating and the resurgence of life.

In another haiku about bird communication Issa's translation may more closely coincide with that of an ornithologist. A "parent sparrow" (*oya suzume* 親雀) chirps a shrill command to her children.

竹に来よ梅に来よとや親雀 (1814; *IZ* 1.128)
take ni ko yo ume ni kiyo to ya oya suzume

"Come to the bamboo!
Come to the plum tree!"
mother sparrow calls

Many readers in Japan who first met the haiku of Issa when they were children continue to think of him as a child's poet and nothing more. This verse of a mother sparrow calling her children would, on the surface, seem to do nothing to dispel this misconception. Such haiku, loved by children, can produce a cloying sweetness for adult readers. Nevertheless, it is possible to view a poem such as this one as Issa's sincere effort to imagine animal life from an animal perspective while at the same time suggesting an essential resemblance between human and animal experience. The parent bird's call might be an urgent warning, which would make Issa's depiction scientifically plausible. Perhaps a cat is prowling nearby, or perhaps the parent bird (I choose to picture a mother) fears that her offspring have wandered too close to a potentially dangerous human observer: Issa himself. Though one doubts that the words "bamboo" or "plum tree" exist in the sparrow lexicon, a warning call certainly must. Considered in this light, the haiku can reveal itself to be more of a snapshot of reality than an exercise in cuteness. Moreover, it affirms that human beings do not have a monopoly on parental concern or parental love—a topic to which we will return in the next chapter.

In other poems, Issa seems to discern more in the communications of animals than could possibly exist in said animals' minds. An example of this occurs in a haiku about frogs in the rain.

蛙なくやとりしまりなき草の雨 (1806; *IZ* 1.158)
kawazu naku ya torishimarinaki kusa no ame

frogs croaking –
"This rain on the grass
is unsanctioned!"

Issa seems to be merely projecting his own thoughts onto the frogs, and yet one might legitimately wonder if frogs can feel annoyed by a hard, falling rain, and that observant Issa has sympathetically perceived and recorded their annoyance. The phrase he uses to translate their croaks, *torishimarinaki* とりしまりなき, is an old expression for being "negligent" or "lax," especially in the sense of lax government. Issa humorously portrays the frogs as citizens protesting a state of anarchy in the weather. A biologist might scoff at this characterization and insist that frogs sing only to attract mates. Issa's view, however, is broader; he accepts the possibility that frogs experience a wide spectrum of perceptions and can express these perceptions in their own way. Once again, as so often is the case in Issa's haiku, the joke is not *merely* a joke. Heavy raindrops hitting the frogs' heads might indeed be a cause of aggravation. Human readers, not being frogs (as Chuang-tzu might admonish them), are wise to keep an open mind on the subject.

A later poem, this one written in Second Month of 1812, again portrays frogs as commentators on natural events, though this time instead of complaining, they appear to be celebrating.

なく蛙溝のなの花咲にけり (1812; *IZ* 1.186)
naku kawazu mizo no na no hana saki ni keri

croaking frogs –
"Rape flowers in the ditch
have bloomed!"

It is up to readers to decide whether there is just one frog singing or a chorus. Another item left to the reader's imagination is the connection between the rape flowers and the frog(s). One clue may lie in the fact that a plant's blossoms and a frog's calls both have to do with sexual reproduction; Issa hints at a deep, real connection between flowers unfurling their blossoms and frogs chanting in a ditch. Though one may doubt that the frogs possess conscious awareness of the fact that a particular flower has bloomed nearby, one can assert with confidence that they are perfectly aware of, and in tune with, the springtime urge to procreate that the flowers, in their way, also are heeding. Issa reveals a subtle truth for readers willing to plumb the depths of his imagery: the frogs do, in fact, celebrate the blooming flowers in the sense that they and the flowers are inseparably part of nature's vernal moment of fertility and rejuvenation.

In the next example, a toad announces his presence as if, in Issa's imagination, he's a visiting aristocrat.

罷出るは此薮の蟾にて候 (1819; *IZ* 1.355)
makari izuru wa kono yabu no hiki nite sōrō

"Allow me to present myself –
I am the toad
of this thicket!"

In his wonderful translation of this poem, Nobuyuki Yuasa has the toad (*hiki* 蟾) introduce himself as "The right honorable Sir Frog" (116). The verse is both funny and truth-telling. It is not a case of the poet anthropomorphically imposing human thoughts into the mind of his amphibian subject. Issa, a sensitive interpreter of animal communication, effectively captures in Japanese the toad's essential message: "I am here! May all females come, and may all my rivals cower in fear!" Issa's translation of the toad's utterance, despite its comically archaic language, is essentially accurate.

This next haiku about frog communication shows frogs behaving not like people—as Issa so often likes to present them—but, in one sense at least, as better than people.

むだ口は一つも明ぬ蛙哉 (1813; *IZ* 1.159)
muda kuchi wa hitotsu mo akenu kawazu kana

never opening
their mouths in vain . . .
frogs

An alternative translation might be: "never opening / his mouth in vain . . . / the frog." Issa notes, wryly, that frogs open their mouths only for good reasons. What might these reasons be? Certainly, we recognize that catching a fly or some other insect justifies this action, but might the poet also be thinking of the frog's love calls? Biologists tell us that frogs sing with their mouths tightly shut, relying on vocal pouches that inflate and resonate at the sides of their heads—a phenomenon of which patient, observant Issa should have been aware. Nevertheless, he could be using "mouth" here to imply speech, suggesting that frogs croak only for the good reason of attracting a mate. Whether we read the haiku as referring to the frog eating or singing, Issa uses it as a vehicle to poke fun at *homo sapiens*: a species filled with far too many individuals who open their mouths, too often, "in vain."

In some cases Issa notices and records in haiku exclusively animal-to-animal utterances, as in the following poems about horses.

秋の夜やよ所から来ても馬のなく (1804; *IZ* 1.444)
aki no yo ya yoso kara kite mo uma no naku

autumn evening –
from elsewhere another horse
neighs in reply

かすむ日の咄するやらのべの馬 (1812; *IZ* 1.84)
kasumu hi no hanashi suru yara nobe no uma

on a misty day
they chat . . .
horses in the field

A key word in the first haiku is *mo* も ("also"), for it indicates that the horse from "elsewhere" isn't the only one neighing in the autumn evening. Though they can't see each other in the gathering darkness, the horses communicate with their neighs, suggesting a sense of fellowship and camaraderie. In the second haiku, the horse conversation is also intimate, wrapped in a cloud of spring mist.[17] In both poems Issa plays the role of eavesdropper, listening in while animals perform what is often misunderstood to be a purely human activity:

speaking to one another, expressing moods and feelings. Horse communication may not be equivalent to human language in its complexity or capacity to convey ideas, but, Issa suggests, it serves the horses well enough—and deserves our acknowledgement.

In many of his poems, nonhuman communication involves, interestingly, creatures of different species.

時鳥馬をおどして通りけり (1815; *IZ* 1.342)
hototogisu uma wo odoshite tōri keri

the cuckoo hurls threats
at the horse
passing by

Whether or not the larger animal is listening, the cuckoo warbles excitedly, probably objecting to the horse's presence in his territory. As in the previous two examples, Issa again appears as an uninvolved listener, simply recording a scene of life. We picture a horse trotting along, indifferent to the small bird hurling threats and, after the dangerous intruder has passed, possibly puffing out his chest, fancying himself a great vanquisher. We smile at the cuckoo but also admire his courageous refusal to back down from a much larger opponent.

In the next haiku Issa sketches a more playful moment of inter-species communication.

狗にここ迄来いと蛙哉 (1813; *IZ* 159)
enokoro ni koko made koi to kawazu kana

"Hey puppy
come here!" croaks
a frog

Six years later, in 1819, he depicts a similar scene, substituting a cicada for the frog.

狗にここへ来よとや蝉の声 (1819; *IZ* 1.384)
enokoro ni koko e koyo to ya semi no koe

"Hey puppy
come here!" sings
a cicada

In both versions, we picture an excited, curious puppy exploring the world. Whether its attention drawn to a frog or a cicada, the former's croak and the latter's chirr summon it. Ironically, the frog and cicada are indeed chanting, "Come here!"—but the intended recipients of their messages are females of their respective species. The puppy, answering the call, gives them more than they bargained for.

In his haiku about animal-to-animal communication, Issa reminds us that human beings are not the only creatures on the planet with points of view, likes and dislikes, and the ability to express such things. At times these animal conversations are friendly (the horses in spring mist), at times they are wildly agitated (the cuckoo hurling threats at a horse), and, at times, as in the following example, the communicators express anger and conflict.

いざこざを雀もいふや村しぐれ (1823; *IZ* 1.629)
izakoza wo suzume mo iu ya mura shigure

even the sparrows
are quarreling –
steady winter rain

With the word *mo* も ("even" or "too"), Issa implies that not only sparrows but people too—forced to stay indoors due to the weather—have been quarreling. One can imagine that these human quarrelers might be the poet and his wife, stuck inside the house while the winter rain pours down. Issa wrote the poem in Tenth Month, 1823; Kiku died earlier that year in Fifth Month. Possibly he is writing from memory, the quarreling sparrows reminding him of his and Kiku's own marital spats. In any case, whoever the implied humans happen to be in the scene, Issa equates their behavior with that of the birds. Huddled together in close quarters in their respective rain shelters, people and sparrows lose their tempers.

In an undated haiku, Issa notes that frogs also quarrel.

今の間に一喧嘩して啼かはづ (undated; *IZ* 1.164)
ima no ma ni hito kenka shite naku kawazu

now they're quarreling
the croaking
frogs

The "now" (*ima* 今) with which he begins the haiku suggests that he has been paying close attention to the frogs previously: listening to their croaking, watching their actions, or both. Now, as can happen just as quickly in human gatherings, the peaceful scene abruptly gives way to belligerence and aggression. People, so much larger than frogs, might consider frog squabbles to be unimportant, and yet, ironically, people often bicker, quarrel, and even go to war over matters of contention that to them seem crucial but would appear petty to an observing deity or Buddha. From the frogs' point of view, their quarrels are extremely important, for they help establish mating territory and mating rights. Little else in life, from a biological and evolutionary perspective, can be as important as this. In any case, regardless of how one chooses to regard the frogs' sudden quarrel, Issa uses it to subtly draw the attention of his readers to a basic similarity between being frog and being human.

Verbal aggression is equally common in human societies and frog colonies, Issa suggests in the next haiku.

江戸川にかはづもきくやさし出口 (1820; *IZ* 1.162)
edogawa ni kawazu mo kiku ya sashideguchi

at Edo River
even among frogs . . .
rude talk

This is one of a series of three haiku that Issa wrote back-to-back in his journal on the subject of Edo River's rude-talking frogs. At least one of these riverside frogs, in Issa's imagination, has made "an un-called for remark" (*sashideguchi* さし出口). Shinji Ogawa suspects that Issa might be making fun of the people of Edo in general or, more specifically, his rival haiku poets. Even if we choose not to view the frogs as stand-ins for the brash and rude-talking, big-city Edoites of the period, or more parti-cularly of jealous, back-stabbing poets; the haiku makes perfect sense on its literal level. If the core of rudeness is self-centeredness—one's refusal to suppress one's own desires in the interest of social harmony—then animals can certainly behave rudely. In fact, when humans do so, this behavior is sometimes ascribed to so-called "animal instincts" that abide despite socialization (Freud's id): primal instincts that motivate people to ignore the wellbeing of others in their own selfish pursuit of gratification. By suggesting that frogs, too, can attack one another not only in action but in speech, Issa reminds us that humans and animals share vices as well as virtues.

Sometimes when animals communicate, Issa can't fathom the topic of conversation but has no doubt that there *is* a topic. In the following haiku he refers to the death anniversary of the "Old Man" (*okina* 翁): the haiku poet Bashō. This anniversary fell on the twelfth day of Tenth Month in the old Japanese calendar and so is considered a winter season word. In haiku, the anniversary is also called "Winter Rain Anniversary" (*shigure ki* 時雨忌) and "Bashō's Anniversary" (*bashōki* 芭蕉忌).

翁忌や何やらしやべる門雀 (1816; *IZ* 1.658)
okinaki ya naniyara shaberu kado suzume

Bashō's Death-Day –
what are you chattering
sparrows at my gate?

Winter sparrows, their feathers fluffed out plumply for warmth, chatter at the gate of a house. In my imagination and translation, it is Issa's house. All we know for certain about their chirping other than the location is that it takes place on Bashō's Death-Day. By inquiring about their topic of conversation on this most meaningful day to haiku poets, Issa playfully hints at a connection. Might the sparrows be remembering and honoring the first great master of haiku? This is the poem's comic suggestion, funny for its absurdity. Of course sparrows aren't keeping track of human dates and anniversaries, so readers will smile at Issa's hint that they might be. However, if readers meditate further on this image of sparrows in relation to Bashō, they might arrive at a keener appreciation of Issa's question to them. Bashō, like Issa, wrote a form of poetry grounded in nature and nature's seasons, a poetry that invites readers to become more attuned to the world's sparrows and seasonal changes. Though the sparrows are certainly unaware of it, their chirping might be connected to Bashō's life and art because *we* see the connection. Issa attends to and writes a poem about the sparrows' communication largely because Bashō came before him and perfected a genre of poetry that requires poets to open their hearts and senses to nature's moments with the attitude of inquisitive explorers. This connection linking Bashō to sparrows to Issa's own poetic disposition lies deep in the haiku. Closer to its surface, Issa simply acknowledges that birds, like people, have consciousness, social lives, and plenty to chatter about, whether we understand them or not.

In the next two examples, Issa listens to and attempts to convey in Japanese the hidden meanings in the coos of pigeons. As if emulating the seasonally sensitive haiku poet, the birds in these poems welcome spring when it comes and mourn its passing.

雪とけるとけると鳩の鳴木かな (1810; *IZ* 1.94)
yuki tokeru tokeru to hato no naku ki kana

"Snow's melting! Melting!"
pigeons celebrate
in the tree

鳩鳴や大事の春がなくなると (1811; *IZ* 1.64)
hato naku ya daiji no haru ga nakunaru to

a pigeon coos –
"That great thing, spring
has passed!"

Both written in the Third Month, these haiku appear a year apart in Issa's journal, *Shichiban nikki* 七番日記 ("Seventh Diary"). On one level, the pigeons are merely mouthing the poet's own ideas and emotions. The

67

melting of snow and the concomitant vernal resurgence of life indeed represent a "great thing" (*daiji* 大事) for the human poet and his readers. Translating the pigeons' cooing in this way, however, Issa suggests that spring is also a great thing for them. If the springtime calls of pigeons primarily express an urge to mate, Issa has not mistranslated them. While they certainly aren't saying, literally, "Snow's melting!" (*yuki tokeru* 雪とける), Issa correctly perceives and captures in human words the instinctual excitement that the seasonal change has triggered. In the second example, a pigeon coos (or, perhaps, several pigeons coo), announcing that spring is now over. Again, the reader is invited to smile at Issa's gentle joke of having a bird (or birds) express regret in human terms. However, also again, the joke contains a nugget of truth, for the pigeons' once excited voices have calmed down. Their mating season has passed; the warmer, slower, less sexually charged days of summer have begun for birds and people alike.

Issa follows the same pattern in hundreds of haiku that portray animals talking. He raises grins by having them express themselves in seemingly human terms, but at the same time he invites his readers to contemplate the deeper truth that animals and humans are not at all very different, as in the following three poems about crows.

出代の己が一番烏かな (1809; *IZ* 1.104)
degawari no ono ga ichiban karasu kana

"I'm the first
of the migrating servants!"
a crow

此時雨なぜおそいとや鳴烏 (1811; *IZ* 1.625)
kono shigure naze osoi to ya naku karasu

"Why's this winter
rain so late?"
the crow caws

ばか長い日やと口明く烏哉 (1818; *IZ* 1.61)
baka nagai hi ya to kuchi aku karasu kana

"It's a foolishly long
day!" . . . the crow opens
his mouth

In springtime in Issa's Japan, old servants were replaced by young ones. The old ones would leave their employers in Edo to return to their home villages; the young ones traveled in the opposite direction. This changing of the labor force originally took place during the Second Month of the old Japanese calendar and, later, during Third Month. In his haiku Issa imagines a crow boasting about being the first migrating servant to hit the road. While the bird isn't literally a servant, he *is* a traveler who faces the same hard reality as his human counterparts. If they wish to eat and survive, crows as well as the servants must migrate. In the second haiku a crow makes a surprising observation (for a crow), wondering why the "winter rain" (*shigure* 時雨) has arrived so late in the season. We smile, yet quickly realize that Issa and the crow *in fact* share the same world and its miseries. No matter when they arrive, early or late in the season, winter rains are always unpleasant. Humans complain in their way; crows complain in theirs—or so Issa suggests. The third haiku follows the same pattern. It seems silly for a crow to be voicing a human-like complaint about the long day of spring, and yet, if we ponder it with open minds, we might come to at least entertain the possibility that crows, like haiku poets, are capable of boredom. Whether this particular crow is, in fact, bored isn't as important as Issa raising the issue, once again narrowing the distance between human and animal realities for his readers.

Sometimes the talking animals in Issa's haiku portraits disclose more about the poet than about their own lives. The following haiku is a case in point.

むさい家の夜を見にござれなく蛙 (1807; *IZ* 1.158)
musai ya no yo wo mi ni gozare naku kawazu

"Come see
the crappy house at night!"
croak the frogs

The house is surely the poet's: the ramshackle abode that he describes, in other verses, as his "Trashy Hut" (*kuzuya* 屑屋). Here, his poetic mask as a poor beggar/hermit firmly in place, he fancies that the frogs are hawking his hovel like carnival barkers. The result is a moment of comedy and self-irony that Issa repeats in several other haiku in which he imagines the disapproval that animals may have for his rundown, ill-kempt abode.

我庵は目に這入ぬかほととぎす (1813; *IZ* 1.341)
waga io wa me ni hairanu ka hototogisu

are you trying not to
look at my hut?
cuckoo

Issa humorously implies that his home is an eyesore beneath the dignity of the cuckoo's gaze, which explains why the bird goes elsewhere to sing. The reader may doubt that frogs or cuckoos in reality disdain, let alone notice, Issa's hut, but by imagining such commentary in their croaks and warbles one is led to consider that animals have their own perspectives; that animals can sometimes be better off than human beings in their living situations; and that the lives of animals and people involve and affect one another.

Many of Issa's haiku emphasize this third point, such as the following in which animal communication proves possibly beneficial to people.

明安き夜を触歩く雀哉 (1814; *IZ* 1.247)
akeyasuki yo wo fure-aruku suzume kana

"Dawn's coming quick!"
cries the town crier . . .
sparrow

The seasonal reference is to the short nights of summer. Issa depicts a sparrow, literally, "walking while announcing" (*fure-aruku* 触歩く) the news of dawn's imminent arrival. Though it is still dark, a new day is about to begin. The chirping sparrow proclaims this fact. Is the poet annoyed at the early wakeup call, or does he share the sparrow's excitement about sunrise and the infinite possibilities of the coming day? However we picture the scene, the sparrow has communicated a message that the human poet and his human readers perfectly understand, and a reality that they and it fully share.

This next haiku requires a greater leap of the imagination to accept the meaning that Issa assigns to a bird's singing.

時鳥鳴けり酒に火が入ると (1822; *IZ* 1.346)
hototogisu naki keri sake ni hi ga iru to

the cuckoo sings
"Watch out! The sake's
burning!"

71

There is a tone of urgency in the song of the cuckoo; Issa fancies that it must be reporting important news. Someone (perhaps Issa) is warming sake over a fire, and the poet connects the cuckoo's song to this action. Unlike the case of the sparrow in the previous example whose singing, we can imagine, might realistically have something to do with its internal clock indicating the coming dawn, we doubt the literal truth of Issa's translation of the cuckoo's song. Nevertheless, a male cuckoo's need to attract a mate can seem, to the cuckoo, truly desperate: an emergency situation akin to a sake-loving poet's sake burning. Though obliquely, Issa understands and expresses, in the haiku, the bird's truth.

In a haiku about a blind man and a butterfly, the supposed interspecies communication—and even the possibility that such communication is, in fact, occurring—is even harder to imagine.

目黒へはこちへこちへと小てふ哉 (1816; *IZ* 1.171)
meguro e wa kochi e kochi e to ko chō kana

"Come this way, this way
blind man!"
little butterfly

Issa portrays a tender scene: a small butterfly seems to be generously guiding a blind person (*meguro* 目黒): literally, a person whose "eyes [have gone] black." The blind person walks in a darkness that doesn't include the butterfly, so how can the latter possibly show the way for the former? The haiku makes sense only when we add Issa, the observing poet, to the equation. From Issa's point of view, the butterfly flits ahead of the man as if serving as his guide. The butterfly and the man are unaware of each other's existence, but the poet, viewing their movements, imagines a leader-follower relationship. Furthermore, he portrays this relationship by attributing a speech act to the silent butterfly, conjuring a scene in which the mute leads the blind. Going deeper, we might consider another level of signification in this scene. Perhaps the butterfly's gentle way of life constitutes the blind man's guiding principle. "Come this way," in this reading, might imply, "*Be* this way." In this interpretation, the butterfly's silent words may ring true.

In most of Issa's haiku about talking animals, they speak plainly about realities that they and people share.

なく蛙此夜葎も伸ぬべし (1805; *IZ* 1.157)
naku kawazu kono yo mugura mo nobinu-beshi

frogs singing –
"Tonight let the weeds
grow taller!"

Issa evokes a springtime mood of unstoppable growth while again casting himself in the role of animal translator. This time, he discerns in frog song a collective plea for the weeds (*mugura* 葎, sometimes translated as "goose-grass") to stretch and grow. We can imagine the poet's heart and mind flooding with springtime excitement, and so, we assume, are the hearts and minds—the *kokoro* 心—of the frogs. In a related haiku written later that same year of 1805, the mood communicated from frogs to poet seems even more ecstatic.

痩藪も己が夜也なく蛙 (1805; *IZ* 1.157)
yase yabu mo ono ga yoru nari naku kawazu

even in a sparse thicket
"This is our night!"
croak the frogs

The thicket isn't dense, but it is the frogs' whole world. Issa captures the happy frenzy of their mating calls in human speech, translating their wild chorus with the words, "This is our night!" It is also, of course, Issa's night, for the frogs' exultations, we can assume, match his own.

If spring symbolizes youth and beginnings in the archetypal round of the seasons, summer stands for the notion of steady growth to maturity. This idea manifests itself in the following haiku about melons.

瓜になれなれなれとや蜂さわぐ (1809; *IZ* 1.414)
uri ni nare nare nare to ya hachi sawagu

"Grow, grow, grow
melons!"
buzz the bees

Readers may doubt that the bees are factually buzzing their encouragement to the slowly swelling melons; the poem might be seen as an exercise in pure imagination. Nevertheless, it might inspire some readers to meditate on the intricate connections between plant and animal life. As hungry visitors to the blossoms and spreaders of pollen, bees are intimately related to plants, including the plants that have produced the melons in question. If their buzzing doesn't directly express the idea, "Grow, grow, grow!"—their existence does. On this deeper level of interpretation, Issa's translation of the bees' message is absolutely accurate.

Animals are just as articulate in Issa's haiku about the changes that autumn and winter bring. The poet hears them grumble when cold weather sets in.

寒いとて虫が鳴事始るぞ (1821; *IZ* 1.538)
samui tote mushi ga nakigoto hajimaru zo

"It's cold!"
the insects' complaining
has begun

Later in the year, in winter, the cries of animals sound more desperate.

霜がれや米くれろとて鳴雀 (1816; *IZ* 1.735)
shimogare ya kome kurero tote naku suzume

frost-killed grass
"Gimme rice!"
a sparrow sings

According to Makoto Ueda, the above poem was written shortly after the death of Issa's friend and patron Natsume Seibi. Since Seibi often fed Issa, the hungry sparrow in the haiku could represent the poet.[18] While there is nothing preventing us from reading this verse in terms of Issa's biography, it is not necessary to do so. Literally, frost has killed the grass, so the sparrow, if it cannot find food, will be next to die. One imagines that gentle-hearted Issa, before or after jotting this haiku in his diary, answered the sparrow's plea.

Earlier, we looked at a haiku of 1813 in which Issa comically presents himself as the famous warrior-monk Benkei. In this next example, from 1819, he alludes to another well-known twelfth century strongman, but this time a bird does the talking.

時鳥蝿虫めらもよつく聞け (1819; *IZ* 1.344)
hototogisu hae mushimera mo yokku kike

cuckoo –
"O flies and worms
listen well!"

Issa prefaces this haiku with the head note, "In the place where Chinzei Hachirō Tametomo tossed around people like small stones."[19] Chinzei Hachirō Tametomo 鎮西八郎為朝 was a twelfth century warrior. The haiku parodies his famous battle cry. Issa's portrayal of the cuckoo as a fearsome samurai in relation to bugs and worms makes for a delightful moment of haiku comedy. And, as usual, the comedy only half-conceals a deeper truth: carnage is carnage, whether it involves soldiers on a battlefield or flying and crawling creatures in a meadow. Issa invites us to smile while at the same time feel sympathy for the fallen: Tametomo's tossed-about people and the flies and worms destined for the cuckoo's beak.

Issa speaks to animals in his haiku, and animals in his haiku speak to each other, to Issa, and to us. The poet identifies with animals, feels kinship with them, recognizes a sameness between their experiences and his, tries to imagine the world as seen through their eyes, acknowledges their perspectives, invites them to share his own visions and excitement, offers advice in matters of digestion and philosophy, sympathizes with their problems, envies their freedom from human conventions and social hierarchy, receives their scolding, wonders how they experience the world, and appreciates their importance to his mission as a haiku poet as well as their roles as fellow poets and wanderers. Sometimes in his haiku Issa purposefully leaves ambiguous who exactly is doing the talking and the listening—which, as we have seen, invites readers to infer deep similarities between human and animal experience and consciousness. In other cases, animals unambiguously talk in his poems, in their own ways, while Issa serves in the role of sensitive listener and translator. Though usually humorous, the resulting haiku are much more than jokes built upon the projection of human ideas onto animals. The more we reflect on them, the more we might discover that these poems are whispering to us, again and again, of human and animal sameness—a theme that, for Kobayashi Issa, is *the* theme.

Chapter 2. ANTHROPOMORPHISM OR REALISM?

I. Animal families

Issa opens himself to the charge of anthropomorphism when he applies human familial terms and relational concepts to animals (mother, father, cousin, sister, brother, stepchild . . .), when he describes the actions of animals in terms of human endeavors (going to work, making love, traveling, playing games . . .), and when he depicts animals as artists, singers, dancers, and poets who create, innovate, improvise, and enjoy beauty. Many readers and critics of the poet conclude that he imposes human terminology and frames of reference onto nonhuman animals for no more profound reason than to create humor and thereby amuse. Such readers and critics accordingly regard Issa's haiku about animals as light poetic trifles unworthy of the serious contemplation that one might properly bring to bear to more usually sober haiku artists such as Bashō and Buson. Such readers and critics are wrong. Subjected to close scrutiny, Issa's animal poems, though often humorous, testify to the essential sameness of all sentient beings, humans included. In Issa's poetic vision, animals realistically deserve their seemingly anthropomorphic treatment because, deep down, their existential situation and that of humans is the same.

In the scientific view, animals select mates in order to procreate and thus ensure the survival of their species. In Issa's warmer but, we shall see, essentially just as valid terms, animals woo, make love, and start families.

留主にするぞ恋して遊べ庵の蝿 (1815; *IZ* 1.374)
rusu ni suru zo koi shite asobe io no hae

while I'm away
enjoy your lovemaking
hut's flies

The words used to describe what the flies are doing, *koi shite* 恋して, denote a tender sentiment in Japanese: what we mean in English when we say that one person "loves" or is "falling in love" with another. In this haiku we find Issa's normal method at work. We grin when we learn that the love-makers who will take advantage of the privacy of the hut when the poet is away are flies! This is vintage Issa: bait-and-switch humor perfectly timed. But the joke's deeper resonance is a reminder that flies are not very different from people. Issa tells the flies to "enjoy themselves," "play," "cavort," "have fun": *asobe* 遊べ. Readers of the haiku know that making love feels good. What those readers might not often contemplate, however, is the probability that houseflies having sex with their mates are also, in their tiny-brained way, enjoying it. Issa's acknowledgement of a fly's feeling of "love" invites us to consider the notion that a fly has consciousness, desires, and a legitimate perspective. A fly, whether we decide to swat it or not, is an sentient individual whose life has value, at least to it.

In 1803 Issa was forty-one, entering a prolific phase of haiku-writing that would span the next two decades and beyond. This next haiku, written that year, alludes to a classic of ancient Chinese poetry.

かりそめの娶入月よやなく蛙 (1803; *IZ* 1.157)
karisome no yomeri tsuki yo ya naku kawazu

a fleeting moonlit
wedding night . . .
frogs singing

Issa prefaces the above with a single word: *cho* 著, which means "literary work" and is the title of a poem from the most ancient Chinese lyrical collection, the Zhou Dynasty's *Shijing* (*IZ* 1.157). This particular poem expresses the point of view of a young woman and begins with the verse, "He was waiting for me between the door and the screen/ The strings of his ear-stoppers were of white silk,/ And there were appended to them beautiful Hua-stones" (Legge). The poem continues for two additional verses that follow the pattern of the first with important variations. In verse 2 the suitor waits for the woman in "the open court" wearing ear-stoppers of "white silk" from which hang "Ying-stones"; in verse 3 he waits for her in "the hall" with ear-stoppers of "yellow silk," again adorned with Ying-stones. The changes of location and costume indicate the passing of time. The lover or would-be lover is persistent, strategically positioning himself on three different occasions in places where the poem's courtly speaker is likely to pass. Issa's haiku about a "fleeting moonlit wedding night" can be read as the romantic culmination of the old Chinese poem. The lovers now enjoy the fleeting pleasures of their wedding night, while (in one way of reading the poem) frogs outside the window entertain them with their singing.

In an alternate reading of the haiku the wedding night refers not to people but to mating frogs. Male frogs sing to attract females. Issa's poem might be celebrating the brief lovemaking of two frogs, brought together by this song. It is indeed comical to describe frog intercourse in terms of a "wedding night" and, on top of that, to connect this action to a scene from courtly Chinese love poetry. But underlying this comedy, Issa challenges readers to examine their assumptions about supposed differences between human and nonhuman experience. If physical desire that involves the releasing of chemicals in the brain is part of human love, even the most poeticized and romanticized love, do not frogs, on their level, love too?

In another haiku written that same year, Issa again alludes to a Chinese classic.

つるべにも一夜過ぎけりなく蛙 (1803; *IZ* 1.157)
tsurube ni mo hito yo sugi keri naku kawazu

even in the well bucket
croaking all night . . .
a frog

The poem has a short head note that harkens back to the ancient Chinese book of divination, *I Ching*: the three words, "Heaven, Wind, Coupling" 天風姤, a reference to *I Ching* Hexagram 44, wherein Heaven (*qian* 天) is the upper trigram and Wind (*xun* 風) is the lower, resulting in *gou* 姤 (Japanese = *kō*), the sign for copulation or "coming to meet."[20] Issa's geomantic joke is on the frog, singing his mating song all night without much chance of success inside the well bucket. However, the frog might be better off alone since, according to the official interpretation of this hexagram, a female met under its influence would not make a good partner. In fact, a marriage with her would be doomed to fail (Blofeld 172). In any case, by framing the male frog's situation in divination terms normally used to help guide human activity, Issa suggests that his unrequited yearning for coupling is exactly the same desire that many, if not most, of his readers have experienced.

His readers can also relate to the pressures of courtship felt by the cat in the following haiku.

81

妻乞や一角とれしのらの猫 (1805; *IZ* 1.120)
tsuma-goi ya hito kado toreshi nora no neko

his looking for a wife
makes him sociable . . .
stray cat

The phrase, *hito kado toreshi* 一角とれし, literally, "round off the angle," is an idiom which means to "become sociable." The stray tomcat, normally rough and wild, is on his best behavior as he comes courting. Issa writes another haiku about the same cat: the poem that precedes the above in his journal for Twelfth Month, 1805.

山猫や恋から直に里馴るる (1805; *IZ* 1.120)
yama neko ya koi kara sugu ni sato naruru

wild cat –
after making love
he's the town pet

Literally, the cat is a "mountain cat" (*yama neko* 山猫). He has wandered into the village looking for a mate, successfully. Basking in the afterglow of this success, he no longer seems or acts wild. Sex has gentled his soul; he grows used to the village and its people. In a later poem, a carousing cat ends up with a new home under similar circumstances.

恋序よ所の猫とは成にけり (1815; *IZ* 1.122)
koi tsuide yoso no neko to wa nari ni keri

love-smitten
my cat becomes
the neighbor's pet

If readers can relate the cat's behavior in these haiku to the actions of human beings, this is because cats and people, Issa suggests, have more in common than is generally acknowledged.

Perhaps his most brilliant portrait of a lover cat—out of dozens—is the following.

恋猫の源氏めかする垣根哉 (1809; *IZ* 1.121)
koi neko no genji mekasuru kakine kana

the lover cat
dandied up like Genji
at the hedge

Murasaki Shikibu's eleventh-century *Tale of Genji* (*Genji monogatari* 源氏物語) is a classic of Heian period literature, a courtly tale of a "shining prince" and his adventures, mostly amorous.[21] Issa's original readers would have instantly recognized the scene in *The Tale of Genji* parodied in this haiku, either from reading the book or from having viewed popular woodblock prints of its key episodes. In Chapter 5, Prince Genji journeys into the hills north of Kyoto in springtime, seeking a cure for his malaria in the cave of a wise healer. While in the neighborhood, he peers through a wattle fence and catches sight of ten-year old Murasaki, a pretty little girl who bears an uncanny resemblance to the woman that Genji most yearns for: the Lady Fujitsubo, with whom he has recently had "an illicit and profitless affair" (Murasaki 90). Genji soon learns that the girl happens to be a daughter of Fujitsubo's brother, Prince Hyōbu—the product of an affair that Hyōbu had with a lady who, thanks to Hyōbu's vindictive wife, was later driven to "a fatal decline" and death (90). Spying on the child, Genji decides instantly that he must "take her into his house and make her his ideal" (90)!

Even to eleventh century readers Genji's behavior must have seemed pedophiliac, since he protests several times in the narrative that his intentions do not stem from "improper motives" (90); that he only wants to serve the best interest of the child by molding her into his perfect woman. Later that year, in autumn, after the death of Murasaki's nurse, Genji abducts the girl and brings her to the west wing of his palace. The next morning, he visits her in her new, opulent chamber only to find her sulking. "Young ladies should do as they are told," he admonishes, and the author adds, wryly, "And so the lessons began" (109).

In Issa's haiku a tomcat steps into the role of this most famous courtly lover of Japanese letters, appearing at a fence in glorious, full adornment: *mekasuru* めかする. Of course, instead of silken, perfumed robes, the cat wears only fur that, perhaps, he has licked and combed for the occasion . . . perhaps not. The haiku elevates the cat or else denigrates Genji—or both—depending on how one chooses to read it. On one hand, Issa suggests that cats, too, can experience on some level the lofty emotion that we humans call love. On the other hand, he implies that Prince Genji, despite all his riches and refinement, is in essence nothing more than a sexually excited animal, a predator. The present moment of a lover cat posing by a fence mingles in the haiku with the literary memory of Prince Genji spying, and mentally staking his claim, on little Murasaki. The long-ago story not only glosses the situation in present time (a cat at a fence), the situation in present time subtly critiques the long-ago story. Just as, in an earlier example, lover frogs can be understood to be playing out a scene of courtly love from the Chinese classic, *Shijing*; here, a cat steps into the role of a famous lover of Japanese tradition. Issa slyly draws an equal sign between feline and human. The lover cat *is* Genji, and Genji, if we strip away his accouterments of culture and courtly refinement, is the cat.

In Issa's universe, even insects can feel love pangs.

鳴な虫別るる恋はほしにさへ (1822: *IZ* 1.501)
naku na mushi wakaruru koi wa hoshi ni sae

don't cry, insects –
lovers part
even among the stars[22]

Issa alludes here to the Tanabata Festival, a celebration of the brief annual reunion of the celestial lovers, the Weaving Princess (the star that Westerners call Vega) and the Cowherd (Altair). One night a year, the night of the seventh day of Seventh Month, they are allowed to cross the Milky Way's river of stars to be together, but before the next night they must part for another year. Issa is aware that the insects that continue chirping and chirring have not yet found mates. He compassionately advises them to accept their lack of amorous success, since lovers can remain separate "even among the stars" (*hoshi ni sae* ほしにさへ). Kai Falkman finds it important that Issa ends the haiku with, as he puts it, "the joyful picture of the stars. The poet's gaze is lifted onto the cosmic plane of understanding" (65). I agree with Falkman's point, except for his characterization of the stars' situation as "joyful." I sense more of a feeling of resignation in Issa's verse. If even celestial lovers must be apart, then mortal ones (including people and insects) should accept the hard reality that their desire for lovemaking may go unrequited.

In a similarly themed haiku Issa presents two cats in the roles of Pyramus and Thisbe.

85

猫鳴や塀をへだててあはぬ恋 (1824; *IZ* 1.124)
neko naku ya hei wo hedatete awanu koi

cats yowling
separated by a wall –
tragic lovers

I end my translation with the phrase, "tragic lovers," in an attempt at expressing Issa's meaning and sense in Western terms. Literally, he writes, "the lovers do not meet" (*awanu koi* あはぬ恋). Since Issa could not have known of the Roman myth of Pyramis and Thisbe (or of Shakespeare's adaptation of it in *Romeo and Juliet*), it's more probable that his scene of lover cats separated by a wall hearkens back to the Asian story of the Weaving Princess and Cowherd. Readers may smile at the cats' frustrating situation while at the same time recognizing a sameness in human and feline "affairs." In another, earlier incarnation of the image, Sumida River instead of a wall separates the cats, calling to mind even more directly the Tanabata legend in which "Heaven's River" of stars keeps lovers apart.

猫なくや中を流るる角田川 (1812; *IZ* 1.121)
neko naku ya naka wo nagaruru sumida-gawa

cats' love calls –
between them flows
Sumida River

This poem follows almost immediately in Issa's journal.

江戸猫のあはただしさよ角田川 (1812; *IZ* 1.121)
edo neko no awatadashisa yo sumida-gawa

the Edo cat
in a frenzy . . .
Sumida River[23]

The cat's frenzy should be familiar to anyone who has
fixated on a distant or, worse, near yet unattainable object
of affection. Issa creates comedy by casting the cats in
these poems in the role of tragically separated lovers of
human folklore, at the same time reminding us that
animals are much like people when they yearn for the
unattainable. They, too, are stirred by body chemistry to
couple. The main difference may be that they write no
poetry about it, unless we interpret, as Issa does, their
chirps, chirrs, and (in this case) yowls—as love songs.

Not all of Issa's lover-animals face insurmountable
barriers to their union. A more common image in his
haiku is that of happy couples starting new lives together.

たのもしやしかも小てふの若夫婦 (1816; IZ 1.170)
tanomoshi ya shikamo ko chō no waka fūfu

brimming with hope
little butterflies . . .
a young couple

はつ蝶やしかも三夫婦五夫婦 (1816; IZ 1.171)
hatsu chō ya shikamo mi meoto itsu meoto

spring's first butterflies –
three couples!
five couples!

When he composed these haiku in Third Month of 1816,
he was three years into his nine-year marriage with Kiku.
For the reader who keeps Issa's biography in mind, it is
tempting to discern in these images of newlywed

87

butterflies the poet's happiness in his own marriage. Kiku was eight months' pregnant with their first child at the time, and no one was more "brimming with hope" (*tanomoshi* たのもし) than she and Issa. Whether or not we view these verses through the prism of Issa's personal life, they exuberantly celebrate the joy of young love. More specifically, Issa describes the paired-off butterflies in both haiku with a word normally reserved for human couples, *meoto* 夫婦: "husband and wife." In this way his portraits particularly call to mind the happiness and promise of married love. Following his usual pattern, Issa invites readers to smile at the application of human terminology to nonhuman animals while at the same time hinting at a deep similarity.

In the same vein, he applies the word *tsuma*妻 ("wife" or "married woman") to a toad.

蟇どのの妻や待らん子鳴らん (1819; *IZ* 1.355)
hiki dono no tsuma ya matsuran ko nakuran

Mister Toad –
the wife may be waiting
your children crying

The haiku parodies a well-known *waka* written by Yamanoue no Okura (山上憶良), a poet of the late seventh and early eighth centuries. On the occasion of leaving a banquet, Yamanoue composed an impromptu poem that contains the lines, "the children may be crying" (*ko nakuramu* 子泣くらむ) and "the wife may be waiting for me" (*haha mo wa wo matsuramu* 母も吾を待つらむ).[24] As we have seen before, Issa delights in literary jokes in which animals merge with figures from Chinese and Japanese classical literature. In this case, a toad replaces the great poet and concerned husband and father, Yamanoue. Beneath the surface of the poem's comedy, it reminds us that animals, too, can have familial bonds.

Cats, for example, have wives in Issa's poetry.

のら猫の妻のござるはなかりけり (1821; *IZ* 1.123)
nora neko no tsuma no gozaru wa nakari keri

the stray cat's wife
fails
to make her entrance

Issa's wording is humorous; he applies ultra-polite language in his report about the nonappearance of the cat's mate. She "fails to make her entrance" (*gozaru wa nakari* ござるはなかり)—despite, we imagine, the tomcat's frustrated yowling. In a happier domestic scene, Issa refers to the wife of a frog.

草陰に蛙の妻もこもりけり (1812; *IZ* 1.158)
kusa kage ni kawazu no tsuma mo komori keri

in grassy shade
the frog's wife also lives
in seclusion

The "frogs" (*kawazu* 蛙) in this example, living in the shade of grasses, might be toads; Issa, not being a stickler for this scientific detail, often refers to toads as such. In any case, here as in the previously cited cat poem, he refers to the female animal in question as a "wife" (*tsuma* 妻). Furthermore, he describes the frog couple as if they are two hermits living in "seclusion" (*komori* こもり). The result is a cozy scene in which sheltering grass serves as a love nest for Mr. and Mrs. Frog.

After lovemaking and settling down—whether this involves animals of the human or nonhuman kind—the next order of business is the production of offspring. Issa's journals are packed with haiku about baby animals: baby monkeys, baby cormorants, nestlings, puppies, kittens, ponies, calves . . . even, as we will see, baby spiders. By far the newborns that figure most prominently in his work are baby sparrows.

むつまじき二親もちし雀哉 (1810; IZ 1.127)
mutsumajiki futaoya mochishi suzume kana

living in harmony –
the sparrow has
both parents!

As an emotionally battered stepchild, Issa seems especially fixated, longingly, on images of happy, intact, animal families; such portraits are legion in his haiku.

親雀子雀山もいさむぞよ (1812; *IZ* 1.128)
oya suzume ko suzume yama mo isamu zo yo

parent sparrows
baby sparrows . . .
a happy mountain

Issa celebrates family love in the above haiku. The mountain is, literally, in "high spirits" (*isamu* いさむ). The joy of the sparrows—of parents and babies—seems to infect everyone on the mountain, including Issa, and, in a wonderful bit of literary exaggeration, the mountain itself. The poet who signed one of his haiku, "Issa the Stepchild" (*mamako Issa* まま子一茶)[25] glorifies the familial bliss of intact animal families, a bliss that he was personally denied in his own childhood.

むら雀さらにまま子はなかりけり (1814; *IZ* 1.129)
mura suzume sara ni mamako wa nakari keri

flock of sparrows –
and not one of them
a stepchild

He wrote this haiku in Third Month 1814; he married
Kiku, his first wife, with high hopes of starting his own
family, just a month later. Knowing the key facts of Issa's
biography, it is difficult to read his verses about happy
sparrow families without sensing in them his own longing
to have a family of his own. This longing, which some
might describe as a "human" impulse, in fact motivates
the behavior of many other creatures that populate the
earth—or so Issa gently reminds us in such poems.

Parent sparrows bring their children, in this next
haiku, to a Buddhist temple.

灌仏やふくら雀も親連れて (1806; *IZ* 1.280)
kuwanbutsu ya fukura suzume mo oya tsurete

Buddha's birthday –
fat little sparrows
and their parents

On the Eighth Day of Fourth Month Gautama Buddha's
birthday is celebrated. Here, Issa reports a scene in which
little sparrows, fat and round due to cold weather, "also"
(*mo* も) are being led by their parents to the celebration,
implying that human children in the scene are undergoing
the same experience. This is another happy haiku about
families—of people and of sparrows—once again underscoring an important yet often overlooked commonality
between humans and other animals. Beyond this, Issa

91

further suggests the possibility that birds can be pious in their fashion—a point to which we shall return in Chapter 4.

Many animals of many species protect their young. This is a fact, not an anthropocentric projection of human values. Issa's depictions of such behavior advance his program of blending the animal and human worlds. Animals and people, in his poetic vision, inhabit the *same* world under strikingly similar conditions.

かはるがはる巣の番したり親雀 (1813; *IZ* 1.128)
kawaru-gawaru su no ban shitari oya suzume

taking turns
guarding the nest . . .
parent sparrows

五六間烏追けり親雀 (1809; *IZ* 1.127)
gorokken karasu oi keri oya suzume

chasing the crow
ten or twelve yards . . .
mother sparrow

The crow-chaser in the second poem might be the mother or father sparrow; Issa only indicates that it is a "parent" (*oya* 親). One of the baby sparrows' parents bravely chases off the larger bird for "five or six *ken* 間," the equivalent of ten or twelve yards, away from (we presume) the nest. A mother dog with her puppies and a "grandfather buck" with his fawns appear just as protective in these next two haiku.

親犬が瀬踏してけり雪げ川 (undated; *IZ* 1.98)
oya inu ga sebumi shite keri yukigegawa

mother dog
testing the depth . . .
snow-melt river

爺鹿の瀬ぶみ致スや俄川 (1819; *IZ* 1.522)
jii shika no sebumi itasu ya niwaka-gawa

grandfather buck
testing the depth . . .
flash flood river

The theme of parent animals guarding their precious charges is so prevalent in Issa—and so natural in most people's experience of the world—an image of a parent doing quite the opposite is shocking.

子を喰ふ猫も見よ見よけしの花 (1814; *IZ* 1. 393)
ko wo kurau neko mo mi yo mi yo keshi no hana

even the cat
who ate her kittens . . .
look! poppies

As in an earlier-cited poem in which he admonishes a stray cat to emulate a butterfly, Issa once again repeats the words, "Look! Look!" (*mi yo mi yo* 見よ見よ), cleverly echoing in Japanese the sound of meowing. The haiku starkly juxtaposes the killing of kittens with the living beauty of summer flowers. The phenomenon of a mother cat devouring her young is rare but not unprecedented; animal behavioral scientists theorize that in some cases a hormonal imbalance fails to trigger the maternal instinct, so the mother cat's hunting instinct kicks in when the kittens arrive. In other cases, they believe, kittens may be born with abnormalities that would reduce their likelihood of survival, triggering a kind of mercy killing.

While Issa doesn't understand or even question why the cat has done what she has done, he suggests that she (and the reader) should focus on the beauty and promise of new life embodied by the blooming poppies.

More often, mother cats in Issa's poetry exhibit solicitous and protective behavior that a scientist might credit to maternal instinct but that most people would describe, more warmly, as motherly love. The tender tone of these verses indicates which side of the debate Issa is on.

親猫が蚤をも噛んでくれにけり (1820; *IZ* 1.378)
oya neko ga nomi wo mo kande kure ni keri

the mother cat
gnawing her kitten's
fleas

蚤かんで寝せて行也猫の親 (1820; *IZ* 1.379)
nomi kande nekasete yuku nari neko no oya

having gnawed their fleas
and put them to bed, she leaves . . .
mother cat

女猫子ゆゑの盗とく逃よ (1823; *IZ* 1.124)
onna neko ko yue no nusumi toku nige yo

mother cat
steals for her kittens . . .
run faster!

人中を猫も子故のぬすみ哉 (1823; *IZ* 1.124)
hitonaka wo neko mo ko yue no nusumi kana

from the human race
for her kittens' sake . . .
mother cat steals

Issa wrote the last two haiku in Eighth Month 1823. A mother cat has stolen a bit of food, and he cheers her on, urging her to "run faster!" (*toku nige yo* とく逃よ) from her human pursuer.

In this next haiku portrait of an animal, set in the New Year's season, a trained monkey dances for a hard-earned reward of *kashi* 菓子, a sweet confection.

御座敷や菓子を見い見い猿が舞 (1821; *IZ* 1.48)
o-zashiki ya kashi wo mii-mii saru ga mau

sitting room –
eyes locked on his treat
the monkey dances

The following haiku, which appears on the same page of Issa's journal, reveals who has been instructing the little monkey.

親猿がをしへる舞の手品かな (1821; *IZ* 1.48)
oya-zaru ga oshieru mai no tejina kana

mother monkey
teaches her baby . . .
dance moves

The mother teaches her baby, literally, "tricks" (*tejina* 手品), a word that suggests that they are both captive performers working for a human master. Their dancing earns money for him, so the fact that the mother is passing on tricks to her offspring must be a pleasing sight to their handler. Looking deeper into the haiku—past this level of exploitation—we see in it the loving ties that bind one generation to the next, as survival knowledge passes from parent to child. The mother-child bond between the monkeys in the poem should be familiar to Issa's primate readers. Once again, he invites them to stop perceiving animals as objectified "others" and instead to understand them as subjects, as belonging to "we."

Issa's portrayals of animals protecting and cherishing their families promote an ethical agenda. He coaxes his readers toward a state of greater consciousness of their own similarities to animals so that they might, in their real lives, relate to their fellow creatures with a heightened sense of compassion. Even the tiniest of creatures deserves our compassion, Issa suggests, because they are like us, and we are like them.

追な追な追な子どもよ子持蚤 (1814; *IZ* 1.377)
ouna ouna ouna kodomo yo ko mochi nomi

don't chase, don't chase
children!
that flea has kids

In Japanese, Issa repeats his admonition, "don't chase!" (*ouna* 追な) three times, making his original text even more emphatic than my English translation. As a Buddhist, he is quite cognizant of Gautama Buddha's edict to respect all life, but he doesn't condemn flea-chasing, in this case, on religious grounds. Instead, he reminds the children, correctly, that even a flea can be someone's mother, urging them (and his readers) to view their harassment and killing as the heinous crime of matricide. The haiku is deviously playful. On one level, Issa is voicing the childish notion that flea killing might make orphans of the flea's offspring—a warning that his adult readers will find (perhaps delightfully) absurd.

Unlike the birds and mammals of previous examples, the endangered flea in the present one certainly has no connection to her brood after the eggs have been laid. Nevertheless, Issa's warning to the children might be read, on a deeper level, as a request for his readers to treat animals of whatever size as they would like themselves to be treated, because even a flea has at least a speck of consciousness and a will to live.

According to Issa's own account, he learned at an early age that animals deserve our compassion; recall that he claimed to have invited an orphan sparrow to play with him when he was six years old, abandoned and lonely. His understanding that animals not only have families but have feelings about their families—the joy of being together, the devastation of separation—provides the basic premise for his ethical concept of how they should be treated. A flea can be someone's mother, and choirs of chirring autumn insects are someone's children.

夜鳴虫汝母あり父ありや (1821; *IZ* 1.538)
yonakimushi nanji haha ari chichi ari ya

insects chirp in the night –
what of your mothers?
your fathers?

And when a mother cormorant's child is taken from her, her cries and agitation indicate what a human being could only describe as a breaking heart.

子もち鵜や門から呼るもどり声 (1818; *IZ* 1.292)
ko mochi u ya kado kara yobaru modori-goe

the mother cormorant
cries at the gate
"Come home!"

Japanese fishermen imprison and use cormorants. Tied to a tether, these sea birds dive for fish that they are subsequently forced to disgorge. In the above haiku, a fisherman takes a young bird through the gate, perhaps to be sold, perhaps to go fishing. Either way, the mother cries pitifully for her child to come back. The emotion that she expresses in her vocalizations should be familiar to Issa's empathetic human readers.

In a scene just as heart-rending, a sold pony is led away from his mother.[26] The pony yearns to return to her, and the mother horse, somewhere in her intelligent equine brain, will miss him. This is truth, not anthropomorphic projection. The cold autumn rain accentuates the haiku's sorrowful tone.

> 売馬の親かへり見る秋の雨 (1804; *IZ* 1.465)
> *uri uma no oya kaeri miru aki no ame*

> the sold pony
> looks back at mother . . .
> autumn rain

A year later, re-imagining the scene, Issa sets it in an equally dreary seasonal context of withering winter fields. The tone and undercurrents of emotion remain the same.

> 冬枯や親に放れし馬の顔 (1805; *IZ* 733)
> *fuyugare ya oya ni hanareshi uma no kao*

> winter withering –
> departing from mother
> the pony's face

Readers aware of Issa's unhappy childhood will find it nearly impossible not to perceive these images of ponies being torn from their mothers and homes as self-portraits. In a third example, the poet alludes to an Eighth Month custom of farmers sending tribute horses from the pastures of Shinano, his home province, to the imperial capital, Kyoto.

駒鳴くやけふ望月のはなれ際 (1816; *IZ* 1.503)
koma naku ya kyō bōgetsu no hanare-giwa

the pony neighs –
under a full moon
led away from his mother

It's a night of full moon, normally an image of divine splendor in haiku, but in this case the light seems cold and unfeeling. The focus of the poem is the pony's neigh; the reader must rely on his or her imagination to conjure its tone of bleak desperation. In Issa's life the loss of his mother occurred when he was three and his exile from home when he was fifteen (actually thirteen, according to the way that Westerners compute age), but this short poem compresses time and merges the two events. Issa perceives and captures—haiku-style, saying so little—his own almost unspeakable pain in losing mother and home while at the same time depicting the apparent sadness of a horse and her pony.

Just as with people, animals separated from their mates miss them, or so Issa suggests in more than one haiku. Sometimes, the separation is permanent.

木に鳴はやもめ烏か天の川 (1804; *IZ* 1.448)
ki ni naku wa yamome karasu ka ama no gawa

cawing in the tree
are you a widow, crow?
Milky Way above

ついついと常正月ややもめ蝶 (1810; *IZ* 1.167)
tsui-tsui to tsune shōgatsu ya yamome chō

she had a husband
when the year was new . . .
widow butterfly

In the first haiku, the phrase, "Heaven's River" (*ama no gawa* 天の川) refers to the Milky Way. The frozen vastness of space provides an appropriate backdrop for the solitary crow. Perhaps Issa detects a note of loneliness in the crow's caw, leading him to wonder if the bird might be a widow. The haiku manifests what Issa's poetic predecessor, Bashō, described as *sabi*寂び: a sense of existential loneliness that for the old master became a key element of his haiku esthetic, embodying an awareness of Buddhist transience. However, Issa's poem about the widow crow contrasts significantly with Bashō's most famous *sabi*-resonant crow portrait.

かれ枝に烏のとまりけり秋の暮[27]
kare eda ni karasu no tomari keri aki no kure

on a bare branch
sits a crow . . .
autumn evening

Whereas Bashō presents a more objective image, Issa inquires into the crow's consciousness and the possibility of broken family ties. The earlier poet regards the crow on the withered branch as an external entity; Issa views his crow as a fellow creature capable of feelings. In the "widow butterfly" haiku, Issa again seeks to under-stand the life of an animal from the inside. It is possible that he recognizes the butterfly as the same one that flitted about with a mate earlier that year but now flies alone. Could the loss of the butterfly's "husband" cause her to feel, on some level, the emotions that humans describe as loneliness and a sense of loss? This question is of course impossible to answer (for us, who are not butterflies), but simply by asking it Issa coaxes readers to regard the butterfly with compassion.

Issa perceives family ties everywhere he turns, it seems.

> むきむきに蛙のいとこはとこ哉 (1813; *IZ* 1.159)
> *muki muki ni kawazu no itoko hatoko kana*

> facing every-which way
> frog cousins
> and second cousins!

The haiku begins with a happy chaos of frogs facing every possible direction but ends with a wonderful revelation: these lookalike clones are *family,* specifically, cousins and second cousins. Issa uses familial terms usually applied to *homo sapiens* to diminish difference between human and nonhuman animals. The frogs, indeed, are cousins and second-cousins to each other and also, Issa hints, to him and to us. In a later haiku he playfully claims personal kinship with animals.

> 起よ起よあこが乙鳥鳩すずめ (1814; *IZ* 1.140)
> *oki yo oki yo ako ga tsubakura hato suzume*

> wake up! wake up! my children –
> swallows, pigeons
> sparrows

Ako あこ is an old word meaning "my child" (*KD* 20); here, Issa uses it to describe swallows, pigeons, and sparrows. This tender attribution suggests that, like a nurturing parent, the poet has come to scatter a breakfast of crumbs or grain for his dear ones. If we consider all of Issa's haiku in which he applies family terms to animals, together they form a sort of syllogism: people have families; animals have families; therefore, people and animals are basically the same. From this conclusion it is only a short further step to decide that people and animals themselves are family. Issa certainly takes this step and invites his readers to take it with him. His human-like treatment of animals goes far beyond mere anthropo- morphic joke-telling. He continuously, consciously wipes away perceived differences between human and animal in order to change our perception of our fellow creatures in a fundamental way, to achieve a more sympathetic view of them, and to conceive of and live in a world where swallows, pigeons, and sparrows are our "children" and frogs our "cousins and second cousins."

II. Animals at work and at play

In addition to presenting animals as lovers and family members, Issa describes their daily lives in terms that would have been quite familiar to his contemporaries of Tokugawa era Japan as well as to readers today: adult animals work to make their living, while their children (and adults, during leisure time) have fun and play games. As usual, these portraits of animals at work and play function on two levels: milking humor from the "human" presentation of nonhuman creatures while, on a deeper level, reminding us that they and people are in essence the same. Human beings have plenty of company on the planet when it comes to the daily and, in some cases, nightly grind.

蜻蛉も起てはたらく夜川哉 (1814; *IZ* 1.291)
tombō mo okite hataraku yo kawa kana

the dragonfly, too
works late . . .
night fishing

In this example "dragonfly" (*tombō* 蜻蛉) might be plural. Whether Issa is referring to one dragonfly or to many, he equates insect and human activity. The grammatical particle *mo* も ("too") indicates that someone else is present in the scene: presumably, one or more human beings who are also "river fishing at night" (*yo kawa* 夜川). Ravenous and efficient carnivores, dragonflies devour smaller insects in mid-flight. Issa's poem asks and answers the question: Is this food-gathering work of dragonflies essentially any different from the labor of fishermen filling their buckets with fish? No, he implies. The fact that a human being will bring his catch home or to market instead of immediately eating it is only a cosmetic difference; the dragonfly and the man both must catch food or starve. For this same purpose they "stay up late to work" (*okite hataraku* 起てはたらく). The haiku paints a picture of common purpose and unspoken camaraderie. The dragonfly and the man, to survive in this world, accomplish the same end though with different means.

Two years later, Issa returned to the image of a hard-working dragonfly, this time (seemingly) without a human counterpart.

蜻蛉の夜かせぎしたり門の月 (1816; *IZ* 1.542)
tombō no yo kasegi shitari kado no tsuki

103

the dragonfly goes about
his night work . . .
moon at the gate

Again, the Japanese verb used to describe the dragonfly's
actions is one normally applied to people: *kasegi shitari* か
せぎしたり: "doing work" in the sense of laboring to
earn a living. This time, Issa doesn't show a fisherman
also working in the scene, but there is nevertheless an
implied human presence: the observing poet, sitting at his
gate, enjoying the moon. This portrait of dragonfly and
man is a study in contrast: the former flits here and there,
busily engaged in the "work" of hunting mosquitoes and
other nutritious insects, whereas the latter, the poet,
relaxes and moon-gazes. Of course, one could argue that
Issa, regarding the moon while at the same time paying
attention to a dragonfly's exertions, is also working, in
that he is performing his job as a haiku poet: opening his
senses, heart, and mind to the world and all its myriad
juxtapositions. In this case, the most impressive juxtaposition in his consciousness and, hence, his poem, is that
of a tiny, ephemeral package of life viewed alongside the
vast, brilliant moon. The dragonfly and Issa both work at
their night jobs. One hunts for food; the other observes,
feels, and makes the haiku—and the moon shines over
both.

In a pair of closely related poems, Issa employs the
same Japanese verb, though this time in its standard
dictionary form (*kasegu* かせぐ), to describe the exertions
of snails.

かたつむり何をかせぐぞ秋の暮 (1808; *IZ* 1.441)
katasumuri nani wo kasegu zo aki no kure

O snail
how do you make your living?
autumn dusk

かたつぶり何をかせぐぞ秋の雨 (1809; *IZ* 1.465)
katatsuburi nani wo kasegu zo aki no ame[28]

O snail
how do you make your living?
autumn rain

What a snail does to survive in this world remains a
mystery to Issa and to most people, other than biologists
who specialize in mollusk behavior, or to Elizabeth Tova
Bailey, who, as mentioned in Chapter 1, patiently observed a woodland snail's daily and nightly life on her
bedside table while confined in her room during a long
illness. Bailey wrote about her snail's remarkably busy,
though snail-paced, life—prefacing many of the chapters
of her book, incidentally, with snail haiku written by
Issa.[29] Although most humans move about at a tempo too
hurried to answer Issa's question, a snail must do *something* to secure the necessities of life, and so, in this
fundamental sense of the term, it indeed "works"—just as
Issa and the vast majority of his readers of the past two
centuries have needed to do. Issa subtly underscores this
fact by using direct address in the poem, thereby
announcing his own presence in the scene. His question
implies a comparison such that, in the English translation, we might place "your" in italics: "How do you make
your living?" The snail's livelihood involves slow, inch-by-
inch foraging, but it is a livelihood nonetheless, Issa suggests. The two share something else in common in these
nearly identical haiku: the seasonal context. Man and
snail alike must endure the colder days of autumn with its
chilling rain and inexorable movement toward winter.

Metaphorically, autumn signals old age and approaching death, suggesting yet another reality shared by poet and snail: death will come for them both. Until that time, they work to survive another day.

Even butterflies—seemingly free of all cares and mundane concerns—must work, Issa notes.

世の中は蝶も朝からかせぐ也 (undated; *IZ* 1.176)
yo no naka wa chō mo asa kara kasegu nari

in this world
from dawn to dusk
even a butterfly must toil

In his original text, Issa writes that the butterfly "works" (*kasegu* かせぐ) "from morning" (*asa kara*朝から) on. To complete the idiom in English, I've added the phrase, "to dusk." Like many people, Issa's butterfly begins its day of labor early in the morning. This understanding of its delicate flitting about the flowers as a form of toil may seem to contradict a previous image that we have considered among Issa's haiku in which a butterfly leading a blind man can be perceived to embody an ideal of otherworldly gentleness. Gentleness and work are not, however, mutually exclusive. Even while their graceful flight can appear to be a symbol for sublime detachment, Issa also recognizes that the nectar gathering of butterflies is essentially their way of eking out a living.

In some haiku, Issa joins the notion of butterfly labor to his earlier-noted motif of butterfly couples starting families.

かせぐぞよてふの三夫婦五夫婦 (1812; *IZ* 1.168)
kasegu zo yo chō no mi meoto itsu meoto

making their living
butterfly couples . . .
three . . . five!

夜明から小てふの夫婦かせぎ哉 (1812; *IZ* 1.168)
yoake kara ko chō no meoto kasegi kana

from dawn to dusk
the butterfly couple
makes their living

However, in one haiku he decides that the butterflies' "work" (*shigoto* 仕事) is actually their playtime.

生れでて蝶は遊ぶを仕事哉 (1821; *IZ* 1.173)
umaredete chō wa asobu wo shigoto kana

from birth on
for butterflies, playing
is their job

"Birth" in the poem of course refers to the butterflies' post-cocoon existence. Flitting from flower to flower may be life-sustaining work, but Issa senses that this work is, to the butterflies, delightful. The same could be said about his own profession as a poet, as he opens himself to moments such as this one, probing their meaning through haiku.

Issa uses the same word, "work" (*shigoto* 仕事), to describe the yowling of a cat.

のら猫が夜永仕事かひたと鳴 (1813; *IZ* 1.446)
nora neko ga yonaga shigoto ka hita to naku

stray cat
all the long night is this your job?
yowling nearby

The poet, we suspect, is trying to sleep, so his joking question to the cat, whining in the darkness nearby, has a sarcastic bite. "Long night" (*yonaga* 夜永) is an autumn season word in haiku, referring to nights growing longer as the shortening days count down to winter and solstice. A cat's calls are connected to mating: female cats in heat yowl to announce their presence to males; tomcats yowl in response. The lovemaking of cats is officially a spring seasonal phrase in haiku, but this activity also occurs in summer and, as in the present example, autumn. The cat's nocturnal singing is not only annoying but, in this autumnal context we can imagine it to be somewhat pitiful and desperate-sounding. The year nears its end, yet the cat in the darkness is still alone, crying for a mate. Issa jokes that its solo performance is its "job," but on a deeper level (as usual with Issa's poetic jokes), he touches on a truth: the cat's noisemaking, connected to mating, *is* its job, biologically speaking. Without the yowling there can be no mate, no coupling, no kittens, and, for the species, no survival.

In Issa's poetic vision, human beings are not the only creatures on the planet who wake up each morning and go to work. Dragonflies hunt, snails and butterflies toil, and cats cry for mates, advancing the important work of reproduction. In the following example, sparrows, too, labor to survive.

雀等がはたらきぶりや草の花 (1814; *IZ* 1.553)
suzumera ga hatarakiburi ya kusa no hana

the sparrows
go about their business . . .
wildflowers

The word *hatarakiburi* はたらきぶり, used here to describe the sparrows' activity, signifies to "toil" or "work at
a job"—and is usually applied to people. In a thematically
related haiku, this one about foraging at low tide,
sparrows and pigeons once again behave like people . . .
or, could Issa's veiled point be that the people in the scene
are behaving like the birds?

人まねに鳩も雀も汐干かな (1820; *IZ* 1.112)
hito mane ni hato mo suzume mo shiohi kana

acting like people
pigeons and sparrows
at low tide

Issa writes that the birds "imitate people" (*hito mane* 人ま
ね) in the scene. Just as the bent-over humans are seeking
shellfish stranded in low-tide pools, pigeons and sparrows
peck the sand and puddles for their share of seafood. Issa
perceives, and helps the reader to perceive, the common
purpose of people and birds; not only their postures but
their actions are basically the same.

Also like human beings, young animals, at some
point in their lives, leave the protection of parents and
home, striking out into the world on their own.

蜘の子はみなちりぢりの身すぎ哉 (1822; *IZ* 1.385)
kumo no ko wa mina chiri-jiri no misugi kana

all the baby spiders
scatter
to make a living

109

There is an expression in Japanese, *kumo no ko wo chirasu yō ni* 蜘蛛の子を散らすように ("like baby spiders scattering"), used to describe people running or fleeing in all directions. Issa plays with this idiom by presenting its literal image in action. The baby spiders, each one a tiny, eight-legged replica of its parents, spread out in all directions in search of, as he puts it, *misugi* 身すぎ: lively-hood. At age fifteen (thirteen by Western calculation) the poet did the same, leaving the intolerably stressful home situation caused by, in his version of events, his mean-spirited stepmother. Like the baby spiders of his haiku, each one wandering off in its own chosen direction, the young Issa found himself suddenly alone in the world, walking the road to Edo and his future. It is not only possible but likely that he recognized an important but traumatic step in his own life's journey in this image of scattering spiders. As their independent lives now begin, their tiny size starkly contrasts with the vastness of the world into which they are vanishing. Bashō, we have noted, would have described the sense of existential aloneness embodied in such a poetic scene with the term, *sabi*. Issa certainly senses and conveys to his readers the *sabi* implicit in this image of spiders leaving their nest, but his deeper point seems to be that it happens to everyone: we are in this together; we are all the same. His use of descriptive language normally reserved for humans— "jobs," going to "work," "making a living,"—is not child-ish anthropomorphism but, instead, truth deeply perceived.

In his haiku portraits of animals Issa notes another point of commonality shared by people and the members of many other species: the necessity to undertake arduous, ambitious travel. Emulating earlier Japanese poets such as Saigyō and Bashō, Issa himself set out on many long and physically taxing literary journeys throughout the course of his life. In one of his earliest haiku-composing treks, he acknowledged at one point in his journal that he was not alone in his wandering. The following haiku of 1795, written at age thirty-three, records that moment. It appears in *Saigoku kikō* 西国紀行 ("Travelogue of My Journey to Western Provinces").

蝶と共に吾も七野を巡る哉 (1795; *IZ* 1.165)
chō to tomo ni ware mo nana no wo meguru kana

a butterfly my companion
through Nana Field
we wander

Issa considered travel to be an essential part of his profession as a haiku poet. In this particular scene, he recognizes a butterfly as his fellow traveler, reminding us of the haiku discussed in Chapter 1, in which he asks a cuckoo, also treated as a comrade in wandering, about the festival in Nikko. Issa feels kinship with the migrating insect whose journeys, scientists have shown, are even more wildly ambitious than any haiku poet's before the age of airplanes. In the same travelogue, Issa provides another image of a butterfly traveling companion.

寝ころんで蝶泊らせる外湯哉 (1795; *IZ* 1.165)
ne-koronde chō tomaraseru soto yu kana

lying down
with a visiting butterfly . . .
outer hot spring

The haiku has the head note, "Close by Dōgo Hot Spring" (*IZ* 5.37). The hot spring Issa enjoyed that day was an open air pool of overflow water just to the west of Dōgo Spa in Matsuyama. Issa later discovered that the pool was intended for horses and cows, not people, but the moment described in his poem is one of luxurious relaxation and intimate camaraderie. After their long journey, poet and butterfly nod off to sleep.

Issa recognizes many other animals as his fellow travelers. Migrating birds, especially wild geese, figure prominently among them.

一度見度さらしな山や帰る雁 (1803; *IZ* 1.150)
ichi do mitaki sarashina yama ya kaeru kari

all eager to see
Mount Sarashina . . .
departing geese

一ッ雁夜々ばかり渡りけり (1819; *IZ* 1.531)
hitotsu kari yoru yoru bakari watari keri

lone wild goose –
fly night after night
on your way

此国のものに成る気か行ぬ雁 (1822; *IZ* 1.155)
kono kuni no mono ni naru ki ka ikanu kari

are you planning
to stay in this province?
goose

Geese migrate according to season in search of hospitable climes and ample food supplies; Issa, also an inveterate traveler, wandered about to stay in touch with his students and to seek poetic inspiration, his own way of finding food. We should note that his economic situation improved greatly in autumn of 1813, at age fifty-one, when he returned to live in his half of the partitioned family home in Kashiwabara. From that point on, what he earned as a haiku teacher was supplemented by the rent paid by farmers working the family lands. For much of his adult life, nevertheless, Issa traveled just as incessantly as the wild geese that he addresses in hundreds of haiku, of which the above-cited poems are just three examples. In the first, the geese leave Japan in springtime en route to northern lands. The verb *kaeru* 帰る ("return") in this context means that the geese in springtime are returning to Siberia. Mount Sarashina, another name for Mount Ubasute or Obasute, is a mountain in Issa's home province of Shinano where, according to legend, old people were "thrown away" (the literal meaning of *ubasute* 姥捨て). Issa asks the geese if they are flying off to see the famous mountain. In the second example the goose resembles Issa even more, for he is traveling—as Issa most often did—alone in the vast world. His heart goes out to the solitary goose, his comrade and double. The third haiku shows a goose—or, perhaps, a flock of geese—lingering, as Issa often did when traveling, in a particular place. He playfully asks the bird if it plans to settle down, quitting the wandering life. Of course, if the goose were to stay it would need to become tame and dependent on humans to feed it in the winter; in other words, it would need to stop being what it is: *wild*. Similarly, though as he aged his journeys became shorter and less ambitious than in his younger years, Issa never stopped traveling, never stopped being what *he* was: an itinerant poet and teacher of haiku—wild in his own way.

He recognizes a fellow traveler even in a cat.

陽炎の猫にもたかる歩行神 (1815; *IZ* 1.92)
kagerō no neko ni mo takaru aruki-gami

a cat in heat shimmers
also follows
the God of Wandering

According to folk belief, the God of Wandering, Arukigami 歩行神, entices people to leave their homes and walk about. The cat's impulse to wander seems inspired, Issa claims, by an irresistible divine force. The particle *mo* も ("also") suggests that someone else is obeying Arukigami in the scene: Issa, of course. The haiku jokingly connects his and the cat's restless journeys to a god's influence, when in reality, as he and his readers must know, the force that compels a cat and a poet to wander is quite worldly: the cat seeks food or sex; the poet seeks inspiration for haiku—which, in turn, makes the attainment of food and sex (whether in marriage or in the brothels of which Issa sometimes writes) possible. They are both doing their jobs, the cat and Issa, two of a kind.

Issa wasn't always traveling. At some points in the year, especially during the hard winters in Shinano's mountains, he hunkered in his "hut" to wait for spring: the so-called *fuyugomori*冬篭 or "winter seclusion," a popular season word in haiku. Animals—especially those that do not migrate—do the same in several of Issa's haiku portraits. A sparrow family, for example, makes their winter "home" (*yado* 宿) in a thicket of bamboo; and a cricket, a dog, and a "mum-gobbling" insect or worm (*mushi* 虫) all avoid the cold weather by moving in with the poet.

春待や雀も竹を宿として (1805; *IZ* 1.617)
haru matsu ya suzume mo take wo yado to shite

waiting for spring
sparrows also make a home
in the bamboo

こほろぎもついて来にけり冬篭り (1824; *IZ* 1.700)
kōrogi mo tsuite ki ni keri fuyugomori

the cricket also
moves in with me . . .
winter seclusion

煩悩の犬もつきそふ冬篭 (1821; *IZ* 1.700)
bonnō no inu mo tsukisō fuyugomori

my sinful dog
at my side . . .
winter seclusion

菊喰虫と云れて冬篭り (1813; *IZ* 1.698)
kiku kurau mushi to iwarete fuyugomori

he's called
the mum-gobbling bug . . .
winter seclusion

The first two haiku express a camaraderie shared by the poet and animals. Issa and the sparrows stay in their respective cold-weather shelters, waiting for spring; and the cricket, singing somewhere in the darkness of his house, appreciates its warm hearth as much as he does. The second two haiku are more humorous. Issa claims that his dog possesses "carnal desire" (*bonnō* 煩悩)—translated here as being "sinful"—but the reader may well suspect that, however true it may be that a dog has bodily urges, Issa is also portraying his own state of mind: like dog, like master. As for the unspecified insect or worm slowly feasting on the chrysanthemum in the last example, Issa identifies it only as a "mum-gobbling bug" (*kiku kurau mushi* 菊喰虫). While the bug is indeed a bug in the literal sense that should always be honored in haiku, the poem is also quite possibly a comic self-portrait; hungry, shut-in Issa is the "bug" that day by day devours the flower's edible petals.

Outside his winter hermitage, bears and boars shelter in their own caves and hollows. In one haiku on this subject, Issa again expresses the notion that "We're in this together."

猪熊と隣づからや冬篭 (1813; *IZ* 1.698)
shishi kuma to tonari-zukara ya fuyugomori

boars and bears
are my neighbors . . .
winter seclusion

Adult animals in Issa's haiku are like human beings in their need to work, to travel, and to seek winter shelter—all in the name of survival. Young animals, in parallel fashion, are like human children in that they love to play. One particular game, in fact, crosses species.

猫の子のかくれんぼする萩の花 (1814; *IZ* 1.573)
neko no ko no kakurenbo suru hagi no hana

the kitten plays
hide-and-seek . . .
in bush clover

In a later haiku, a mother cat joins in the game.

親としてかくれんぼする子猫哉 (1817; *IZ* 1.124)
oya to shite kakurenbo suru ko neko kana

mother cat
plays hide and seek . . .
with her kittens

The kittens and mother in these haiku are not anthropomorphically playing a human game; they are playing a cat game named "hide and seek" in English and *kakurenbo* かくれんぼ in Japanese. The cats may have no word for it, but the game belongs to them as much as it does to people and, as we will soon see, to sparrows and frogs as well. By calling it "hide-and-seek" Issa is not straining simply to please his younger readers; he is, in fact, observing and recording the kind of real behavior that in our time has been the subject of a plethora of scientific books and studies. When animals play, Oliveira notes, they tend to have good health, adequate nutrition, and a stress-free environment (1-5). In other words, to apply a human term, they are happy. Scientists have studied the play of ravens, kangaroos, pronghorn deer, squirrel monkeys, turtles, and countless other species.[30] Issa's haiku portraits of animals at play are as valid as a biologist's field notes.

Animals besides cats and kittens play hide and seek in Issa's poetry. A group of sparrows and a solitary frog also practice this important game that one day might save them from a predator.

茶の花に隠んぼする雀哉 (1813; *IZ* 1.738)
cha no hana ni kakurenbo suru suzume kana

playing hide-and-seek
in tea blossoms . . .
sparrows

草の葉にかくれんぼする蛙哉 (1813; *IZ* 1.159)
kusa no ha ni kakurenbo suru kawazu kana

in leaves of grass
playing hide-and-seek . . .
a frog

On the other side of the survival equation, predators also play in Issa's haiku to sharpen their survival skills. A cat catching flies at a window performs this action *nagusami ni* なぐさみに: a Japanese expression denoting "for amusement," "for recreation," "for entertainment" or "for pleasure." In my translation, it's "for fun."

なぐさみに猫がとる也窓の蠅 (1822; *IZ* 1. 375)
nagusami ni neko ga toru nari mado no hae

just for fun
the cat catches them . . .
window's flies

On some occasions, Issa observes animals of different species playing together. A turtle plays with whitebait, a type of small, white fish.

白魚に大泥亀も遊びけり (1808; *IZ* 1.178)
shirauo ni ōdoro-game mo asobi keri

among the whitebait
a big mud turtle
plays too

Sparrows play with a mouse.

菜の花や鼠と遊ぶむら雀 (1815; *IZ* 1.187)
na no hana ya nezumi to asobu mura suzume

flowering rape –
the sparrows play
with the mouse

And a dog and a butterfly have a good time together,
according to Issa.

がむしやらの犬とも遊ぶ小てふ哉 (1815; *IZ* 1.170)
gamushara no inu to mo asobu ko chō kana

playing with
the rambunctious dog . . .
little butterfly

The state of nature is not every minute a tooth-and-claw
struggle for survival. These tender images of peaceful,
playful, coexistence suggest a community of life whose
members can ignore, at least in some moments, the
boundaries of species: a community to which human
beings also fully belong. Issa reminds us in his poetry that
animals and people share not only the need to work but
also the same inclination to enjoy, in leisure time, the
pleasures of play. While it is true that the play behavior of
animals prepares them for the serious "work" of survival—hiding from predators or, for the predators,
hunting and pouncing on prey—this is equally true of the
game-playing of human children, who through this
activity hone skills they will need in adult life—these
days, more often than not, involving computers. Issa's
approach is consistent: he raises smiles by showing
animals engaged in supposedly human actions while,
deeper, planting the suggestion that they are like us, and
we are like them. We are, essentially, the same.

III. Animals and beauty

In a revealing essay published on the Dana Foundation's website, animal behavior researchers Gisela Kaplan and Lesley J. Rogers observe,

> Creation and appreciation of art are aspects of consciousness that we have traditionally viewed as purely human activities, ones that express our highest cognitive abilities. If animals share at least some aspects of this ability, we will have to look upon them with more respect and perhaps change the ways we treat them.

Issa was not a scientist. He never studied the implications of elephants or chimpanzees that paint; he most likely never posed questions that scientists today are asking, such as, "Are spider web decorations, so elaborately beautiful to us, also beautiful to spiders?" or, "Is birdsong 'music' to birds?" It was as a poet and as a keen observer of all manner of creatures, not as a scientist, that Issa plainly and repeatedly claimed that animals appreciate nature's beauty, and that animals are more than capable of creating their own music and poetry. Kaplan and Rogers believe that an acknowledgement of an esthetic sense in animals could radically change the way that we regard and treat them. Two centuries ago, Issa suggested that animals indeed recognize beauty on some level; he regarded and treated them as equals in their ability to make and enjoy art, music, poetry, and dance.

We have already considered examples of toads having wives and children in Issa's poetry. In one such portrait, we noted, Issa had a toad mouth the words of the medieval *waka* poet, Yamanoue no Okura, implying that this particular toad was, in his way, a poet. The toad in the following example also seems to have a poet's heart, savoring nature's beauty.

福蟾ものさばり出たり桃の花 (1804; *IZ* 1.235)
fuku-biki mo nosabari detari momo no hana

Lucky the Toad, too
swaggers out . . .
peach blossoms

"Lucky" (*fuku* 福) is an endearing pet name for toads in Japan and—in the Kamo District of Shizuoka Prefecture, among other places—a colloquialism for "toad" (*IZ* 2.205; 6.169). The compound word, *fukubiki* 福蟾, a pun on the Japanese word for "lottery" (*fukubiki* 福引), might be translated, "Lucky the Toad." Here, Lucky emerges from grasses or some other leafy hiding place, exhibiting an attitude that Issa describes as *nosabari* のさばり, an old verb for behaving selfishly or in an arrogant manner (*KD* 1292). Issa suggests, without stating it overtly, that the reason for the toad's swagger is his sense of pride for, hence his implied ownership of, the peach blossoms. The toad's attitude seems to be, "This is mine, all mine!" As we have seen in earlier examples, the grammatical particle *mo* も ("also") is crucial. The toad claims credit for the blossoms *too*. The unidentified other proud claimant, we can assume, is Issa or, perhaps, some gardener who planted, pruned, and loves the tree in question. We can imagine that this human in the scene is puffed with pride because *his* tree has bloomed so gloriously. By equating Lucky's attitude to the person's, Issa implies that people do not have a monopoly on appreciating and responding to natural beauty. We share the world and its splendors with fellow creatures, fellow blossom lovers . . . toads included.

A scientifically minded reader might issue the challenge: Is the toad—an extremely nearsighted creature, biologists tell us—even *aware* of the peach blossoms? And, if he is, could he plausibly be swelling with pride for their beauty, as Issa suggests? At first view, this portrait of a blossom-proud toad seems an extreme anthropomorphic joke. Attributing the human attitude of selfish possession and arrogant entitlement to a toad seems wonderfully absurd, but, if we look deeper into the poem we might perhaps discern an undercurrent of truth. The toad's demeanor as depicted by Issa could be interpreted to declare: "I am part of all this; all this is part of me. The peach blossoms are splendid! *I* am splendid!" On some level Lucky the Toad might be conscious that he belongs in this world of textures, patterns, shapes, and colors; and this world—as blurry as it may be to his eyes—belongs to him. Read in this way, the haiku teaches a lesson to human beings who too often feel themselves to be separate and alienated from the natural universe that created, surrounds, and sustains them. Because we are, all of us, part of nature, the peach blossoms do, in a real sense, bloom for *us*. They are ours; they are Lucky's—and we all should be proud of them.

At times the animals in Issa's haiku portraits not only appreciate beauty; they create it.

わざわざに蝶も来て舞ふ夏花哉 (1806; *IZ* 1.283)
waza-waza ni chō mo kite mau gebana kana

a butterfly deigns
to come and dance . . .
summer flowers

A butterfly (or, possibly, several butterflies) comes to dance among the summer flowers. The fact it "deigns" to do so (*waza-waza ni* わざわざに) suggests that it lives a higher, more spiritual existence than other creatures and yet, despite this fact, has descended to earth, lured by the flowers decorating a summer retreat (*gebana* 夏花).[31] Issa, in turn, has also been lured—in his case by the compelling scene of summer retreat, flowers, and dancing butterfly. Writing the haiku, he invites his readers, too, to enjoy and contemplate this picture of serene, earthly beauty. The image is not only pleasant but instructional: Issa seems to be saying as subtext, "See how flowers attract the butterfly, causing it to dance!" Nature's beauty, he suggests, delights all sorts of animals, not just the human kind.

We have already noted that Issa approaches the natural universe not as a scientist but as a poet. However, even though he is a poet relying on observation and imagination rather than hypothesis and experiment, one wonders if what he writes about beauty-loving animals could possibly be true. Butterflies consume the nectar of flowers, so what seems to be their beauty-drunk "dance" is actually a feeding frenzy. Still, this does not necessarily mean that flowers are *only* food to butterflies. After all, they are drawn to flowers for the same reason that many garden-visiting humans are: because of their colors. With pentachromatic eyes containing five different color-sensitive cell types, butterflies perceive even more of the come-hither colors of flowers than we do, extending into the ultraviolet range beyond human eyesight. Butterflies apparently experience a sense of excitement when perceiving the color-coded flowers, their symbiotic partners in evolution, and this sense of excitement *might be*, on its most elementary level, the esthetic sense.

In one of Issa's early works, undated but written at some point in the 1790s, he reveals that at the time he was already trying to see the world through butterfly eyes, to gain insight into their floral excitement.

てふてふのいまだにあかぬ木槿哉 (undated; *IZ* 1.591)
chōchō no imada ni akanu mukuge kana

> butterflies never
> tire of them . . .
> roses of Sharon

Roses of Sharon (*mukuge* 木槿) were considered autumn blooms in the old Japanese calendar. According to Issa, butterflies never grow tired of these delicate white flowers with their deep, inviting, pink centers. Survival-based attractions—to food that is nourishing, to mates that are suitable—exist in all species. For human beings, a chef's succulent dishes and good-looking members of the opposite sex can trigger primal desires linked to survival while, simultaneously, inspiring what we often think of as our "higher" sense of beauty. What we are attracted to is hard-wired in the human brain as shown, for example, in studies that have linked sex appeal to near-symmetry in faces.[32] People are genetically programmed to be repulsed by the smell of rotten food, to be excited by the smell of good food, and to be attracted to partners whose faces and bodies exhibit symmetry that indicates health and might therefore ensure the passing of one's genes to the next generation. If our human sense of beauty evolved from such primal impulses, we might come to suspect that nourishing flowers excite and draw butterflies to them because, to butterflies, they are beautiful.

In this next haiku a frog seems to relish the light of fireflies on a summer evening.

蛍火や蛙もこうと口を明く (1809; *IZ* 1.357)
hotarubi ya kawazu mo kō to kuchi wo aku

sparkling fireflies –
even the frog's mouth
gapes

Does the frog's gaping mouth signify an esthetic appreciation, or is he merely waiting for a firefly to flit into
range of his grasping tongue? At least one other mouth
gapes in the scene, as indicated by Issa's *mo* も ("also").
He might be talking about himself specifically or referring
to some other person's mouth. As he describes in other
haiku, Japanese people like to "call" (*yobu* 呼ぶ) for
fireflies to come to them—at times to catch them but
usually just to enjoy their flickering light show. This
means, the frog and the person in the scene are
performing the same action motivated by the same desire:
both want the fireflies to come to them, although perhaps
for different reasons. Nevertheless, both are excited by the
fireflies. Roses of Sharon attract butterflies; fireflies interest a frog . . . food can be beautiful.

In this next animal haiku Issa has fun with the dual
nature of flowers as being both lovely and tasty.

さをしかの口とどかぬや杜若 (1814; *IZ* 1.402)
saoshika no kuchi todokanu ya kakitsubata

the young buck's
mouth can't reach . . .
the iris

The young buck, in Issa's version of the Tantalus myth,
gazes longingly at a blooming iris. To flower-loving humans such as the poet Issa, the iris is an object of
admiration; to the buck of the poem, it is a potential
snack. Unlike the butterflies in earlier examples, the buck
betrays no sense of delight ("a butterfly deigns/ to come
and dance") or excitement ("butterflies never/ tire . . ."),

only hunger. The poem can be read as satirical, its target being the buck that follows his belly alone, oblivious to the iris's beauty. That some animals in Issa's haiku exhibit a lack of esthetic sense doesn't change that fact that others do. Even human beings, as shown in several of Issa's haiku, are capable of crass indifference to nature's beauty and may even choose to desecrate it.

夕顔の花で洟かむおばば哉 (1812; *IZ* 1. 391)
yūgao no hana de hana kamu o-baba kana

blowing her snot
on the moonflower . . .
granny

In this comic haiku that exploits the pun of *hana* as "blossom" and *hana* as "nose," the old woman exhibits no more esthetic appreciation for the moonflower than the buck does for his out-of-reach iris. Issa's point in both haiku is to gently admonish all who ignore natural beauty—deer and human alike.

He drives the same point home—as almost always, veiled in humor—in three haiku about dogs.

里犬の尿をかけけり菊の花 (1807; *IZ* 1.556)
sato inu no bari wo kake keri kiku no hana

watered by
the village dog . . .
chrysanthemum

赤犬の欠の先やかきつばた (1813; *IZ* 1.402)
aka inu no akubi no saki ya kakitsubata

before
the red dog's yawn . . .
irises

里犬のなぐさみなきや梅の花 (1813; *IZ* 1.198)
sato inu no nagusami naki ya ume no hana

nothing special
to the village dog . . .
plum blossoms

For humans, the chrysanthemum is a thing of beauty; for
the dog in the first poem, it's exactly as significant as a
fire hydrant. The irises that inspire reams of haiku poetry
are met with the second dog's yawn of boredom. And
plum blossoms, the delicate blooms that signal the beginning of spring in Japan—luring droves of human con-
noisseurs into the countryside for flower-gazing picnics—
are "nothing special" (*nagusami naki* なぐさみなき) as far
as the third dog is concerned. In all three cases, Issa's
humor derives from the way that the dogs' attitude
diametrically opposes that of flower-loving humans,
especially flower-obsessed haiku poets like himself and
many of his readers. To butterflies, flowers may arguably
be beautiful, but to dogs they serve only as functional
landmarks upon which to leave their scent markings. In
regards to the esthetic sense, animals, like people, vary in
their tastes.

In these next haiku Issa presents more esthetically
aware creatures: a horse and a frog.

あさぢふや馬の見て居る梅の花 (1807; *IZ* 1.194)
asajiu ya uma no mite iru ume no hana

cogon grass –
the horse gazes
at plum blossoms

葉隠の椿見つめてなく蛙 (1807; *IZ* 158)
ha-gakure no tsubaki mitsumete naku kawazu

in leafy shade
gazing at the camellia . . .
croaking frog

The horse stares at plum blossoms in a place where cogon (*asaji* あさぢ), an early spring grass, is growing (*KD* 25). In the second poem, the frog seems to pay just as rapt attention to a camellia in bloom. As he often likes to do, Issa startles us with bait-and-switch humor predicated on animals performing actions normally expected of human beings. "Cogon grass –/ the horse gazes . . ." raises the expectation that the horse will be gazing at something of interest to horses (perhaps the tasty grass itself?), but in his punch line Issa reveals instead that the object of attention is "plum blossoms"—thus depicting the horse joining in with human blossom-admirers such as the poet and, most likely, others in the scene. Similarly, the second haiku begins with the phrases, "in leafy shade/ gazing at the camellia," leading the reader to expect that a human being will be identified as the gazer. Instead, the agent of action turns out to be a "croaking frog." As we have seen many times before, there are two levels to such haiku jokes: their humorous surfaces and their more serious depths. The surface level in these two cases may inspire readers to smile at a blossom-gazing horse and a camellia-gazing frog. Deeper, Issa implies that these animals, as much as humans, may be entranced by the delicate, colorful blooms that this living planet provides. Of course,

Issa (being no scientist) offers no proof of this possibility; he simply, pointedly, raises it in his poems.

Two years after portraying his frog admiring the camellias, Issa describes another (or the same?) frog gazing, this time, at cherry blossoms.

つくづくと蛙が目にも桜哉 (1809; *IZ* 1. 226)
tsukuzuku to kawazu ga me ni mo sakura kana

even the frog's eyes
can't turn away . . .
cherry blossoms!

The frog watches the blossoms as "attentively" (*tsukuzuku to* つくづくと) as someone else in the scene, presumably Issa. As we noted earlier, frogs are nearsighted creatures; their vision is quite blurry beyond six inches. Their eyes surely focus more on the movement of prey or predators than on the beauty of flowers. Even so, does this fact disprove Issa's attribution of an esthetic sense to them? While they stare, hoping a fly might swoop into range, might they not also be enjoying the colors and shapes of this world? Who are we, who have never been frogs, to say that they don't?

Another frog in a haiku by Issa appears almost swallowed up by beauty, once again raising the question of what such an animal perceives and enjoys.

ちる花にあごを並べる蛙哉 (1813; *IZ* 1.159)
chiru hana ni ago wo naraberu kawazu kana

chin-deep
in the fallen blossoms . . .
a frog

The word "blossoms" (*hana* 花) in this context means "cherry blossoms." Fallen cherry blossoms may remind us of how ephemeral is beauty, is life. For Issa's original readers, the association of this image with the Buddhist teaching of transience (*mujō* 無常) would have been natural and obvious. The brevity of the cherry blossoms' glory is precisely what makes them precious. In fact, the brevity of life itself is an essential element of beauty and its appreciation, as Kenkō Yoshida 兼好吉田, an early fourteenth century Japanese monk and essayist, understood: "If man were never to fade away like the dews of Adashino, never to vanish like the smoke over Toribeyama, but lingered on forever in the world, how things would lose their power to move us" (7)! Like Issa's frog, we find ourselves chin-deep in a world that owes much of its beauty to the fact that nothing in it will last. Humans and frogs abide here for only a short time to enjoy life's textures, colors, sounds, smells, shapes, and flavors. In this particular scene, is the frog aware or impervious to the fragile delicateness of the fallen cherry petals? Most people would probably surmise that frogs are no more interested in the beauty of flowers than the dogs portrayed in previous examples. Nevertheless, Issa invites his readers to at least wonder about a frog's consciousness, which in itself constitutes a giant step toward acknowledging its essential value.

Once we begin to accept Issa's premise that animals, on some level, notice and respond to the colors, shapes, and smells of the world as pleasures beyond the survival imperative; our vision of the world and its creatures transforms. Planet Earth becomes suddenly a place vibrantly alive with consciousness, as animals, our fellow travelers, celebrate and revel in nature's splendor alongside us. The sparrows in the next haiku, for example, seem to share Issa's joy at the blooming of a flower.

咲ぼたん一日雀鳴にけり (1809; *IZ* 1.394)
saku botan ichi nichi suzume naki ni keri

the peony has bloomed!
the whole day
sparrows chirping

And a monkey, Issa suggests, enjoys it as much as humans do when spring's blossoms unfurl.

大江戸や芸なし猿も花の春 (1810; *IZ* 1.28)
ōedo ya geinashi-zaru mo hana no haru

great Edo –
even for a monkey without tricks
spring blossoms

The blooming of a peony and chirping of sparrows may seem unconnected to some readers, but Issa purposefully links them in his poem, intimating that the opening of a summer flower may be the cause of celebration for birds. Whether this is literally true is beside the point; Issa paints a picture of the universe in which the heart strings of animals are tugged hard by nature's splendors, giving his readers greater cause to identify and empathize with their fellow creatures. In the second haiku the shogun's city appears splendid in springtime, a fact that Issa repeats in many poems. The difference in the present scene is that even a "monkey without tricks" (*geinashi-zaru* 芸なし猿) sees and seems to appreciate the glorious textures and colors. Readers familiar with Issa's penchant for multiplying layers of meaning might suspect with good cause that the "monkey without tricks" is not only a real monkey but also, figuratively, the poet himself.

In this next haiku, has blooming bush clover drawn a cat, as it has Issa, to stop at a roadside inn?

のら猫も宿と定る萩の花 (1811; *IZ* 1.573)
nora neko mo yado to sadamuru hagi no hana

the stray cat also
picks this inn . . .
bush clover blooming

The stray cat "also" (*mo* も) chooses the inn where autumn flowers are blooming, implying that there is a human in the scene who has done the same, most probably Issa. The cat and the poet are both wanderers, sharing the same deep connection that we noted earlier in our discussion of poems about wandering geese and that feline devotee of the God of Wandering. The cat in this haiku and Issa are essentially the same: resting from their travels for a while in a pleasant place where bush clover blooms. Issa's joke, as usual, coaxes us to contemplate the serious possibility that even a cat, on some level, may be stirred by the beauty of flowers. Merely to consider this possibility is important, for it requires us to set aside our stereotyped image of animals as being lesser, unconscious, and inconsequential.

Sometimes Issa presents animals with what seems to be purposeful ambiguity. For example, in this next haiku, does the frog's wide-open mouth imply a sense of awe at the delicate beauty of the falling flowers, or might he be yawning with boredom? Or—a third possibility—does he regard the flitting petals as potential food?

ちる花を口明て待かはづ哉 (1808; *IZ* 1.158)
chiru hana wo kuchi akete matsu kawazu kana

his mouth open
for the falling blossoms . . .
a frog

Issa lets his readers arrive at their own conclusions, but the first interpretation—that the frog gapes in wonderment at the beauty of the scene—is certainly on the table in light of Issa's many other haiku that present animals appreciating nature's glory, especially in the form of blossoms. This theme crops up in a later haiku, again couched in ambiguity, about another frog and a different flower.

山吹の御味方申す蛙かな (1812; *IZ* 1.159)
yamabuki no o-mikata mōsu kawazu kana

the yellow rose's
honorable ally . . .
a frog

*Yamabuki*山吹 has two meanings in Japanese: a type of yellow rose and an old gold coin, otherwise known as a *koban* 小判. Literally, the *yamabuki* of the haiku is a spring flower, but its other meaning as a coin adds a satirical resonance. The samurai-frog gallantly or avariciously pledges his support to the golden rose/coin, possibly because of its beauty, possibly because his sword is for sale to the highest bidder.

Issa is perhaps the first poet in the world to suggest that even a chicken has a connoisseur's eye for nature's splendors.

鶏の抱かれて見たるぼたん哉 (1819; *IZ* 1. 395)
niwatori no dakarete mitaru botan kana

sitting on her eggs
the hen admires
the peony

Animal behavioral scientists report on the inquisitiveness and intelligence of chickens. Two centuries ago, Issa went a step further, asking us to consider the possibility that a mother hen might pass her time looking at and enjoying a peony's color and shape. Following his typical modus operandi, Issa's humorous depiction of an animal invites his readers to acknowledge an animal's consciousness and at least to wonder what the contents of that consciousness might include.

In an earlier haiku that we considered, a buck longed to eat an iris just out of reach, suggesting that its value, for the animal, was strictly culinary. In this next example, Issa shows a deer adopting a more art-for-art's-sake attitude.

さをしかの桜を見てや角落る (1813; *IZ* 1.125)
saoshika no sakura wo mite ya tsuno otsuru

the buck looks
at cherry blossoms . . .
shedding his antlers

In my World Literature class at Xavier University of Louisiana, I occasionally ask students to pick one of Issa's haiku and expound on it. Recently, a group of such students picked this poem to present. Their insightful explication goes as follows (I paraphrase):

The buck literally loses his antlers, but there's a deeper symbolism. Antlers are used to fight for a mate, so they stand for aggression, but shedding antlers implies a softer, gentler, benevolent attitude—just right for viewing cherry blossoms.

My students are correct to equate the shedding of antlers with the end of rutting season. No longer needing their imposing antlers to fight off rivals in defense of mates and territory, bucks in this peaceful time of year shed these weapons. The intensity and struggle of the rut give way to a more liesurely time that, as my students note, is perfectly conducive to blossom-viewing. Issa hints that the buck in this more relaxed frame of mind gazes at and, it would seem, *appreciates* the dazzling pink or white blossoms. The deer's mating season is over, but the cherry trees' precious weeks of blooming and pollination are at their peak. Soon, like the buck's antlers, the blossoms, too, will fall . . . but life goes on. Issa loads his poem with rich symbolism and resonance, but its ultimate effect, in my view, is to challenge readers to see the universe through the eyes of a fellow creature.

Issa wrote the above haiku in First Month, 1813. The seventh verse that follows in his journal presents yet another contemplative animal gazing at natural beauty, in this case, a frog.

いうぜんとして山を見る蛙哉 (1813; *IZ* 1.159)
iuzen to shite yama wo miru kawazu kana

serene and still
the mountain-viewing
frog

The haiku appears without a head note, but Issa copied it six years later in his poetic journal *Oraga haru* with this prose preface: "In the summer evening, spreading my straw mat, I call 'Lucky! Lucky!' and soon he comes crawling out from his nook in the thicket, enjoying the evening cool just like a person" (*IZ* 6.143). "Lucky" (*fuku*), as we noted earlier, is a colloquialism and a pet name for toads, suggesting that many of Issa's "frogs" (*kawazu* 蛙) might actually be toads. In any case, the first and second phrases of the poem echo a well-known, pre-

Tang Dynasty Chinese verse by Tao Qian 陶潛 (also known as Tao Yuanming 陶淵明). His poem, "I Built My House Near Where Others Dwell," has the lines: "I pluck chrysanthemums under the eastern hedge/ And gaze afar towards the southern mountains" (66). The ancient Chinese poem is about a hermit poet gazing at distant mountains and soaring birds, sensing within these sights an ineffable "hint of Truth" (66). Tao Qian's tone is serene and refined, but Issa comically shatters this tone in the concluding phrase of his parody, descending swiftly from classical heights down to . . . a frog. However, like so often with Issa, the joke might not be *only* a joke, for the serene hermit-frog in Issa's vision of reality is on the path to Buddhist enlightenment—an idea that we will explore further in Chapter 4. For now, we can note that these poetic images of a mountain-gazing frog and a blossom-gazing buck drive home the notion that animals, on some level, might be attuned to nature's beauty and grandeur.

A frog, in Issa's view of things, can look up at the full moon as well as any haiku poet may do.

元の座について月見る蛙哉 (1820; *IZ* 1.163)
moto no za ni tsuite tsuki miru kawazu kana

in his regular seat
for moon gazing . . .
a frog

And, he notes elsewhere, a frog gazing skyward can notice a star.

一ッ星見つけたやうになく蛙 (1814; *IZ* 1.160)
hitotsu boshi mi-tsuketa yō ni naku kawazu

like he just now
spotted a star . . .
croaking frog

Issa writes that the frog is singing "as if" or "like" (yō ni
やうに) he has suddenly caught sight of a star. Of course,
biologists who inform us of the frog's poor eyesight might
doubt that such a creature could possibly notice such dim,
distant light. One suspects, however, that Issa, if
presented with this challenge, would smile. The deeper
truth of his not purely whimsical poem is that frogs, just
as much as humans, are fully part of this universe and, in
their way, might appreciate its wonders. Moreover,
human beings grow in their own humanity largely to the
extent that they grow in their empathy, in this case,
learning to imagine how other creatures view this world
and cosmos.

IV. Animal artists

Earlier, we looked at a haiku in which Issa equated a
cuckoo's act of singing with the making of poetry,
suggesting that animals not only appreciate beauty but
can create it.

俳諧を囀るやうなかんこ鳥 (1814; IZ 1.349)
haikai wo saezuru yōna kankodori

like warbling pure haiku
mountain
cuckoo

Written in Third Month, the last month of spring in the
old Japanese calendar, this haiku has a one-word preface

in Issa's journal: "Summer" (*natsu* 夏), for its focus is the song of a summer bird, the *kankodori* 閑古鳥 or Himalayan cuckoo. (I refer to this bird as a "mountain cuckoo" in my translations to distinguish it from the "little cuckoo" or *hototogisu*.) The cuckoo's name in Japanese, as in English, is an onomatopoetic approximation of its song, *kankodori* signifying "the *kanko* bird," whose distinctive call sounds to Japanese ears like *kakkō-kakkō*. Today, it is more commonly known, simply, as the *kakkō* 郭公. In his haiku, Issa recognizes a brother poet in the cuckoo, specifically a brother haiku poet. Before writing this off as anthropomorphic fantasy, the reader might consider that, like a good haiku, the cuckoo's song is a one-breath burst of consistent length tied to a particular season. Moreover, it is an eloquent expression of what might be considered emotion, if we admit that the primal desire for a mate is, to a bird, a feeling. If poetry is a musical language that expresses feeling and thought, the cuckoo's call perfectly fits this definition, for it is a structured sequence of tones that communicate the same basic urge that moved Petrarch to write sonnets for Laura.

In a similar poem, Issa recognizes the poetic talent of an owl.

梟も一句侍れ此時雨 (1816; *IZ* 1.658)
fukurō mo ikku hanbere kono shigure

you too, owl
dedicate a haiku . . .
this winter rain

The phrase, "this winter rain" (*kono shigure* 此時雨), alludes to the death anniversary of Bashō in Tenth Month. On this day, every poet worth his salt composes a verse in Bashō's honor. Issa invites an owl—another short-form poet, like the cuckoo—to join in.

Birds are not the only animal poets in Issa's universe. Frogs also receive this recognition.

星の歌よむつらつきの蛙かな (1826; *IZ* 1.500)
hoshi no uta yomu tsura tsuki no kawazu kana

looks like he's composing
a "Star Poem" . . .
the frog

This haiku refers to the Tanabata Festival, which, as we noted earlier, honors two celestial lovers who one night of the year cross the Milky Way's starry river to be together. In honor of these lovers, a "Star Poem" (*hoshi no uta* 星の歌) is written on mulberry leaves. In Issa's comic haiku, a frog has an intent expression of concentration on his face, as if composing his own poem. In a similar vein, a decade earlier Issa wrote,

西行のやうに居て鳴蛙 (1816; *IZ* 1.160)
saigyō no yō ni suwatte naku kawazu

like Saigyō
squatting, croaking
frog

Saigyō Hōshi, we have noted, was a famous Japanese poet-monk of the twelfth century whose many wanderings inspired Issa's own haiku-writing journeys. In one journal in which he describes himself setting off on a poetic trek, Issa writes,

When I hung a beggar's satchel around my neck and hoisted a little cloth-wrapped bundle onto my back, I saw that my shadow was looking laudable, like Saigyō's. But our hearts so completely opposite:

139

his, white as snow; and mine, the sleeve of a black robe."[33]

In the above haiku, Issa pays a frog the supreme compliment of comparing him to the great, pure-hearted Saigyō. The iconoclastic depiction of a squatting, singing frog as a venerable poet of Japanese tradition is sure to raise smiles. One wonders, though: By elevating a frog to Saigyō's level, does Issa also, at the same time, lower the great poet to the status of a frog, thereby suggesting that his honored poetry is nothing better than a frog's croaking? Once again, Issa's joke raises questions. Who is to say that human poetry is any better, any more *important* than frog song? Who can say that frogs do not also have their Saigyōs, their Shakespeares, their Issa's? Issa helps his readers to imagine a universe with a level playing field on which a haiku is no better, no worse, than a cuckoo's call or a frog's croak.

In his prose-and-haiku journal, *Oraga haru*, Issa notes that frogs can not only be poets but also judges of poetry. As we saw earlier, in a prose head note for his haiku about a "mountain-viewing frog," Issa writes about a particular frog that on summer evenings boldly crawls out of a thicket to join him, enjoying the cool air like a person. He then alludes to the book, *Mushi uta awase* 虫歌合 ("Poetry Contest of the Insects") by Chōshōshi 長嘯子 (1569-1649), in which a toad serves as the judge of a *waka* contest involving insects.[34] We can imagine Issa relating this "fact" with a smile, especially when he goes on to note that the experience, for the world's frogs, was—as Yuasa puts it in his charming translation of the passage— "the crowning glory of their race" (72). Once again Issa's humor leads the reader to reflection and insight: if frogs create one-breath poetry in their mating calls, they surely must be able to discriminate good croaking from bad croaking; their chances of attracting lady frogs, after all, depend entirely on their "poetic" sensibility.

In addition to animal poets, animal singers also appear in Issa's collection of haiku portraits. In the following examples he describes bird calls using the verb *utau* (諷ふ; 唄ふ) and the noun *uta* (唄), "sing" and "song"—words normally applied to human activity.

君が代を鶏も諷ふや餅の臼 (1803; *IZ* 1.52)
kimi ga yo wo tori mo utau ya mochi no usu

the rooster also sings
to Great Japan . . .
on the rice cake mill

君が代を雀も唄へそりの唄 (1806; *IZ* 1.693)
kimi ga yo wo suzume mo utae sori no uta

"Great Japan!"
join the snow sled song
sparrows

椋鳥が唄ふて走る小春哉 (1813; *IZ* 1. 613)
mukudori ga utōte hashiru ko haru kana

the gray starling
rushes his song . . .
a spring day in winter

明六を鳩も諷ふや春の雨 (1818; *IZ* 1.71)
akemutsu wo hato mo utau ya haru no ame

the pigeon too
sings at six a.m.
spring rain

In the first haiku, a rooster sings a New Year's praise-song to the emperor's reign: *kimi ga yo* 君が代, a phrase that begins the Japanese national anthem. In the second haiku, Issa invites sparrows to join in this same patriotic song, now being sung by sled riders. In the third, a gray starling rushes his song on a spring-like winter's day, and in the fourth, a pigeon sings at the time of *akemutsu* 明六, which roughly corresponds to six in the morning (*KD* 20). The rooster's crow, the sparrows' chirp, the starling's call, and the pigeons' coo all are presented in these haiku as songs (*uta*), indicating that Issa considers their crowing, chirping, calling, and cooing to be musical efforts.

As with any music, birdsong can be good or bad, depending on the skills of the particular performer. In these next four haiku, Issa chides the poor singing of certain nightingales (*uguisu* 鶯). He describes their songs with the word *heta* 下手: "unskilled" or "not good," translated here as "off key."

窓あれば下手鶯も来たりけり (1804; *IZ* 1.131)
mado areba heta uguisu mo kitari keri

to every window
an off-key nightingale
comes too

痩藪の下手鶯もはつ音哉 (1804; *IZ* 1.131)
yase yabu no heta uguisu mo hatsu ne kana

in a sparse thicket
an off-key nightingale too . . .
first song

来るも来るも下手鶯よ窓の梅 (1804; *IZ* 1.193)
kuru mo kuru mo heta uguisu yo mado no ume

one by one they come
off-key nightingales
to the plum blossom window

鳴けよ鳴けよ下手でもおれが鶯ぞ (1813; *IZ* 1.133)
nake yo nake yo heta demo ore ga uguisu zo

sing! sing!
though off key
my nightingale

In the final example and several others in my online
archive, I translate the command form of *naku* (*nake* なけ)
as, "Sing!"—even though in Japanese the verb more
specifically denotes a kind of animal call: a goose's honk,
a duck's quack, or, in this case, a nightingale's warble.
One might argue that a translation of *nake* as "Sing!" adds
a semantic feature not found in Issa's Japanese, injecting
an anthropomorphism not evident in the original. I reject
this argument based on two reasons: my reading of other
haiku, such as the earlier-cited ones in which Issa
understands the calls of animals to be esthetic acts,
referring to them as *uta* ("song" in the human sense); and
the fact that birdsong can be "off key" or "poorly done"
(*heta*) in Issa's opinion means that birds are performers
whose performances should be judged on the basis of
esthetic criteria. In Issa's universe a nightingale doesn't
simply "warble" or "trill"; he *sings*.

In the same vein, Issa brings an attitude of
discriminating connoisseur to evaluate the singing of
autumn insects.

世の中や鳴虫にさへ上づ下手 (1820; *IZ* 1.538)
yo no naka ya naku mushi ni sae jyōzu heta

in this world
among insects too . . .
good singers, bad singers

Like people, like insects: not everyone is a virtuoso.
However, some insects deserve our admiration not just
for their musical talent but for their tenacious dedication
to their art, as in the following poems.

虫干や吹かれて鳴やきりぎりす (1814; *IZ* 1.317)
mushiboshi ya fukarete naku ya kirigirisu

airing out the bedding –
he's blown away, still singing
katydid

仰のけに寝て鳴にけり秋の蝉 (1816; *IZ* 1.540)
aonoke ni nete naki ni keri aki no semi

lying belly-up
yet still singing . . .
autumn cicada

きりぎりす紙袋にて鳴にけり (1818; *IZ* 1.549)
kirigirisu kamibukuro nite naki ni keri

the katydid
in the paper bag . . .
still singing

きりぎりす売られ行手で鳴にけり (1821; *IZ* 1.549)
kirigirisu urare yukute de naki ni keri

katydid –
on his way to being sold
still singing

鳴ながら虫の乗行浮木かな (1822; *IZ* 1.538)
naki nagara mushi no noriyuku ukigi kana

> still singing the insect
> is swept away . . .
> floating branch

The last example is perhaps the most dramatic and poignant. Issa introduces it with the head note, "Flood" (*kozui* 洪水). The insect may be floating to his death, yet he keeps singing. Perhaps Issa sees himself in the insect; perhaps he sees in it the fate of all living creatures, for all are equally, eventually doomed. The important thing isn't the inevitable death to which the currents of the universe sweep us; what matters, Issa implies, is to embrace the present moment . . . and sing.

Animals also dance in Issa's poetry. We have already considered his haiku of 1806 in which a butterfly dances among summer flowers. Two decades earlier, in 1788 when Issa was just twenty-six, he wrote his first haiku on the topic of butterflies (or, perhaps, a single butterfly) dancing.

舞蝶にしばしは旅も忘けり (1788; *IZ* 1.165)
mau chō ni shibashi wa tabi mo wasure keri

> dancing butterflies –
> my journey forgotten
> for a while

This lovely vision appears in a collection titled *Fifty-three Post Towns* (*Gojūsan eki* 五十三駅), referring to post towns along the Tōkaidō highway from Edo to Kyoto: towns where travelers could spend the night and, if on horseback, continue the next day with fresh horses. Issa's perception in this haiku is a common one: the delicate, whirling flight of butterflies appears, to human eyes, as dance. If one considers the question deeply, to call butterfly flight "dance" might not be an anthropomorphic fantasy. Renowned scholar of dance history, Curt Sachs, notes that apes such as chimpanzees dance in the true sense of the word with rhythmical foot-stamping, whirling, hopping, head-bobbing, and forward and backward paces (11). He goes on to observe that an early form of human dance still performed by cultural groups, the so-called "mimetic dance," rigidly imitates the movements of animals in rituals intended to cause life-sustaining animals to flourish and to ensure successful hunting (57). Reflecting on the evolution of human dance, Sachs describes a "great process of change which has gradually transformed the dance from an involuntary motor discharge, from a state of frenzied movement and a ceremonial rite, into a work of art conscious of and intended for observation" (218). The dancer's knowledge that he or she is dancing is, therefore, a later development in its history. Dancers danced, Sachs argues, before they were aware of it or invented a word for it. Jamake Highwater further describes dance as, originally, a "primal activity" that emerged as "a complex extension of animal impulses" (39-40). In light of Sachs' and Highwater's speculations, one might reasonably conclude that many animals dance, whether conscious of it or not, and that human dance developed in large part through imitation of the movements of fellow creatures. The butterflies that help Issa forget his journey transport themselves through space, moving from flower to flower; we can safely assume that they are not trying to embody a message. Nevertheless, they are dancing in the sense of movement caused by "animal impulses," and this dancing, to human eyes, is beautiful. Whether they know it or not (and one suspects that they don't know it) butterflies dance, and *because* they dance, Issa reminds us, yet again, animals are not very different from people.

In Issa's poetry butterflies dance, sparrows dance, and, at times, they dance together.

起よ起よ雀はをどる蝶はまふ (1812; *IZ* 1.168)
oki yo oki yo suzume wa odoru chō wa mau

wake up! wake up!
sparrows, butterflies
are dancing

In a magical autumn scene a kitten dances with falling leaves.

猫の子のくるくる舞やちる木の葉 (1820; *IZ* 1.730)
neko no ko no kuru-kurumai ya chiru konoha

the kitten dances
round and round . . .
falling leaves

In the next haiku, Issa urges a frog to dance.

其声で一つをどれよなく蛙 (1819; *IZ* 1.162)
sono koe de hitotsu odore yo naku kawazu

as long as you're singing
go ahead, dance!
frog

And even fleas dance, Issa claims, in his little house.

よい日やら蚤がをどるぞはねるぞよ (1813; *IZ* 1.377)
yoi hi yara nomi ga odoru zo haneru zo yo

a good day, eh?
fleas dancing
and hopping

In the next example, Issa imagines a butterfly dancing to musical accompaniment: the plucking of a samisen, a long-necked, three-stringed banjo-like instrument plucked with a plectrum.

舞は蝶三弦流布の小村也 (1818; *IZ* 1.172)
mau wa chō samisen rufu no ko mura nari

butterfly dance –
someone plays samisen
in the little village[35]

The butterfly's dance, of course, does not directly connect to the music of the samisen, at least not in the same way that a human dancer's movements respond to a song's rhythm and flow. The deeper truth of the poem, however, is that butterflies and people share the music of the world and, consciously or not, dance to it. A little over a century later, Irish poet William Butler Yeats writes the lines, "O body swayed to music, O brightening glance,/ How can we know the dancer from the dance" (117)? Issa's vision of a harmoniously interconnected universe in which life responds to other life, in which a butterfly flits to the tune of a samisen, perhaps answers Yeats's profound question. Issa and his readers can see the butterfly as both dancer and dance. The butterfly doesn't need to realize that it participates in a universal dance—of atoms, molecules, spirals of genetic code, star-born energy, and intrinsic physical and biological connection—because not knowing these things is part of the role it plays.

Issa's portrayals of animals as creators of beauty reinforce his perennial theme that they are more like humans than most people realize. His poems narrow the perceived distance between human and nonhuman inhabitants of this planet, inspiring his readers to adopt, as he has done, a warmly compassionate appreciation of animals that are (whether they realize it consciously or not) poets, singers, and dancers. Issa's portraits of animal artists, animal parents, animal workers, animals at play, and animals excited by nature's beauty are not shallowly anthropomorphic; they are deeply realistic poetic sketches of a broader reality of animal existence that many people, indoctrinated to believe in human exceptionalism, fail to acknowledge.

Chapter 3. WHERE ANIMALS BELONG

In the previous chapter we considered a few haiku in which animals venture indoors to join Issa in his winter seclusion, including a cricket and a "mum-eating" bug or worm. Animals share human spaces and involve themselves in human activities throughout Issa's poetry. Most of the time these encounters are superficially comic while sparking a deeper insight that people and animals belong together. One might construe Issa's cricket and flower-eating *mushi* as intruders in his human habitat, but in Issa's presentation of such scenes no one is intruding. The animals and Issa cohabitate. The question of which one of them owns the house or pays the rent, of such importance to people, is immaterial. When a spider builds a web in one of the corners in his home, Issa writes,

隅の蜘案じな煤はとらぬぞよ (1821; *IZ* 1.669)
sumi no kumo anjina susu wa toranu zo yo

corner spider[36]
rest easy, my soot-broom
is idle

We smile at Issa's laziness. Fortunately for the spider, the poet depicts himself as a poor housekeeper who neglects the domestic chore of winter soot-sweeping. Beneath this comic self-portrait, however, one detects a feeling of tenderness toward the spider. Issa's laziness might not be the only reason that his broom is idle. His tone can be construed to be one of affection for a tiny creature whose life, he recognizes, has value.

When Issa prepares rice cakes in his "secluded house" (*kakurega* かくれ家), these treats are guarded, he claims, by resident cats.

かくれ家や猫が三疋もちのばん (1820; *IZ* 1.674)
kakurega ya neko ga sambiki mochi no ban

secluded house –
three cats guard
the rice cakes

Issa's humor, again, arises from a deeper sentiment. While we can safely assume that the cats have no real interest in guarding rice cakes from thieves, the poem tacitly acknowledges that they belong in the secluded house as much as the poet does. His cakes are their cakes.

In a similar haiku Issa playfully suggests that a chicken will stand guard over his newly grafted tree.

鶏の番をしているつぎ木哉 (1813; *IZ* 1.119)
niwatori no ban wo shite iru tsugiki kana

the chicken
is standing guard . . .
my grafted tree

He has painstakingly joined the base or rootstock of one fruit tree with the scion or upper part of another. Now, satisfied that his work is done, he leaves the tree to its biological task but not before assigning (at least in his mind) a chicken to watch over it. The guard-chicken, even more nonsensical than a guard-cat, raises a smile, but beneath Issa's humor lies a reminder that the chicken, too, has a stake in the tree's future. The latter will grow, blossom, and produce fruit, some of which will ripen and fall for the chicken's pecking pleasure. The chicken belongs in this space and deserves to reap its seasonal rewards as much as does Issa.

In one poem Issa opens his home even to bats, but for a good reason.

我宿に一夜たのむぞ蚊喰鳥 (1825; *IZ* 1.335)
waga yado ni hito yo tanomu zo ka kui tori

I entrust my home
for the night
to mosquito-eating bats

Literally, he welcomes in the "mosquito-eating birds" (*ka kui tori* 蚊喰鳥), a Japanese euphemism for bats. While many people would be upset to have such visitors, Issa, plagued by mosquitoes, perceives the flying rodents as valuable company. In related poems, he entrusts his abode and possessions to a Himalayan cuckoo (*kankodori*) and to a puppy.

帰る迄庵の番せよ閑古鳥 (1817; *IZ* 1.349)
kaeru made io no ban seyo kankodori

till I return
guard my hut . . .
mountain cuckoo

犬ころが火入れの番や夕涼み (1818; *IZ* 1.323)
inukoro ga hi-ire no ban ya yūsuzumi

the puppy guards
my pipe lighting tool . . .
evening cool

In Issa's day a *hi-ire* 火入れ was a small ceramic holder used to pick up a burning charcoal with which to light one's pipe (*KD* 1373). Of course, the puppy has no interest in pipe smoking or its utensils except, perhaps, to gnaw on them, nor does a mate-seeking cuckoo concern himself with the comings and goings of a hut's human owner. They are not *intentionally* the guardians of Issa's objects or home. However, by assigning them this role the poet suggests that these animals belong in and around his living space. There is no sharp dividing line between the human property line and the territorial one of animals. The two interpenetrate in Issa's poetic vision. Issa's home is the puppy's; Issa's yard is the cuckoo's.

As if to underscore this point, the dividing wall between indoors and outdoors in Issa's house is porous, allowing for the comings and goings of all sorts of creatures.

うす壁や鼠穴よりみそさざい (1822; *IZ* 1.716)
usu kabe ya nezumi ana yori misosazai

thin wall –
from the mouse's hole
a wren!

This is one of Issa's most delightful haiku surprises that, beyond its humorous punch line, speaks volumes about his attitude toward animals. He not only maintains an open door policy for nonhuman guests; he has an "open wall" policy as well, suggesting once again that his domestic space is not exclusively his. In fact, his guests are not guests, if we believe, as Issa repeatedly leads us to believe, that he and animals share a common space. As a haiku poet, he delights in the surprises that the universe offers with open-eyed, open-minded receptivity. This esthetic attitude of joyful acceptance is perhaps at least partly responsible for the feeling of welcome rather than

annoyance perceivable in this portrait of a little bird entering the poet's house through a hole.

Issa writes some marvelous haiku about the large
sitting room (*ōzashiki* 大座敷) of a house or, perhaps, a
Buddhist temple; and the animal visitors that pass
through it as if they have as much right to the place as the
humans who built it.

昼ごろや雉の歩く大座敷 (1813; *IZ* 1.148)
hiru goro ya kigisu no aruku ōzashiki

around noon a pheasant
passes through . . .
the big sitting room

山蝉や鳴々抜る大座敷 (1813; *IZ* 1.383)
yama semi ya naki naki nukeru ōzashiki

mountain cicada –
singing, singing passes through
the big sitting room

The middle phrase of the second haiku has a playfully
alliterative sound in Japanese to match the playfulness of
the image: *naki naki nukeru* 鳴々抜る ("singing, singing
passes through"). Both the pheasant and the mountain
cicada lay claim to the supposedly human space, unfazed
by the presence of the observing poet. The first boldly
struts through; the second crosses the tatami mat while
chirring for a mate. The human-made room, suddenly,
reveals itself to be a wild place. In a third example, Issa
presents the most incongruous visitor of all.

入梅や蟹かけ歩大座敷 (1817; *IZ* 1.259)
nyūbai ya kani kake-aruku ōzashiki

rainy season –
a crab strolls into
the big sitting room

The rainy season has erased the boundary between dry
land and sea. In this world of flooding and puddles, a
crab scuttles into the sitting room, following the path
blazed for it in earlier poems by a pheasant and a cicada.
Even a sea creature claims the room as its own, at least
for the moment. The deeper effect of these micro-
comedies is to call into question the supposed separation
between civilization and nature. In Issa's imagination,
planet Earth is a living space shared by all.[37]

Issa usually appears in haiku self-portraits as an accepting, welcoming roommate for the nonhuman inhabitants of his house.

庵の蚤かはいや我といぬる也 (1812; *IZ* 1.377)
io no nomi kawai ya ware to inuru nari

my hut's fleas
how cute!
they sleep with me

狭くともいざ飛習へ庵の蚤 (1814; *IZ* 1.378)
semaku to mo iza tobinarae io no nomi

though it's cramped
practice your jumping!
hut's fleas

In one haiku, however, he confesses to the inhospitable
act of flea-killing.

あばれ蚤我手にかかつて成仏せよ (1813; *IZ* 1.377)
abare nomi waga te ni kakatte jōbutsu seyo

155

> pesky flea
> caught in my hand
> become a Buddha!

As he ends its life he humorously attempts to justify the deed as an act of compassion, claiming that he is hastening the flea's karmic evolution toward becoming a Buddha. Even Issa's most pious Buddhist readers must recognize the hollowness of such an excuse, and we should assume that the poet did as well. The haiku is a self-ironic reflection of a man who sins for a selfish reason (the flea has been "pesky": *abare*あばれ), then seeks to cover up his transgression with a religious excuse. On a deeper level, Issa is admitting to an essential truth about human nature that Shinran, the founder of Jōdoshinshū Buddhism, avowed: that people are corrupt; sin is inevitable.

His more typical attitude vis-à-vis the fleas in his abode is one of "Live and let live," as shown in the first two examples above. Fleas are his "cute" (*kawai* かはい) bedmates in the first poem, and in the second he encourages them to practice their jumping with due caution about the narrowness of his room, lest they bump their tiny heads. In the vast majority of his scores of haiku about fleas, Issa expresses a similar concern for their wellbeing. In one such verse, he provides potentially lifesaving advice, should the flea in question happen to understand Japanese.

> とぶな蚤それそれそこが角田川 (1819; *IZ* 1.378)
> *tobu na nomi sore-sore soko ga sumida-gawa*

> don't jump flea!
> that's Sumida River
> over there

Though most people view fleas as undesirable pests, Issa usually regards them as intimate comrades in haiku that, while admittedly comic, nevertheless suggest that their lives have value. He even learns to appreciate the subtle thumping music of their leaping and landing in the darkness of his room.

夜の庵や蚤の飛ぶ音騒々し (1822; *IZ* 1.379)
yo no io ya nomi no tobu oto sōzōshi

evening hut –
the fleas jumping
bumpity-bump

Not many people are willing to accept Issa's suggestion that a flea has a point of view and a right to live. When I prepared an anthology of his haiku for an English-Hindi edition, my collaborator, Angelee Deodhar, advised me to keep our book, *The Distant Mountain*, flealess. Indian readers, she said, would not appreciate Issa's sympathetic treatment of "vermin." I complied with Angelee's advice, though it underscored for me an important implication of Issa's poetic treatment of animals that many people are not ready or willing to understand: that even the smallest and least desirable among living creatures are fellow travelers deserving our compassion.

Like fleas, katydids—an autumn insect in haiku—also occasionally found themselves spending their nights in Issa's living space.

庵の夜や棚捜しするきりぎりす (1810; *IZ* 1.547)
io no yo ya tana sagashi suru kirigirisu

night in the hut –
a katydid forages
for food

きりぎりす庵の柱をかじりけり (1816; *IZ* 1.549)
kirigirisu io no hashira wo kajiri keri

the katydid
on my hut's post
gnawing away

寝返りをするぞそこのけきりぎりす (1816; *IZ* 1.549)
negaeri wo suru zo soko noke kirigirisu

turning over in bed –
move aside!
katydid

In the first haiku, the phrase *tana sagashi suru* 棚捜しする, "searching for something on the shelf," denotes, in this context, "looking for something to eat." The katydid helps himself to whatever he can find to eat in the house. This might include Issa's food or, as Issa writes in the second haiku, the house itself, as a hungry katydid gnaws on the "hut's post" (*io no hashira* 庵の柱). The third haiku, the most comic, shows Issa once again sharing his futon with a tiny visitor, whom he solicitously warns before turning over. We smile but also learn a lesson in gentleness.

In his poetry Issa often presents animals as friendly and sociable. A butterfly flits from gate to gate, as if paying social calls to the people in the neighborhood.

門々を一々巡る小てふ哉 (1806; *IZ* 1.166)
kado kado wo ichi-ichi meguru ko chō kana

gate after gate
making the rounds . . .
little butterfly

As usual, Issa constructs the poem like a joke. Its first two phrases, "Gate after gate/ making the rounds," set up an expectation of human activity and human agency. Then, in the third phrase, he surprises us by presenting a "little butterfly" (*ko chō* 小てふ) as the scene's busy protagonist. On the surface he simply replays his favorite haiku jest of showing animals in human terms. Deeper, however, he suggests the consciousness and autonomy of the insect. A butterfly has places to go, people to see. In addition, because it approaches its fellow creatures with gentle friendliness, it becomes more than a peer for the humans who live behind the gates; it becomes an ideal, a role model. Issa repeats this image of a "social butterfly" in an undated composition.[38]

一人茶や蝶は毎日来てくれる (undated; *IZ* 1.168)
hitori cha ya chō wa mainichi kite kureru

drinking tea alone –
every day the butterfly
stops by

Animals populate Issa's world in haiku, appearing as participants in seasonally based human rituals, beginning with New Year's celebrations. He perceives and portrays the excitement of a new year, new spring, even in the faces of horses and cows.

古郷や馬も元日いたす顔 (1810; *IZ* 1. 23)
furusato ya uma mo ganjitsu itasu kao

159

my home village –
even the horse
with a New Year's face

牛馬も元日顔の山家哉 (1810; *IZ* 1.23)
ushi uma mo ganjitsu kao no yamaga kana

even cows and horses
with New Year's faces . . .
mountain home

These portraits may seem merely the fanciful inventions of a poet: Issa projecting his own feeling of joy on spring's first day onto farm animals. We can safely assume that horses and cows had no idea that a new year had begun on a particular day marked on the calendars of the Japanese people of Issa's time. However, springtime with its promise of warmer weather and delicious (to horses and cows) plant life is something that such animals certainly sense, on some level, and definitely value. Issa captures their true perspective; he is not simply projecting his own onto them.

The participation of animals in scenes throughout the round of seasons reminds us that humans and other beings are equally affected by the natural cycles of life and, therefore, deserve to enjoy the fruits of these cycles. Accordingly, people are not alone in savoring special New Year's treats in Issa's poetic scenes.

かれらにも元日させん鳩すずめ (1814; *IZ* 1.23)
karera ni mo ganjitsu-sasen hato suzume

for them too
a New Year's feast . . .
pigeons, sparrows

Issa feeds birds on New Year's Day, so his haiku is factually accurate. Though they don't understand the reason, pigeons and sparrows receive extra food on this most auspicious day on the Japanese calendar. But deeper, as in his haiku about the horses and cows with New Year's faces, Issa reminds us that the season of plentiful food for *all* creatures has begun. His food-sharing signals not only his generosity but also a feeling of springtime optimism applicable to all concerned—birds and poet alike.

A cat also benefits on the day that the humans of Japan calculate to be the beginning of spring.

かくれ家や猫にも一ッ御年玉 (1819; *IZ* 1.41)
kakurega ya neko ni mo hitotsu o-toshidama

secluded house –
even for the cat
a New Year's gift

門礼や猫にとし玉打つける (1821; *IZ* 1.40)
kadorei ya neko ni toshidama uchi tsukeru

"Happy New Year!"
at the gate, tossing the cat
a present

In a related haiku, a sleeping cat sprawls on the New Year's presents intended for people, an image that reiterates Issa's conviction that animals belong, front and center, in our so-called human world. The cat world and the human world are, in fact, one in the same for Issa.

とし玉の上にも猫のぐる寝哉 (1821; *IZ* 1.41)
toshidama no ue ni mo neko no gurune kana

161

on top
of the New Year's gifts . . .
cat curled asleep

Japanese people cherish the start of a new year too much to celebrate it with only a single day's festivities. The first several weeks of a year constitute a New Year's season—separate from the usual four—full of celebrations and pastimes. Kite-flying is one of the latter but, as we see in this next haiku, not at all restricted to human beings.

猿引は猿に持せて凧 (1807; IZ 1.45)
saru hiki wa saru ni motasete ikanobori

the trainer lets
his monkey hold it . . .
New Year's kite

The monkey, at least in this moment of New Year's celebration, doesn't need to dance or perform tricks for the financial benefit of its human handler. Instead, it is allowed to hold the *ikanobori*凧, also called *tako*: a colorful traditional kite shaped like *ika* ("squid") or *tako* ("octopus"). Of all the citizens of Issa's poetic republic of animals, monkeys (specifically the macaques indigenous to Japan) most closely resemble people. It is fitting, then, that a monkey holds the kite just as any human adult or child might do. Issa's implication is that the joyous New Year's season belongs to the monkey as much as it does to its human trainer. For one splendid moment, in Issa's poetic vision, the two are perfectly equal.

In a haiku about another New Year's tradition, pigeons and sparrows mingle with human spectators.

万ざいや門に居ならぶ鳩雀 (1811; *IZ* 1.47)
manzai ya kado ni inarabu hato suzume

begging actors at the gate –
pigeons and sparrows
in a row

The haiku refers to *manzai* 万ざい, a traditional form of stand-up comedy in which two performers, a straight man and a jokester, travel from house to house to deliver messages from the gods in a routine filled with puns and misunderstandings. The birds, Issa notes, are present in the scene; in fact, they appear "seated in a row" (*inarabu* 居ならぶ) as if they are an attentive part of the comedians' audience. In another haiku of the same year, a horse receives a blessing from these same jokesters.

万歳や馬の尻へも一祝 (1811; *IZ* 1.47)
manzai ya uma no shiri e mo hito iwai

begging actors –
even the horse's rump
gets a blessing

The fact that the pigeons, the sparrows, and the horse will not understand the humor or physical antics of the *manzai* performers is immaterial. Issa recognizes and shows that they are fully part of these scenes, participants in a New Year's ritual that celebrates the new life of spring that, clearly, matters to them all, whether they know it or not.

In a haiku set in early springtime when plum trees bloom, a dog plays an important, though not starring, role.

梅さくや犬にまたがる桃太郎 (1813; *IZ* 1.197)
ume saku ya inu ni matagaru momotarō

plum blossoms –
riding a dog
the Peach Boy

According to a Japanese legend, an old woman was washing clothes in a river one day when she found a large floating peach. She took the peach home, thinking to eat it, but cutting it open, she and her husband amazingly discovered a little boy inside. They immediately adopted Momotarō, the Peach Boy. Momotarō became a great boy-hero whose most famous quest involved a journey to an island of devils, where he subdued the devils with the help of three animal allies: a dog, a monkey, and a pheasant. He returned triumphantly to his parents' home with hard-won treasure and the devil chief as his prisoner (Ozaki 244-61). Issa portrays a child riding a dog as this unstoppable hero of folklore. In two undated haiku, he rewrites the scene with slight variations. In one, the opening phrase is "peach blossoms" (*momo saku ya* 桃咲や) and the dog rider is a "naughty boy" (*akutarō*悪太郎); in the other, the blossoms are plum and the child is identified as "Golden Boy" (*kintarō* 金太郎).[39] Kintarō, the Golden Boy, is another boy-hero of folktales, an exaggerated depiction of the Heian Era samurai, Sakata no Kintoki, in his childhood. In all three versions of this haiku, the boy, a treasured child, rides a dog like a proud little warrior, the spring blossoms symbolically underscoring his youth and vigor. My Japanese advisor, Shinji Ogawa, notes that a doll of Kintarō riding a bear is a popular gift for the Boy's Festival of fifth day, Fifth Month. Changing the tiny hero's mount from bear to dog is a brilliant stroke of haiku humor. As so often is the case, Issa's joke reminds readers of an important, underlying truth: people *need* animals. Every great samurai needs a great "horse."

In another springtime scene Issa shows a butterfly lighting repeatedly on *kusamochi*草もち, a type of rice cake eaten during the Girl's Doll Festival, celebrated on the third day of Third Month.

蝶とまれも一度留れ草もちに (1816; *IZ* 1.170)
chō tomare mo ichi do tomare kusamochi ni

stop, butterfly
once more, stop!
on the festival rice cake

The butterfly apparently enjoys the sweet cake, suggesting that the festival is not for people alone. In another butterfly haiku Issa reiterates the idea that animals belong in scenes of seasonal human activity. In this case, the activity in question is the summer transplanting of rice stalks into flooded paddies.

早乙女におぶさつて寝る小てふ哉 (1824; *IZ* 1.328)
saotome ni obusatte neru ko chō kana

rice-planting girl –
on her back a butterfly
sleeps

The sight of a butterfly asleep on a girl's back visually reminds readers, especially readers of Issa's time and place, of a baby bundled on the back of his or her mother. In this way, the poet hints of a deep, family connection between peasant girl and sleeping insect.

In springtime the days grow longer, giving rise to a popular seasonal expression in haiku: "the long day" (*hi naga* 日永). In the following verse Issa suggests that people are not the only ones for whom the days are growing long.

165

鶏の人の顔見る日永哉 (1807; *IZ* 1.60)
niwatori no hito no kao miru hi naga kana

the chicken stares
at the man . . .
a long day

In an earlier example, we encountered a crow complaining that the day was "foolishly long." Here, a chicken says nothing but gives a man—presumably Issa—a hard, cold stare. Later, he writes similar haiku depicting "staring contests" with a frog (1819) and with a gargoyle (1824), but this early one is perhaps the funniest. The chicken gazes steadily at a man's face, as if holding him personally responsible for the long day. Or, perhaps the chicken simply stares without thought, mirroring the poet's own feeling of stasis and boredom. However we interpret the bird's stare, the haiku suggests that the lengthening of daylight hours, the topic of so many human poems, also affects chickens.

In a haiku about summer rice transplantation, a toad is just as much a part of the scene as its human participants.

大蟾ものさのさ出たり田植酒 (1822; *IZ* 1.328)
ōhiki mo nosa-nosa detari taue-zake

even a big toad
boldly joins the fun . . .
rice-planting sake

The haiku's key expression, *nosa-nosa* のさのさ, has several meanings in Issa's Japanese; in this case it denotes the performance of an action without dread.[40] While the rice planters enjoy their hard-earned rest, lubricating their ease with sake, a toad emerges from some nearby clump of vegetation as if expressly to join the party. Superficially, the haiku derives humor from the image of a toad at a human drinking party. On a deeper level, however, Issa reminds his readers that rice fields and their surroundings belong to the toad as much as they do to the planters. Even if the toad will not plant, reap, or partake of the sake being passed around, he boldly (*nosa-nosa*) joins the fun . . . for he, too, belongs there.

In Issa's early travelogue, *Saigoku kikō*, a snail participates, in its way, in a summer festival.

御旅所を吾もの顔やかたつぶり (1795; *IZ* 1.385)
o-tabisho wo waga mono-gao ya katatsuburi

temporary shrine –
acting like he owns it
a snail

This haiku has a head note in which Issa explains that at a place called Mitsu-no-mura, a purification ritual takes place each year in Sixth Month. *O-tabisho*御旅所signifies the temporary resting place for a portable shrine known as a *mikoshi* 神輿, an ornately decorated palanquin carried by the local men. On festival days, a god is transported inside the *mikoshi* from his or her usual shrine and installed somewhere along the route in an *o-tabisho*: a roofed, wooden structure. The snail in Issa's poem seems to be laying claim to this holy place; its face, Issa writes, looks as if it is saying, "This is mine!" (*waga mono-gao* 吾もの顔). The image is at once humorous and profound. A lowly snail substituting for a god in an *o-tabisho* seems the height of presumption. However, its quiet presence may suggest that the snail fully belongs amid these human festivities; after all, the god of the *mikoshi* is its god too. Beyond this idea, Issa might even be hinting that the

167

snail, in its humble way, *is* the god of the place. In Shinto belief all living creatures carry a divine spark in them—a topic to which we will return in the next chapter. For now, it is sufficient to note that the snail in the haiku not only belongs in the summer festival, it inhabits its most important, sacred space.

Turning now to autumn rituals, we again find animals figuring prominantly in Issa's haiku portraits. At the end of the rice-growing cycle, when the grain is ready for harvest, farmers break the dikes that kept their fields nicely flooded. In the following poem, a fish that lived in such a paddy all summer escapes with the draining water.

落し水魚も古郷へもどる哉 (1793; *IZ* 1. 513)
otoshi mizu uo mo kokyō e modoru kana

draining the rice field –
a fish also
heads home

Literally, the fish is returning to its "native village" (*kokyō* 古郷)—yet another playful example of Issa's portrayal of animal behavior in human terms. Moreover, he states that the fish goes home "also" (*mo* も), drawing the reader's attention to the fact that its return to the stream or lake of its origin parallels the journeys of itinerant farm workers heading back to their villages at this time. Farm workers and fish alike find the rhythm of their lives dictated by the seasons of the agricultural year.

Another autumn ritual in the human world is the sport of sumo, as immensely popular in Japan in Issa's time as it is today. The following pair of haiku appear back-to-back in his journal, *Hachiban nikki*, as Eighth Month entries. In them, he suggests that human beings are not sumo's only fans. As in the previous example of the homeward-bound fish, the particle *mo* も ("too") is significant.

宮角力蛙も木から声上る (1823; *IZ* 1.508)
miya-zumō kawazu mo ki kara koe ageru

sumo match –
from trees the frogs, too
cheer

松の木に蛙も見るや宮角力 (1823; *IZ* 1.508)
matsu no ki ni kawazu mo miru ya miya-zumō

from the pines
frogs watch, too . . .
sumo match

The sumo tournament (*miya-zumō* 宮角力) is taking place on the grounds of a Shinto shrine. The frogs in the trees seem to enjoy the clash of the blubbery giants "too"— watching and, Issa imagines, cheering. We recognize in both haiku the kind of comic exaggeration typical of Issa's animal portraits; he invites us to smile at the image of frogs croaking their support for one wrestler or another. The humor deepens when we consider the physical resemblance of big-bellied wrestlers and frogs. Issa simultaneously reminds his readers, especially his contemporary readers, of the "animal-person caricatures" (*chōjū-jinbutsu-giga* 鳥獣人物戯画) of Toba Sōjō 鳥羽 僧正 (1053-1140), particularly a famous, playful scroll depicting bipedal frogs and a rabbit competing as sumo wrestlers. Issa's haiku also recalls Edo period *netsuke* 根付 figures: small, whimsical statues attached to kimonos that included sumo frogs. However, amid the levity of Issa's scene with all its artistic resonance, he reminds us yet again that animals are inextricably part of the human world, or, more accurately, that animals and humans share a world.

In an earlier chapter we considered a haiku that shows sparrows chattering on the 12th day, Tenth Month death anniversary of Bashō. In this next poem, Issa again juxtaposes the great poet's death-day and birds.

芭蕉忌や鳩も雀も客めかす (1821; *IZ* 1.659)
bashōki ya hato mo suzume mo kyaku mekasu

Basho's Death-Day –
pigeons and sparrows
dressed for company

Issa humorously describes the pigeons and sparrows as if they are decked out in their finest clothing suitable for social calls. This "clothing," of course, consists only of feathers, but these appear, Issa implies, clean and perfectly preened as if to honor the special day. The birds' lack of consciousness of the importance of the day on the human calendar is less important than their lively presence in the scene. In another haiku about a winter ritual, Issa portrays a disgruntled pigeon.

ぶつぶつと鳩の小言や衣配 (1807; *IZ* 1.677)
butsu-butsu to hato no kogoto ya kinu kubari

grumble, grumble
the pigeon nags . . .
no gift of new clothes

Alluding to a Twelfth Month custom of providing gifts of new clothes for one's relatives, Issa imagines that the cooing pigeon is complaining for being left out of the seasonal gift-giving. In another poem, he imagines that a cat harbors hope of being included.

其次に猫も並ぶや衣配 (1813; *IZ* 1.677)
sono tsugi ni neko mo narabu ya kinu kubari

next in line
the cat . . .
gifts of new clothes

Even if the pigeon and the cat fail to receive the clothes that people in the scene are doling out to one another, their presence reminds us that animals belong wherever and whenever human beings gather. My mentor, Paul A. Olson, offers a further reflection on the above two haiku. As the year progresses, the pigeon and the cat will grow new feathers and new fur. People, pigeons, and cats all renew their wardrobe in accordance with the cycle of seasons, and in this sense they are the same.

A feline also participates in an end-of-year drinking party.

御仲間に猫も坐とるや年わすれ (1819; *IZ* 1.678)
o-nakama ni neko mo za toru ya toshiwasure

the cat joins
the party . . .
drinking away the year

More literally, the cat "also takes a seat" (*mo za toru* も坐とる) along with the people at the party. Even if it has no taste for sake, the cat chooses to take part in the friendly gathering. It belongs in the scene as much as the people do.

Issa also shows animals present in scenes of human activity not directly tied to seasonal observances, for example, the year-round business of prostitution. At Yoshiwara, the licensed pleasure district on the outskirts of Edo, boisterous men and women are not the only ones making noise.

吉原やさはぎに過て鳴かはづ (1824; *IZ* 1.164)
yoshiwara ya sawagi ni sugite naku kawazu

Yoshiwara –
passing time raising a ruckus
frogs

Frog song, Issa reminds us in this haiku, has a sexual meaning, and so the frogs croaking for mates provides an appropriate soundtrack for the famous neighborhood of brothels. The haiku is a riotous celebration of passion—human and amphibian—as the people and the frogs share not only the space but the reason for being there. In another haiku written in the same Fifth Month of 1824, Issa takes us from the elegant "floating world" of Yoshiwara to a more desolate scene involving a *yohochi* 夜ほち or "nighthawk": a low-grade streetwalker waiting for customers on a roadside in the evening. Because of an annoying nonhuman presence, she is not alone.

かはほりや夜ほちの耳の辺りより (1824; *IZ* 1.335)
kawahori ya yohochi no mimi no atari yori

a bat –
buzzing the ear
of the hooker

In this and a few other haiku of 1824, Issa makes a playful connection between human "nighthawks" and bats: kindred creatures of the night. It's a wonderful pun that, unfortunately, doesn't carry over in English translation. Deeper than the fun of his language play, Issa suggests a sameness and a shared space: the bat flits in the night in search of food; the streetwalker does the same, in her way. The prostitute and the swooping bat equally belong in the darkness.

Animal participation in human celebrations and rituals is the norm, not the exception, in Issa's haiku.

酒好の蝶ならば来よ角田川 (1808; *IZ* 1.167)
sake suki no chō naraba ko yo sumida-gawa

if you like sake
butterfly, come!
Sumida River

When he invites the butterfly to join the riverside drinking party, Issa plainly indicates that the happiness and fellowship of the occasion can and should be shared with creatures beyond his own species. In a haiku about butterflies and hot tubs he repeats this idea.

湯入衆の頭かぞへる小てふ哉 (1816; *IZ* 1.171)
yu iri shū no atama kazoeru ko chō kana

counting heads
in a hot tub . . .
little butterfly

Issa makes use of his familiar two-part joke structure in this poem. The first two phrases, "counting heads/ in a hot tub. . . ." lead us to expect a human agent, but then in the third phrase he surprises us, identifying the head counter as a "little butterfly." The butterfly shares in the happiness of the people who soak away their aches and troubles in the hot water, sucking salty sweat (delicious, to a butterfly) from the bathers that it lights upon. It flits from head to head, sharing the moment and fully part of it.

湯の中のつむりや蝶の一休[41] (1821; *IZ* 1.173)
yu no naka no tsumuri ya chō no hito yasumi

in the hot tub
on someone's head . . .
butterfly's rest stop

湯の滝を上手に廻る小てふ哉 (1825; *IZ* 1.175)
yu no taki wo jyōzu ni meguru ko chō kana

skillfully skirting
the hot tub waterfall . . .
little butterfly

In the last verse, hot water slops over the edge of a tub, but the little butterfly adroitly avoids this "waterfall" (*taki* 滝), reminding us of Issa's "piss waterfall" haiku of 1812 in which he imagined the perspective of a frog. In all of these poems about humans bathing amid flitting butterflies, Issa implies that these delicate insects are important and integral to the scene, adding life, grace, and beauty to luxurious moments of soaking. In a late poem he returns one last time to the image.

湯けぶりのふはふは蝶もふはり哉 (1826; *IZ* 1.175)
yu keburi no fuwa-fuwa chō mo fuwari kana

hot tub steam
wafts softly, softly . . .
as does a butterfly

In a related haiku, Issa reminds us that healing baths are not only for people.

春風に猿もおや子の湯治哉 (1822; *IZ* 1.78)
haru kaze ni saru mo oyako no tōji kana

spring breeze –
monkey families, too
take healing baths

A more literal translation would be, "In the spring breeze
even monkeys—parents and children—take healing hot
baths." This is not a fantasy, for a quick Internet image
search for "macaque" and "hot springs" will attest that
Japanese monkeys derive as much pleasure as their human couterparts from soaking in springs at resorts such as
Yamanouchi. The particle *mo* も ("too") makes the scene
even more communal, indicating that human families are
doing the same thing that the monkey families are doing.
Two of Issa's favorite themes—that animals are like us,
and that we and animals share a world—resonate strongly
in this haiku.

Examples of Issa's inclusive vision of people and animals could easily fill the remaining pages of this book. I
will close this chapter with just two more.

野ばくちや銭の中なるきりぎりす (1814; *IZ* 1.548)
no bakuchi ya zeni no naka naru kirigirisu

gambling in the field –
in the pot
a katydid!

野ばくちの銭の中より小蝶哉 (1821; *IZ* 1.173)
no bakuchi no zeni no naka yori ko chō kana

        gambling in the field –
        from the pot
        a little butterfly

The gamblers care only about their game and their
winnings, but in the first haiku a katydid boldly hops onto
their pile of coins as if announcing that the field is a
shared space. In the second, a butterfly rises from the
money and flies away. Issa lampoons the gamblers, so
narrowly focused on the game that they usually pay no
attention to nature's treasures such as a robustly singing
katydid or a delicate, pretty butterfly. Only when these
creatures land in their pot, their center of interest, do they
get noticed, if at all. Metaphorically, the gamblers can
represent most people, too caught up in the business of
daily striving and earning to notice or appreciate their
animal cohabitants. Issa's poetic mission, in large part, is
to cure this blindess by calling attention in haiku after
haiku to the presence and importance of the nonhuman
creatures among us. His clear message in hundreds of
such poems is that animals truly belong here, and that life
without them wouldn't be much of a life.

Chapter 4. SHINTO AND BUDDHIST ANIMALS

I. Killing Animals, Animals Killing

In his poetry Issa draws our attention to the value of animals—potential gods in Shinto belief and future Buddhas in the Buddhist perspective. However, despite the spark of divinity within them and the supreme enlightenment that they one day might achieve, animals in Issa's haiku portraits (including the human kind) at times exhibit the antithesis of spiritual behavior: hunting, killing, and eating what they kill.

> 初蝶もやがて烏の扶食哉 (1808; *IZ* 1.167)
> *hatsu chō mo yagate karasu no fujiki kana*

> first butterfly –
> before long some crow's
> bite

The Japanese language often leaves to the reader's imagination whether a noun is singular or plural. Such is the case with this haiku. Depending on how one decides to read it, it might refer to one butterfly and one crow, to many butterflies and one crow, or to many butterflies, many crows. Jean Cholley chooses the latter option in his French translation, making both the butterflies and the crows plural—an image that suggests a widespread slaughter (77). I have chosen the first option: picturing a single butterfly destined to become food for a particular, hungry crow. I prefer to imagine Issa focusing attention on single creatures for two reasons. First, Occam's law of

177

parsimony applies to haiku as much as it does to science: one butterfly and one crow in the scene suffice to convey Issa's meaning and feeling; more butterflies and crows would be superfluous (this, incidentally, is why most critics choose to interpret the *kawazu* 蛙 in Bashō's famous "old pond" haiku as a single frog, not several). Secondly, the one-butterfly, one-crow image is more emotionally loaded than Cholley's vision of a general massacre. If we picture a single butterfly's impending demise and a single crow's feeding, we are likely to care more about both animals, victim and victimizer, than we care about masses of doomed butterflies and ravenous crows.[42]

A key word in the poem is *fujiki* 扶食, which Cholley translates as *la pittance*, "food." It combines the characters for "help" or "support" (*fu* 扶) with "food" (*jiki* 食). The butterfly supports the crow's diet. In Issa's original text the particle *mo* も ("also") indicates that the butterfly is one of many things that the crow eats; a more literal English translation—though less effective, I believe—would read: "first butterfly –/ also before long some crow's/ bite." If we choose to sympathize with the butterfly, Issa's referring to it as a mere diet supplement seems insensitive and demeaning. However, if we adopt the crow's point of view, the butterfly is exactly just one bite of food among many needed to support its survival. In the haiku, prey and predator appear in juxtaposition, inviting the reader to consider both perspectives, both ways of understanding one event: as a disturbing act of violence or as a happy snack time. Issa presents a brutal fact of animal existence while still inviting readers to sympathize with both involved parties—the butterfly that must be eaten and the crow that must eat it.

One might object that my own eye on this haiku is not cold enough, that I have allowed my reading of Issa's other poems to color my perception of this one, "discovering" in it sympathy that is really only mine. The objection is a fair one, but as I stated in the Introduction, a deep understanding of an individual haiku often requires the shaping of one's perception of it by hundreds or thousands of other haiku written by the poet. Writing as he does with such profound sympathy for an orphan sparrow, a scrawny frog, a swallow in a mosquito swarm, and a katydid that shares his bed, Issa can hardly be expected suddenly to invoke for readers an attitude devoid of compassion in this image of a crow eating a butterfly. In light of countless other poems in which he expresses sympathetic concern for his fellow creatures, one might well suspect, as I do, that in this case Issa's compassion extends not only to the butterfly but also to the crow, a victim of its own nature. Gautama Buddha prohibited the taking of life for those who would follow him to enlightenment. Issa's unlucky crow, living wild, cannot live without killing, and for this reason may well deserve a Buddhist poet's sympathy.

In a prose section of his 1819 journal, *Oraga haru*, Issa addresses the topic of killing animals directly. He begins by telling the strange story of a doctor named Nakamura from his home province of Shinano, who one fateful day killed an entwined pair of snakes engaged in procreation. That night, feeling a sharp pain in his private parts, the doctor dropped dead. Nakamura's son, Issa relates, also became a doctor but his penis, previously a robust "mushroom" (*matsutake* 松茸), failed him on his wedding night, resembling a useless, limp "candle wick" (*tōshin* 灯心). He spent the rest of his life impotent and alone. Issa notes the resemblance of this supposedly real-life story to popular tales found in *Uji shū monogatari* 宇治拾遺物語 ("Tales of Uji Gleanings")—Uji being a town near Kyoto—stories that, before, he never thought credible. In light of what became of the Nakamuras, he goes on to say, it would seem that such stories may have some truth in them: what happened to father and son must have been "the vengeance of the snakes" (*hebi no shūnen* 蛇の執念). He concludes, "All creatures, even fleas and lice, enjoy life, which is just as precious to such creatures as it is to people. It is a deep sin to kill other living things, even more so when they are coupling."[43]

In the following haiku Issa returns to the topic of animals killing animals, once again inviting his readers to consider more than one perspective.

蛤や在鎌倉の雁鴎 (undated; *IZ* 1.179)
hamaguri ya zai-kamakura no kari kamome

O clams
meet the geese and gulls
of Greater Kamakura!

The scene takes place in the outskirts (*zai* 在) of Kamakura, where wild geese and sea gulls are feasting on the clams. Issa surely feels sympathy for the clams, for life, as he noted in his prose passage about the coupling snakes, is precious to every living thing. His haiku, in this light, may be read as a warning to the clams. However, it might also be read as a high compliment paid to the deadly-efficient birds. More likely, Issa is inviting his readers to consider both perspectives: that of the hungry, effective geese and that of the hapless clams.

Issa belonged to Jōdoshinshū, the popular True Teaching Pure Land sect founded by Shinran. He evidently was a fervent follower of Shinran, given the number of haiku and prose passages in his journals devoted to two of the core themes of Pure Land Buddhism: the notion of rebirth in the Western Paradise, where even in this corrupt age of *mappō* 末法 Buddhahood can be achieved; and the reliance on the "Other Power" (*tariki* 他力) of Amida Buddha's "Original Vow" (*hongan* 本願), which will enable that happy rebirth, despite one's inescapable sinfulness.[44] Issa frankly admits his own sinfulness in his 1819 journal, *Oraga haru*, where he compares himself unfavorably, in spiritual terms, to his baby daughter Sato—his second child who would die of smallpox later that year.

> I don't yet know how to trust in Amida's way to enlightenment, heedlessly wasting my nights and days, shamed even by my two year-old child (who is closer to enlightenment than I); as soon as I leave my prayers I right away start sowing seeds of hell, hating the flies that swarm my lap, swatting the mosquitoes that cross my table—and, on top of all this, drinking the sake that Buddha has forbidden.[45]

He chides himself for regularly breaking two of Buddha's Five Precepts: the First Precept against killing and the Fifth against imbibing fermented drink. However, in a later passage of the same journal he advises readers that the key to enlightenment is to "simply trust" (*o-tanomi mōsu bakari* 御頼み申すばかり) in Amida Buddha's saving power. He writes, "One need not constantly strain to raise one's voice, reciting the *nembutsu*—such is not needed, for the Buddha deigns to protect us. Hence, the so-called great peace of spirit."[46] Many Pure Land Buddhists recite the *nembutsu* 念仏 prayer, "*Namu Amida Butsu*" ("All praise to Amida Buddha!"), as if the words by themselves constitute a magical incantation that will assure their rebirth in the Pure Land. Shinran, however, insists—and Issa agrees—that rebirth in the Pure Land has nothing to do with chanting a prayer. In his major doctrinal work, *Kyōgyōshinshō* 教行信証 ("True Teaching, Living, Faith, and Realizing of the Pure Land"), Shinran writes that the "mind of Amida" enters the believer's corrupt mind once it has been opened in an attitude of faith. It is Amida's mind, not the ego, that enables one to enter the Pure Land (mythically, in the next life but metaphorically in this one), thus giving rise to *anjin* 安心, a deep and abiding feeling of inner peace (59-60).

Because of his devotion to Jōdoshinshū, Issa believed that his mosquito-swatting and sake-guzzling would not prevent his rebirth in Amida's Western Paradise, as long as he trusted completely in the Buddha's saving vow. Taking the life even of a tiny mosquito may indeed be a sin in the strictest interpretation of Buddhism, but Issa understood that such sinning is an inescapable part of human and animal nature. When a dog joins a group of people to enjoy the first bonito of the summer, one can imagine that Issa's tone, without losing sympathy for the fish, is one of acceptance of the inborn, shared sinfulness of dogs and humans.

> 大家や犬もありつくはつ松魚 (1824; *IZ* 1.388)
> *ōie ya inu mo aritsuku hatsu-gatsuo*

> a big house –
> even for the dog
> summer's first bonito

Issa's perspective of sympathy for both predator and prey flows naturally from his Buddhism: he feels for the fish because it is a fellow traveler and a cousin; he feels for the fish eaters because no one can completely avoid sinfulness in the present, fallen age. In an earlier haiku on the same subject, he writes,

> 門川や逃出しさうな初松魚 (1817; *IZ* 1.388)
> *kado-gawa ya nigedashi sō na hatsu-gatsuo*

> river at the gate –
> summer's first bonito
> look fresh enough to swim away

In the old Japanese calendar, migrating bonito passed near Edo in summer, so "first bonito" (*hatsu-gatsuo* 初松魚) is a summer season word in haiku, though in the modern calendar this bonanza of fish catching and eating occurs in spring. Issa gives no indication that he will not be among the many Buddhists who, despite Buddha's first edict, will participate in the killing and eating of the fish. In fact, in this scene—evidently of a riverside fish market—the fresh-caught bonito are already dead, ready for purchase and the kitchen. Nevertheless, the poet's observation that they look as if they could "swim away" subtly tugs at the reader's heart. Issa invites us to consider the scene from both perspectives: that of people who have waited all year for the savory bonito to return, and that of the victim fish, looking almost alive—reminding us that they have been snatched from the ocean where they once swam free.

In the next example, Issa's word choice would seem to leave no doubt as to where his sympathy lies.

大毛虫蟻の地獄におちにけり (1823; *IZ* 1.365)
ōkemushi ari no jigoku ni ochi ni keri

big caterpillar –
into the ants' hell
it has fallen

Ants swarm and devour the poor, writhing caterpillar while it still lives—though not for long. By describing its condition as "hell" (*jigoku* 地獄), Issa underscores the creature's suffering and makes that suffering vivid for his readers. All but the most hard-hearted readers of this haiku will feel sorry for the unlucky caterpillar, whose butterfly days will never come. The ants, from the caterpillar's perspective, are tormenting devils. Issa's use of the term "hell," however, evokes a cosmic vision in which devils play a necessary role. According to a Japanese Buddhist belief system, when a person or animal dies there are six possible "ways" of rebirth, the so-called *rokudō* 六道: (1) as a sufferer in hell, (2) as a hungry ghost, (3) as an animal, (4) as an angry demon, (5) as a human being, or (6) as a heavenly being.[47] In this scheme of things, bad karma needs to be punished, so hell's devils (in this case, the ants) serve a necessary function. Furthermore (though Issa would not have realized this next point, many of his readers today will), contemporary biology exonerates the ants, noting that they serve the necessary function of helping to maintain nature's balance by reducing the number of plant-devouring caterpillars. Although he casts the ants in the role of devils in his haiku, Issa, ironically, might not be demonizing them. His poetic language leaves the door open for readers to appreciate both perspectives: a caterpillar suffering hellish torture and necessary ants enjoying a feast.

In film terms, the violence of this next haiku occurs off camera.

蛇の穴阿房鼠が入にけり (1820; *IZ* 1.535)
hebi no ana ahō nezumi ga iri ni keri

into the snake's hole
O foolish
mouse

Snakes entering their holes is an autumn reference in haiku. Here, Issa switches things around by having a rodent enter the hole instead. He leaves to the reader's imagination what happens next: disaster for the mouse, a home-delivered meal for the snake. He clucks his tongue in the poem at how "foolish" (*ahō* 阿房) this mouse is, and invites readers to do the same. By describing the mouse in this way, Issa seems to attribute some of the blame for what will become of it to the mouse. He gives no hint in the haiku that the snake that will eat the mouse should bear any guilt. Readers may feel sympathy for and even identify with the mouse, because it is so easy in this world to find oneself suddenly in a dangerous place, but the poem also leaves space for them to sympathize with the snake, minding its own business in its hole, following its nature.

As mentioned earlier, Shinran, the founder of Jōdo-shinshū, recognized that sentient beings in this corrupt, present age of *mappō* cannot live without sin. In the next haiku Issa alludes to this religious idea.

花咲て祖師のゆるしの肴哉[48] (1811; *IZ* 1.211)
hana saite soshi no yurushi no sakana kana

cherry blossoms –
with the Founder's blessing
eating fish

Someone, most likely Issa himself, is enjoying the freedom to break Buddha's precept against taking life, thanks to Shinran, who scoffed at following rules and precepts, insisting instead that rebirth in the Pure Land can only by brought about through the Other Power of Amida Buddha. Six years later, Issa writes a related haiku about a cat.

山寺や祖師のゆるしの猫の恋 (1817; *IZ* 1.122)
yamadera ya soshi no yurushi no neko no koi

mountain temple –
with the Founder's blessing
cats make love

Just as the Founder has exempted people in the earlier poem from the First Precept against killing, in this haiku he exempts a cat from the Third Precept against sexual misconduct—a comical allusion to Shinran's waiving of celibacy as a requirement for priesthood. The temple cat may have sex; Issa may eat a fish. Underlying the humor of these twin haiku is the key insight of Jōdoshinshū's Founder: sin is unavoidable in the corrupt age of *mappō*. Even the desire to escape desire and attain enlightenment by following Buddha's Five Precepts is tainted with egoistical craving. Instead of striving, Shinran and Issa recommend surrender to, and trust in, the Buddha's saving grace.

While he presents the killing and eating of animals as a forgivable sin, Issa consistently shows sympathy for fellow creatures that will end up in someone's bowl—even, often, his own. In the next haiku he helps us to imagine the experience of pond snails in a cooking pot. This haiku is poem 1 of a six-poem series on the "Six Ways" (*rokudō* 六道) of reincarnation. It has the head note, "Hell" (*jigoku* 地獄)—the least fortunate of the six possible existences.[49]

夕月や鍋の中にて鳴田にし (undated; *IZ* 1.179)
yūzuki ya nabe no naka nite naku tanishi

evening moon –
pond snails singing
in the kettle

Debi Bender, a visitor to the *Haiku of Kobayashi Issa* website, theorizes that the "singing" of the snails might be the hissing of their shells, "making a noise, something like air escaping a tea-kettle." Another visitor, Colleen Rain Austin, agrees.

They have a hard shell at the end of their "foot" that they can pull up and use to seal themselves in with when they are threatened. As they are grilled or boiled, they steam in the shells, and the loss of moisture causes their bodies to shrink, and steam escapes through the edges of the seal, causing a shrill whistling noise like a high-pitched scream. It isn't something you are likely to forget . . . The whelks are done when the button-like seal pops out and the shrieking stops.

My Japanese advisor, Shinji Ogawa, believes that the "singing" might instead be the sound of snails peacefully spitting water before the kettle has gone onto the fire. He writes,

> The kettle may have been prepared for tonight, and the pond snails may not have tomorrow. But, the pond sails are singing. This seemingly tranquil scene well deserves to be described as Hell. Issa, in his well-disciplined way, keeping it low key, using plain everyday words and common settings without any adjective, without a drop of blood . . . describes Hell. Hell is not a matter of the next world, but here. It is a reality in which we must kill others in order to survive. Worse, we may call it a feast.

Of the two interpretations of the snails' "singing"—the hissing of steam shriveling and killing them, or the playful squirting of water—the former seems more deserving of its title, "Hell." By describing their experience as such, Issa clearly sympathizes with the snails. However, as usual, a second perspective also is implied. Under the tranquil evening moon, human beings sip their drinks while enjoying a pleasant aroma rising from a kettle.

Issa's poem evokes hellish torment; Issa's poem makes one's mouth water.

In the next example, the idea of being cooked haunts a turtle's dream.

大釜の湯やたぎるらん亀の夢 (1812; *IZ* 1.745)
ōkama no yu ya tagiruran kame no yume

maybe water's boiling
in the big kettle . . .
turtle's nightmare

This haiku would appear to be far more flippant than the previous one. Issa attempts to read a turtle's mind, in fact, a *sleeping* turtle's mind, and in so doing conjures the horrible image (to a turtle) of water boiling in a kettle. However, despite its humor, the haiku again illustrates the poet's desire to understand the reality of an animal from an animal point of view. Whether or not turtles actually dream is beside the point.

としの暮亀はいつ迄釣さるる (1807; *IZ* 1.614)
toshi no kure kame wa itsu made tsuru saruru

the year ends –
how long will that turtle
hang there?

This other turtle-related haiku has the head note, "At Ryōgoku." According to Maruyama Kazuhiko, Issa is referring to a famous east-west bridge in Edo where people would gather to enjoy the cool of evening (132, note 637). Shinji Ogawa points out that *tsuru saruru* 釣さ るる in this context means "to be hanged." He adds that Issa must be describing a market scene at Ryōgoku.

Turtles, he notes, are symbols of longevity: appropriate food for the New Year's celebrations. Ironically for the turtle, its reputation for long life may have condemned it to becoming a holiday meal. Jean Cholley, however, believes that the turtles are being suspended by shop owners along the bridge prior to a Buddhist ceremony of releasing them: the Release of Captive Animals ceremony (*hōjō-kuyō* 放生供養). Cholley fancies that Issa sees himself in the tortured, hanging creatures (237). However one chooses to read this haiku, Issa's sympathy for the turtle is palpable.

In a thematically related haiku Issa draws our attention to an animal's obliviousness to the danger posed by humans.

> 初雪や今に煮らるる豚あそぶ (1819; *IZ* 1.638)
> *hatsu yuki ya ima ni niraruru buta asobu*
>
> first snowfall –
> soon to be boiled
> the playful pig

The pig will die soon, but for now, fully alive in the moment, it plays in the snow. The haiku is tender but also wise in a Buddhist sense, for as Gautama Buddha taught, nothing abides—a universal transience expressed by the Japanese word *mujō*. Issa's image of a happy pig is reminiscent of Bashō's well-known haiku about an octopus or octopi trapped in a pot.

> 蛸壷やはかなき夢を夏の月 (1688; Matsuo 1.205)
> *tako tsubo ya hakanaki yume wo natsu no tsuki*
>
> octopi in a pot –
> ephemeral dreams under
> a summer moon

Like Bashō's octopi, Issa's pig is living on borrowed time. The tones of the two haiku, however, differ greatly. Bashō's haiku strikes a tone of detached observation: the captured octopi, destined to be food for humans, enjoy brief dreams of life without awareness of their fate. Issa's pig, on the other hand, though equally unaware, *plays*. Pathos mingles with joy in this portrait of a pig in the snow: the pathos felt by the human poet (and perhaps his readers) and the joy of a playful pig. Once again, Issa invites readers to consider multiple perspectives.

In this next, very early haiku, the killer of a chicken seeks instant atonement.

冬篭り鳥料理にも念仏哉 (1793; IZ 1.697)
fuyugomori tori ryōri ni mo nebutsu kana

winter seclusion –
cooking a chicken
praising Buddha

This haiku refers to the *nembutsu* prayer of thanksgiving for, and praise of, Amida Buddha's "Original Vow." Eons ago, Amida promised that all who rely on his saving power will be reborn in the Western Paradise or Pure Land. This means that even a sinner who kills and cooks a chicken (and perhaps that sinner is Issa?) can reach Amida's Pure Land—both a mythic place and a metaphor for enlightenment. In typical form, the poem suggests two perspectives and evokes two tones. On one side, we have the human perspective and a comic tone: we can smile at the cook, casually rattling off a prayer to justify his transgression. On the other side of this poetic diptych, we can sympathize with the poor chicken. The seasonal context of "winter seclusion" (*fuyugomori* 冬篭り) under-scores the cold-heartedness of taking a life while excusing one's self karmically with a quick *nembutsu*. The coldness of winter, the coldness in the cook's heart, the coldness of the chicken's carcass before it goes into the pot—speak volumes about the nature of a violent and merciless existence in which, as Shinji Ogawa noted earlier, "Hell is not a matter of the next world, but here."

Two other of Issa's haiku about chicken killing deserve attention.

鶏〆る門の柳の青みけり (1808; *IZ* 1.239)
tori shimeru kado no yanagi no aomi keri

killing a chicken –
the willow at the gate
so green

鶏の小首を曲げる夜寒哉 (1820; *IZ* 1. 434)
niwatori no kokubi wo mageru yozamu kana

twisting the chicken's
neck . . .
a cold night

The first haiku presents a stark, intense image of life and death side by side: the green spring willow and the dying chicken. The second haiku with its cold autumn night setting reminds us of the earlier "winter seclusion" poem. The temperature outside perfectly accords with the cold-blooded killing indoors.

Issa has a favorite expression for people who behave monstrously in their treatment of animals; he calls them *hito oni* 人鬼: "human devils" or "human goblins." A parent sparrow (it could be a mother or father; Issa doesn't specify) raises an alarm and bravely attacks these dangerous monsters. In my translation, I have chosen to envision the parent as a mother.

人鬼に鳴かかりけり親雀 (1810; *IZ* 1.127)
hito oni ni naki-kakari keri oya suzume

she cries and attacks
the human goblins . . .
mother sparrow

The above haiku appears in Issa's journal *Shichban nikki* in a Third Month entry. Later that same month, he returns to the image.

人鬼よおによと鳴か親雀 (1810; *IZ* 1.127)
hito oni yo oni yo to naku ka oya suzume

"Beware the human goblins!"
is that what you're chirping?
mother sparrow

To a bird guarding its nest, a human being is, indeed, a dangerous beast. Issa, though a human being himself, seems almost ashamed of this fact at times.

人鬼をいきどほるかよ鰒の顔[50] (1813; *IZ* 1.722)
hito oni wo ikidōru ka yo fugu no kao

are you mad
at the human goblins?
face of the pufferfish

From a human point of view, a pufferfish's bloated, spiky face may be the definition of ugly. However, in this humorous poem with serious undertones Issa imagines the captured fish's perspective. To the *fugu*, human beings—vendors in a fish market, diners at a table—look evil and monster-like, he suggests. They, after all, will be eating it .

. . not the other way around. Is it cosmic justice that, occasionally, the gourmets who feast on *fugu* ingest a deadly toxin and die? Though he frames it in the form of a question, Issa's statement to the fish suggests that it feels "angry at" or "indignant about" (*ikidōru* いきどほる) the human goblins. Issa implies that the fish has every right to feel this way. In a haiku written ten years earlier, faces of people look "shameful" (*asamashi*浅まし) to *fugu*.

浅ましと鰒や見らん人の顔 (1803; *IZ* 1.711)
asamashi to fugu ya miruran hito no kao

looking shameful
to the pufferfish . . .
people's faces

The way that we often treat animals, Issa suggests— beneath the poem's surface level of quirky humor—is shameful indeed.

His compassion for animals, the driving force behind his poetic efforts to imagine the world from their per-spective, plainly informs Issa's haiku about hunting. The following three haiku appear as First Month 1812 entries in *Shichiban nikki*, the second two written back-to-back.

蝶まふや鹿の最期の矢の先に (1812; *IZ* 1.168)
chō mau ya shika no saigo no ya no saki ni

butterfly dances
'round the arrow
in a dying deer

猪ねらふ腕にすがる小てふ哉 (1812; IZ 1.168)
shishi nerau kaina ni sugaru ko chō kana

clinging to
the boar hunter's arm . . .
little butterfly

鉄砲の三尺先の小てふかな (1812; *IZ* 1.168)
teppō no san jaku saki no ko chō kana

three feet
from the musket's barrel . . .
little butterfly

Issa juxtaposes the butterfly with the hunter and his instruments of violence: arrow and musket. In the second poem we can imagine the gentle butterfly clinging to the arm of the hunter just as he takes aim at the boar. The butterflies in all of these poems wordlessly chide the hunter . . . and all readers who hunt. They represent an alternative and spiritually more evolved way of being in the world than that of the stalking killer: an attitude of peace, harmony, and acceptance of fellow creatures. In fact, in a haiku on reincarnation Issa praises the possibility of returning to this world as a butterfly.

むつまじや生れかはらばのべの蝶 (1811; *IZ* 1.168)
mutsumaji ya umare kawaraba nobe no chō

such sweet harmony
to be reborn
a meadow butterfly!

Perhaps, as Shinji Ogawa envisions the scene, Issa is referring to the friendly intimacy of a butterfly couple. He uses the same word, *mutsumaji* むつまじ ("harmonious friendliness"), to describe the gentle, tame deer in a temple town, possibly Nara.

足枕手枕鹿のむつまじや (1814; *IZ* 1.521)
ashi makura temakura shika no mutsumaji ya

my feet for a pillow
and my hands . . .
the friendly deer

The friendly, harmless butterflies and deer of these haiku follow a markedly different way of life than that of the hunters, fishermen, and killers of poultry and pigs who appear in many of Issa's other poems. Gentle creatures, however, can fall victim to violence, as we recall from Issa's haiku about a crow snacking on a butterfly, and as we can see in the next example.

人なつき鶴よどちらに矢があたる (1819; *IZ* 1.744)
hito natsuki tsuru yo dochira ni ya ga ataru

which one of those
tame cranes
will the arrow hit?

A hunter takes aim at an unsuspecting, tame bird. Ironically, like the turtle hanging on Ryōgoku bridge, cranes are traditional symbols of longevity, and yet one of them in this poem is about to die. Issa refrains from moralizing; instead, he asks a simple question and leaves his reader to feel outrage at the injustice of slaying a tame animal.

Issa acknowledges that animals kill other animals and that people do the same, but even though his sect of Pure Land Buddhism can forgive killers—placing the key to their eligibility for the Pure Land beyond the pale of ego-tainted actions—he cherishes the perspective of victims and coaxes his readers to do the same. Every victim deserves the mourning that people normally reserve for close family members. Even clams in a kettle, Issa suggests in one haiku, are worthy of funeral rites.

蛤のつひのけぶりや夕時雨 (1814; *IZ* 1.626)
hamaguri no tsui no keburi ya yūshigure

the clams' cremation smoke
rises . . .
evening's winter rain

The rising steam from the pot, Issa imagines, is the clams' *tsui no keburi* つひのけぶり, literally their "last smoke"—an old Japanese expression for cremation smoke (*KD* 1099). Describing their cooking in this religious fashion, he indicates his profound respect and sympathy for the clams. He even suggests kinship with them, recognizing them as members of the family of life whose cooking is a rite of cremation. The fact that he will possibly eat them does not negate the depth of his feeling.

II. Shinto Animals

Shinto and Buddhism, the two great spiritual traditions in Japan, count animals as their members and celebrants . . . according to Issa. By his time, the Shinto-Buddhist syncretism established in the Heian period was a thousand years old. The esoteric Buddhist schools of Shingon and Tendai mixed the earlier Japanese animism with Buddhist elements—a mingling so successful that, in Issa's time, Shinto gods or *kami-sama* 神様 existed alongside Buddhas and bodhisattvas in the imaginations of most Japanese people. In fact, as Thomas P. Kasulis points out, "the term 'Shinto' had no popular use in Japan until the development of state ideology in the middle of the nineteenth century" (102). In Issa's Edo period there was no pressure to disentangle the native tradition from the Buddhist one imported from India via China. This is why, in one haiku, a sparrow can sing a Buddhist-style sutra dedicated to a god, Tenjin 天神, without surprising his original audience in the least.

梅咲や天神経をなく雀 (1822; *IZ* 1.204)
ume saku ya tenjinkyō wo naku suzume

plum blossoms –
singing Tenjin's sutra
a sparrow

Sugawara no Michizane (845-903) was a Heian period scholar and poet, posthumously deified and renamed Tenjin: a god of literature and learning. The Tenjin cult, popular in Issa's time, included a worship service that ended with a recital of the "Tenjin Sutra" (*tenjinkyō*天神経), a prayer invoking Tenjin's name in language modeled after Buddhist sutras (Borgen 330). This is the holy text that the sparrow chirps among the plum blossoms, Issa claims, implying that worship is not for humans alone.

If a sparrow prays in one of Issa's haiku, it should come as no surprise that a dragonfly, in another, undertakes the *hyakudo mairi* 百度参り—a practice that involves praying while moving back and forth one hundred times between a shrine or temple and some fixed point in that shrine or temple's precincts, or else visiting a shrine or temple on one hundred consecutive days.

蜻蛉の百度参りやあたご山 (undated; *IZ* 1.543)
tombō no hyakudo mairi ya atago yama

the dragonfly's
100 prayers pilgrimage . . .
Mount Atago

The location of the pilgrimage suggests a third possible meaning for the dragonfly's hundred-fold journey. Atago is a mountain near Kyoto with a major shrine at its summit. In Issa's time, pilgrims who climbed to it on the 24th day of Sixth Month would reap the benefits of one thousand climbs, the so-called *sennichi mairi* 千日参り. Possibly, Issa's lucky dragonfly is visiting the temple on a similar, special day that multiplies the spiritual benefit of the visit by one hundred. On one level, as we have seen often in Issa, the haiku functions as a joke: the inclusion of a dragonfly in the religious ritual of humans in a particular location on a particular day can seem a case of whimsical anthropomorphism. Deeper, however—again, as we have noted so many times—Issa challenges our assumptions. If one believes in the benevolent power of a shrine's god, is it not possible that a dragonfly—though unaware of it—will be blessed for arriving on this auspicious day?

He writes other haiku in which dragonflies not only attend Shinto festivals; they seem dressed for the occasion.

御祭の赤い出立の蜻蛉哉 (1817; *IZ* 1.542)
o-matsuri no akai dedachi no tombo kana

departing for the festival
all in red
dragonfly

連立つて御盆御盆や赤蜻蛉 (1821; *IZ* 1.543)
tsuredatte o-bon o-bon ya aka tombo

coming along
to the Bon Festival . . .
red dragonfly

In his discussion of Shinto *matsuri* 祭 ("festivals"), Kasulis writes,

> On the social level, the festivities bring people together to celebrate their commonality. The *matsuri* participants sense their perhaps unknown but assumed connectedness. On the religious level, it is an entry point for highlighting the people's intrinsic inseparability from the *kami* and at least potentially evokes the sense of living within a *kami*-filled, *tama*-energized world. (63-64)

Tama 霊 is the Japanese term for the spiritual power that infuses matter, resembling the English words, "spirit" and "soul." In these two haiku Issa extends the net of soul-connectedness to include a red dragonfly along with the human celebrants at the *matsuri*. Its festive color, he implies, is like a special robe for the special occasion.

Once again, these haiku function as jokes with deeper implications. Readers may smile at the image of an insect festival-goer; yet, upon reflection, they might at the same time come to suspect that the immanent gods of this world are just as much the dragonfly's gods as they are gods for people. In the second example, the particular gathering that the dragonfly joins is the Bon Festival of the Dead, an Eighth Month event in the old Japanese calendar. At this time, people light lanterns to guide their ancestors' spirits back home—a ritualized acknowledgement of the continuing connection between the living and the dead. Issa reminds us that the dragonfly, too, has ancestors: countless generations without which it would have never existed. Its presence at the festival can therefore be interpreted, by Issa and his readers, as an unconscious act of piety. The fact that the insect certainly lacks awareness of the spiritual meaning of Shinto festivals does not negate their importance and relevance to its life. It is enough that Issa and his readers perceive this importance and this relevance.

In the next example animals don't merely celebrate the sacredness of the world; they *are* sacred. However, as with the red dragonflies, they remain unaware of their role in Shinto belief and ritual.

神の猿蚤見てくれる小春哉 (1824; *IZ* 1.613)
kami no saru nomi mite kureru ko haru kana

sacred monkeys
pick each other's fleas . . .
a spring day in winter

Literally, the monkeys are "the god's monkeys" (*kami no saru* 神の猿), implying that the scene takes place within the precincts of a Shinto shrine. Issa wrote the poem in late summer (Sixth Month) in his home province of Shinano, prefacing it with the head note, "Winter" (*fuyu* 冬). "Little spring" (*ko haru* 小春) refers to mild, clear weather in the Eleventh and Twelfth Months of the old calendar. Since the image is a product of imagination or memory—not based on immediate, local experience and therefore impossible to locate based on where Issa was living at the time—the reader is free to imagine its geographical setting. Many Japanese readers will automatically associate the poem with Mount Hiei near Kyoto, where some of the most famous sacred monkeys of Japan reside. The principle god of the mountain is Sannō (山王), one of whose avatars is a monkey. In Issa's haiku, these god-infused protectors of the mountain's Tendai Shinto-Buddhist temple complex appear unaware of their spiritual status and importance, casually grooming each other. Sacred power, he implies, can fill a creature even while it is doing the most mundane thing in the most mundane, natural way. A monkey doesn't need to realize it is sacred to be sacred.

In two other haiku about monkeys, Issa again depicts them quite naturally.

明神の猿遊ぶや秋の山 (1814; *IZ* 1.488)
myōjin no mashira asobu ya aki no yama

the great god's
monkeys are playing . . .
autumn mountain

小猿ども神の御留主を狂ふ哉 (1821; *IZ* 1.656)
ko-zaru domo kami no o-rusu wo kuruu kana

little monkey –
with the gods all gone
he's running amuck

The first haiku raises the point that divine avatars, too, like to play. The monkeys do not meditate, participate in a religious ritual or, like the earlier-cited sparrow, sing prayers. Instead, they honor the mountain's god (once again, we can imagine Mount Hiei's Sannō), simply by playing, exuberantly enjoying the spark of divine life—the *tama*, the spirit—that animates them. Their playing is their praying. The second, more comic haiku alludes to the Shinto belief that in Tenth Month (the first month of winter in the old calendar) all of Japan's gods vacate their shrines to congregate at the Izumo-Taisha Shrine. With its deity absent, one little monkey seems to have lost all sense of decorum. "When the cat's away . . ."

A haiku about a buck strikes a more reverent tone.

さをしかや社壇に角を奉る (1824; *IZ* 1.125)
saoshika ya shadan ni tsuno wo tatematsuru

on the shrine's altar
the buck offers
his antlers

The image recalls the earlier-discussed haiku of 1813 of a buck shedding his antlers amid blooming cherry trees. This time, the antlers take on a more plainly religious significance: a sacrifice offered to the god of the shrine. In the poem following this one in his journal, *Bunka kuchō* 文政句帖 ("Bunka Era Poem Collection"), Issa rewrites the scene, deliberately shifting from Shinto to Buddhist associations.

御仏の山に落すや鹿の角 (1824; *IZ* 1.125)
mi-hotoke no yama ni otosu ya shika no tsuno

on Buddha's mountain
he sheds them . . .
the buck's antlers

Issa's image of a buck shedding his antlers on a temple mountain is highly symbolic. Like monks who shave their heads, the buck apparently is relinquishing worldliness. Moreover, shedding the weapons with which he earlier battered rivals in the struggle to win and keep a mate further suggests a notion of celibacy. The buck, Issa hints, has become a monk, taking an important step on his road to enlightenment.

We will examine more closely Issa's conviction that animals can be Buddhists in the next section of this chapter. For now, to continue our investigation of animals and Shinto, the following haiku presents a cat and a New Year's "auspicious direction shelf" (*ehōdana* 恵方棚).

> とぶ工夫猫のしてけり恵方棚[51] (1821; *IZ* 1.34)
> *tobu kufū neko no shite keri ehōdana*

> the cat considers
> jumping up . . .
> New Year's offering shelf

The haiku alludes to the custom of visiting a shrine located in an auspicious direction on New Year's Day. At home, a shelf decorated with flowers and offerings is positioned so that while facing it one faces the direction of the shrine where that year's Toshitokujin 歳徳神, the Auspicious Direction Goddess, is located—a Japanese New Year's ritual that originated in Chinese Yin-Yang divination (Japanese: *onmyōdō* 陰陽道). Issa's cat takes aim at the goddess's shelf perhaps out of curiosity or, perhaps, because he plans to steal a food offering. Whatever his motive, the cat, tensing to leap, faces the spiritually beneficial direction. Once again, Issa implies that religious consciousness might not be a prerequisite for reaping religious blessings.

In a related haiku, he portrays a cat making himself at home on a Bon Festival altar.

> 玉棚にどさりとねたりどろぼ猫 (1825; *IZ* 1.491)
> *tama-dana ni dosari to netari dorobo neko*

> on the ancestors' altar
> flopping down to sleep . . .
> thieving cat

The *tama-dana* 玉棚 is a home altar honoring the visiting spirits of ancestors during the Eighth Month Bon Festival. Issa describes this particular cat as a "thief" (*dorobo* どろぼ), revealing that his motive for visiting the altar has been to steal food from it, after which he brazenly curls up to sleep at the scene of the crime. The image is comic while at the same time suggestive of a deeper religious truth. Despite the cat's thievery, one can imagine that he might enjoy the spiritual protection of Issa's ancestors.

In this next haiku about sparrows enjoying a special dish of Bon Festival rice, one might picture the birds swooping in and stealing their portion or, as I prefer to imagine the poem, Issa generously offering it.

雀らもせうばんしたり蓮の飯 (1815; *IZ* 1.492)
suzumera mo shōban shitari hasu no meshi

even the sparrows
partake . . .
Bon Festival rice

During the Bon Festival, as the spirits of ancestors are welcomed home, devout followers of Shinto also honor the souls of living parents, grandparents and, sometimes, elder brothers and sisters. "Lotus rice" (*hasu no meshi* 蓮の飯) is a special festival dish consisting of cooked rice on a lotus leaf. In 1815, the time of the haiku's composition, Issa and Kiku entered their second year of marriage. Since Issa had no living elders left on his side of the family, he is possibly referring in the haiku to lotus rice cooked for Kiku's relatives. In any case, his attitude toward nonhuman animals is, once again, inclusive. The sparrows *too* partake of the special food to honor living elders, and so in a sense Issa invites the birds into, or else recognizes them as already being a part of, his family. To the sparrows the rice is just food, but Issa and his readers understand the spiritual significance of the offering. As in previous examples, the animals' lack of religious consciousness might not negate their blessing.

In a haiku about a butterfly Issa connects its pure whiteness to Shinto purification.

神垣や白い花には白い蝶 (1818; *IZ* 1.171)
kamigaki ya shiroi hana ni wa shiroi chō

shrine fence –
on a white flower
a white butterfly

The *kamigaki*神垣 is a decorative fence surrounding a shrine, a symbolic barrier between the ordinary world and the divine. The white butterfly and white flower are emblematic of the purified world of the *kami-sama*. Issa wrote this haiku in Third Month 1818; later that same month he returned to the image of a white butterfly but switched the religious context from Shinto to Buddhist— just as he did earlier with the back-to-back haiku about the buck sacrificing his antlers.

祝ひ日や白い僧達白い蝶 (1818; *IZ* 1.171)
iwai-bi ya shiroi sōtachi shiroi chō

festival day –
white robed monks
and a white butterfly

Again, the butterfly embodies spiritual purity, its color this time matching the festival robes of Buddhist monks. Whether we look at it through the prism of Shinto or Buddhism, the butterfly, without conscious effort, achieves a purity of being that Issa appreciates, and praises, in religious terms.

This next haiku about a butterfly recalls an earlier-cited one about counting heads in a hot tub.

参詣のつむりかぞへる小蝶哉 (1821; *IZ* 1.173)
sankei no tsumuri kazoeru ko chō kana

counting heads
of the shrine visitors . . .
little butterfly

Pilgrims are visiting a shrine. The butterfly, flitting from head to head, seems to be counting them—serving as an unofficial greeter and census taker of the holy place. For Issa, the gentle butterfly is an apt ambassador for the shrine's god.

Even a frog can play a religious role in Issa's haiku.

御社へじくなんで入るかはづ哉 (undated; *IZ* 1.165)
o-yashiro e jikunande iru kawazu kana

taming the flesh
he enters a shrine . . .
frog

The frog appears (comically) as a flesh-taming ascetic, willingly undertaking "self-suffering" (*jikunan* じくなん) as a religious discipline. The image of a suffering holy man, or in this case "holy frog," does not directly pertain to Shinto but rather to Shugendō 修験道, the ancient practice of asceticism in the mountains. Issa places his flesh-taming frog in the setting of a Shinto shrine, suggesting a spiritual connection between its mortification and the local deity. Conflating Shugendō and Shinto ideas, he suggests that the frog's suffering is meant to honor the *kami-sama*. The reader might wonder how the frog suffers as it enters the shrine. I believe that a haiku of 1826 explains the situation: the frog is gamely crawling through a thorn bush.

じくなんで茨をくぐる蛙哉 (1826; IZ 1.164)
jikunande ibara wo kuguru kawazu kana

taming the flesh
he moves through thorns . . .
a frog

Because of their unusual depictions of ascetic frogs, these two haiku must have been closely connected in Issa's mind. The frog endures its path of thorns for what humans can understand to be a religious purpose: to enter the divine space presided over by the shrine's god, even though it has no conscious awareness of this purpose. Once again and not coincidentally, the image of an animal being simply itself is charged with spiritual significance in Issa's poetry.

In the next example, he directly addresses one of the Shinto deities, drawing her attention to a butterfly.

一姫の神笑み給へ草のてふ (1806; *IZ* 1.166)
ichihime no kami emi tamae kusa no chō

O goddess Ichihime
smile!
a meadow butterfly

Kamu O-Ichihime is an important Shinto goddess, the mother of O-Toshi no Kami, the great harvest god and guardian of rice fields (Jordan 237; 298). She has an important shrine in Kyoto, the Ichihime Jinja. In his poem Issa politely asks the goddess to deign to smile

207

upon a butterfly flitting over the grasses. By suggesting that a great *kami-sama* should pay attention to—and delight in—a mere winged insect in a meadow, Issa strongly implies that his readers would do well to do the same. Although the butterfly doesn't grasp human concepts of deity and religion, this goddess of nature, Issa imagines, will behold it approvingly . . . and smile.

The following haiku brings us back to a frog, clearly one of Issa's favorite animals.

住吉の神の御前の蛙哉 (1816; *IZ* 1.161)
sumiyoshi no kami no mimae no kawazu kana

in the divine presence
of Sumiyoshi's gods . . .
a frog

Sumiyoshi Grand Shrine (*Sumiyoshi Taisha* 住吉大社) is a major Shinto shrine in Osaka about which Issa wrote over a dozen haiku, starting in the last decade of the eighteenth century—the period of his earliest poem-writing journeys. This later haiku of 1816 must be a work of memory and imagination, since Issa was staying in Shinano Province at the time of its composition in First Month 1816, far to the north of Osaka. It is possible that he observed a frog in a local shrine but decided to change the setting to Sumiyoshi; it is equally possible that he imagined the whole scene. Either way, he purposefully situates the action in a shrine that houses some of Japan's most powerful and sacred *kami-sama*, most notably Hachiman-shin, the god of war and the country's protector. Issa's comic-serious construction of the scene invites readers to proceed in two steps: firstly, to smile at the incongruity of a frog appearing in such an exalted setting; and, secondly, to reflect on the possibility that even without consciousness of the shrine's religious meaning, the pilgrim frog has indeed been blessed.

Issa invites readers to experience the same two steps of laughter followed by a deep realization of religious truth in two haiku about a crow.

旅烏江戸の御祓にとしよりぬ (1810; *IZ* 1.284)
tabikarasu edo no misogi ni toshiyorinu

traveling crow
at Edo's purification . . .
now you're old

旅烏江戸の御祓にいく度逢ふ (1814; *IZ* 1.284)
tabikarasu edo no misogi ni iku tabi au

traveling crow
at Edo's purification . . .
how many years?

The poems refer to a purification ritual that took place in Sixth Month in the traditional Japanese calendar. Shinji Ogawa notes that a *tabikarasu* 旅烏 ("traveling crow") can metaphorically denote travelers, especially frequent travelers, or outlaws. The term would certainly apply to Issa, an incessant wanderer. In these haiku he draws an equal sign between himself and the crow: both are travelers; both find themselves in Edo for the purification ceremony for yet another year; both are growing old. The pilgrim crow in these haiku functions much like the pilgrim frog at Sumiyoshi, causing readers first to smile but then to reflect. If Issa belongs in this scene, so does his double, the vagabond crow.

He indicates in his journal *Shichiban nikki* that he was indeed traveling in Sixth Month 1814, the month he wrote the above haiku. Starting in Edo, he journeyed north and east into Shimōsa Province, today's Chiba Prefecture, reaching the town of Fukawa in time for its Daimyōjin Festival, an annual celebration in honor of the local god that took place from the fourteenth to sixteenth (*IZ* 3.69). Though he and Kiku had married just two months earlier in Fourth Month—he at age 52, she at 28—his new status as a husband didn't prevent him from his customary wandering, in this case to visit his haiku students and his patron, Natsume Seibi. He must have felt a special kinship with the old, traveling crow.

Shinto purification rituals have ancient and even mythical precedents. According to an account in the eighth century *Kojiki* 古事記 the great *kami-sama* Izanagi and his sister-wife Izanami created many of Japan's islands and gods. However, after Izanami died, Izanagi (like Orpheus in search of Eurydice) attempted to retrieve her unsuccessfully from the Land of the Dead. In that dark place he witnessed her corpse, thus breaking a grave taboo, so when he emerged from the darkness Izanami purified himself in the river-mouth of Tatibana—in the process spawning fourteen new deities (68-70). This is one mythic source for the Shinto practice of *misogi* 御祓: purification by water. *Misogi* can take many forms, from washing one's hands and rinsing one's mouth before entering a shrine to extreme physical rituals involving immersion in cold water or waterfalls. *Misogi* or *harai* 祓 can also involve using the water of a river to float away impurities, diseases, and bad luck, embodied in paper boats (*katashiro* 形代). Issa often refers to this rite of exorcism, as in the following example.

疱瘡のさんだらぼしへ蛙哉 (1813; *IZ* 1.159)
hōsō no sandara-boshi e kawazu kana

onto a straw lid
marked "smallpox"
hops a frog

Sandara-bōshi さんだらぼし is another word for *san-dawara*: a round, straw lid used on both ends of rice bags. In place of a paper boat—as my Japanese advisor Shinji Ogawa envisions this poem—the straw lid has been released onto a river to carry the smallpox god away. Six years later, in 1819, Issa made use of a similar ritual in an attempt to cure his baby daughter Sato. He writes, "We made a boat with bamboo grass, sprinkled it with sake and released it to carry away the Smallpox God, but she only became weaker and weaker . . ."[52] In the haiku of 1813 his tone is lighter. A frog has chosen to climb aboard the smallpox god's boat. Like the captain of a tiny ship, he drifts away, heroically taking with him the disease of a city or village.

Frogs, according to Issa, display the proper *gravitas* at a Shinto ritual.

しかつべに蛙も並んで夕はらひ (1821; *IZ* 1.285)
shikatsube ni kawazu mo narande yū harai

with grave seriousness
frogs line up too . . .
evening's purification

The particle *mo* も ("also") indicates that there are others in the scene lining up with the seriousness befitting the occasion: human participants, including, one assumes, Issa. "Evening's purification" (*yū harai* 夕はらひ) can involve a number of specific rituals, the two most common being the launching of paper boats to carry away disease (as in the previous haiku) or crawling through a hoop of reeds at a shrine, another way of securing divine protection from infectious diseases. In this case, Issa evokes the latter: the image of frogs "also" lining up suggests people in a queue soberly waiting their turn to crawl through the sacred hoop. The haiku that immediately follows the above in Issa's journal mentions such a "purification hoop" or *chinowa* ちの輪.

蝶々の夫婦連してちの輪哉 (1821; *IZ* 1.286)
chōchō no meoto-zure shite chinowa kana

two butterflies
pass through together . . .
purification hoop

The butterflies, literally "husband and wife" (*meoto* 夫婦), fly through the disease-preventing hoop together. As in other haiku that we have previously considered, their consciousness of the meaning of the religious ceremony into which they have injected themselves might not be required for them to reap its benefits. In a sense, their unconsciousness makes their participation in the rite even more exemplary. Unlike human believers who crawl through the *chinowa* due to an egoistic desire to prolong their own lives, the happy butterfly couple flits through it expecting, and asking for, nothing. This act of "natural piety"—to borrow a phrase from Issa's faraway English contemporary, William Wordsworth—might not go unrewarded by the *kami-sama*, or so Issa hints.

In another haiku, a cat uses the occasion of evening's purification ritual to purify his fur.

痩蚤を振ふや猫も夕祓 (1821; *IZ* 1.285)
yase nomi wo furuu ya neko mo yū harai

rousting his skinny fleas
the cat too . . .
evening's purification

Issa comically sets the cat's flea-scratching and nibbling in a religious, Shinto context. Yet still, despite the poem's humor, the reader may suspect that the cat, as much as any human pilgrim, genuinely deserves divine blessing. Issa suggests the same in a haiku about a dog.

春風や御祓うけて帰る犬 (1813; *IZ* 1.76)
harukaze ya o-harai ukete kaeru inu

spring breeze –
purified at a shrine
the dog comes home

In this and in many similar haiku, Issa suggests, firstly, that the indigenous gods of Japan bestow their blessings on human and nonhuman animals alike, and, secondly, that the ancient religious practices that would later fall under the umbrella term, Shinto, indeed benefit all creatures of this shared earth.

III. Buddhist Animals

Animals in Issa's haiku also pay visits to Buddhist temples. For example, a cow leads the way to Zenkōji in the following poems, one set in winter and the other in spring. Zenkōji is a major temple in Issa's home province of Shinano.

しぐるるや牛に引かれて善光寺 (1803; *IZ* 1.623)
shigururu ya ushi ni hikarete zenkōji

213

winter rain –
led by a cow
to Zenkō Temple

春風や牛に引かれて善光寺 (1811; *IZ* 1.76)
haru kaze ya ushi ni hikarete zenkōji

spring breeze –
a cow leads the way
to Zenkō Temple

These poems allude to a popular folktale. One day, a sinful woman left a piece of cloth to dry in the garden behind her house, but a passing cow snagged it with a horn and trotted off. The woman followed the beast all the way to Zenkōji, where it disappeared. She found herself standing before the image of Amida Buddha, a famous bronze statue flanked by the statues of two bodhisattvas—a spiritually powerful icon that, in Issa's time, was displayed approximately once a year (McCallum 169). From that point on, she became pious. In both of its forms, the haiku pays tribute to the tenets of True Teaching Pure Land Buddhism. According to Jōdoshinshū's founder, Shinran, rebirth in the Pure Land (both actual and metaphorical) is a gift that comes from beyond the ego's calculations. The woman in the story takes giant steps toward her enlightenment without thinking about it, simply by following a cow, the embodiment of Amida's rescuing power. Issa, too, follows the cow to Zenkōji (and spiritual rescue) in his imagination. Perceptive readers will follow her there too.

此方が善光寺とや蝶のとぶ (1815; *IZ* 1.170)
kono kata ga zenkōji to ya chō no tobu

"Follow me to Zenkō Temple!"
a butterfly
flits

In this later haiku, he substitutes a butterfly for the cow and even gives the former a speaking role. The religious message, however, remains the same: animals are capable of guiding people to Buddha's enlightenment.

Throughout this book we have noted how Issa likes to present animals as relatives and fellow travelers. In hundreds of haiku with Buddhist themes, he reveals the spiritual thinking that shapes this perception: the notion that all creatures, human and nonhuman, find themselves on the same karmic road to Amida's Pure Land: a mythic place beyond this corrupt world and age where enlightenment may be achieved. In addition to the cow and butterfly, Issa depicts families of sparrows making the pilgrimage to Shinano's major temple. Though not affiliated with a particular sect, Zenkōji is administered by two sub-temples: Daihongan, a Pure Land temple, and Daikanjin, a temple affiliated with Tendai (McCallum 168). Because, as we have noted, Amida Buddha is its main icon, Issa strongly associates Zenkōji with the promise of rebirth in Amida's Western Paradise.

善光寺へ行て来た顔や雀の子 (1816; *IZ* 1.129)
zenkōji e itte kita kao ya suzume no ko

faces looking like
they've been to Zenkō Temple
baby sparrows

雀らもおや子連にて善光寺 (1818; *IZ* 1.130)
suzumera mo oyako-zure nite zenkōji

sparrow parents too
bring their children . . .
Zenkō Temple

The central statue of Amida Buddha, located in the Main
Hall, is believed to possess enough spiritual power to
guarantee one's rebirth in the Pure Land just by laying
eyes upon it, so excited pilgrims throng to Zenkōji on
those rare days when the curtains that normally hide it
are drawn back. While superficially these two haiku seem
to be merely charming portraits of birds mirroring the
human world, considered more deeply, they suggest that
rebirth in Amida's Paradise, a prelude to Buddhist enlightenment, is a possibility for all creatures.

The next poem implies the same Mahayana Buddhist
truth with an even more delicate tone.

負さつて蝶もぜん光寺参かな (1822; *IZ* 1.173)
obusatte chō mo zenkōji mairi kana

riding piggy-back
a butterfly too is a pilgrim . . .
Zenkō Temple

Here, a butterfly hitches a ride on the back or shoulder of
one of the temple's human visitors. Issa reverses the roles
of his earlier butterfly/Zenkōji haiku of 1815; in this later
one, the butterfly no longer appears as the guide but as
the one being guided; in fact, it is physically carried to the
temple. This time, a person brings an animal to Buddha's
grace.

In Issa's time, pilgrims at a Buddhist temple would
sleep on straw mats called *shikine* 敷寝. In this next haiku,
he imagines that a frog's *shikine* is the flower upon which
he sleeps. The image is tender and full of religious significance.

木母寺の花を敷寝の蛙哉 (1813; *IZ* 1.159)
mokuboji no hana wo shikine no kawazu kana

at Mokubo Temple
bunking on a flower . . .
a frog

Mokuboji, located in Edo on Mukojima Island near the
Uchigawa Inlet of Sumida River, was reachable only by
boat in Issa's time (the frog, of course, could swim there).
On the fifteenth day of Third Month, "The Great Amida
Prayer Ceremony" (*Dainembutsu Kōgyō* 大念仏興行) took
place, attracting pilgrims from far and wide. Issa envisions the frog as one of these devout visitors.

Issa's quintessential haiku about an animal pilgrim
portrays a snail creeping up the side of Japan's most
sacred mountain.

かたつぶりそろそろ登れ富士の山 (undated; *IZ* 1.284)
katatsuburi soro-soro nobore fuji no yama

little snail
inch by inch, climb
Mount Fuji!

Issa composed this poem at some time in the Bunsei
period, probably the mid-1820s. In it, he refers not to the
real Mount Fuji but to an imitation Fuji: a small, sculpted
hill (*tsukiyama* 築山) constructed in the garden of a shrine
such as the Asakusa Jinja in Edo. On the first day of Sixth
Month, pilgrims—especially the elderly and infirm who
were unable to climb the real mountain—reaped spiritual
benefit by climbing the pseudo-Fuji. Issa's encourages a
snail to continue climbing such a hill, *soro-soro* そろそろ
("slowly, slowly"—or, as I have translated it here, "inch

by inch"). Its climb has both Shinto and Buddhist significance. For Shinto, Mount Fuji is the home of the great goddess Konohanasakuya-hime, enshrined near the summit. For Buddhists, it is the abode of Dainichi Nyorai 大日如来, the Buddha of All-Illuminating Wisdom, and its snowy peak represents a supreme state of meditative concentration or *zenjo* 禅定. Figuratively, the snail climbs to the goddess's blessing; the snail climbs to enlightenment.

Elsewhere, Issa paints a portrait of quite a different animal on an artificial Fuji.

浅草の不二を踏へてなく蛙 (1813; *IZ* 1.159)
asakusa no fuji wo fumaete naku kawazu

trampling Asakusa's
little Fuji . . .
a croaking frog

The imitation Mount Fuji referenced in this haiku, which today no longer exists, attracted throngs of pilgrims to Asakusa Shrine during the Edo period. The situations in this poem and the previous one about the snail are similar—but not their tones. Whereas Issa encourages the little snail to climb Mount Fuji, intimating a slow and gradual pilgrimage to blessing and enlightenment, the frog recklessly treads upon the hill, showing neither respect nor concern. Issa's verb in Japanese to describe this stomping is *fumaete* 踏へてなく: "treading on" or "stamping on." The snail appears persistent and pious; the frog appears brazenly indifferent. Nevertheless, paradoxically, the frog may be the better Buddhist of the two, in light of Shinran's teaching that enlightenment is not a thing to be attained through the private "self-effort" (*jiriki* 自力) of obeying Buddha's precepts. The frog doesn't understand the sacredness of Fuji or the spiritual reward that climbing its miniature simulacrum might garner; he simply hops along, croaking for a mate. Nevertheless, albeit unconsciously, he *does* climb Mount Fuji and so progresses, in Issa's eyes if not his own, toward a future enlightenment.

In this next example a butterfly delivers a wordless Buddhist sermon just as unconsciously as Issa's frog on Asakusa's Fuji.

かいだんの穴よりひらり小てふ哉 (1818; *IZ* 1.171)
kaidan no ana yori hirari ko chō kana

from a hole in the temple's
pulpit, swish!
little butterfly

A *kaidan* (a word that Issa writes in *hiragana* かいだん instead of the *kanji* 戒壇) is an "ordination platform" or "sanctuary" found in large temples. Standing on this dais, priests impart Buddhist precepts, and so I have chosen the English word, "pulpit," to approximate its meaning (*KD* 318). Faithful spectators expect to hear Buddha's truth preached from atop a *kaidan*, but instead, in the wonderful moment evoked in the haiku, a butterfly emerges from somewhere in its interior. Issa hints that the butterfly *is* the sermon, inviting his readers to contemplate what its particular message might be. Perhaps he wants us to consider how the butterfly was once an earthbound caterpillar that has been reborn to become an embodiment of the hope of fortunate reincarnation and nirvana. Or, perhaps he wants to remind us that words are empty, but Buddha's power to bring about our enlightenment, like the butterfly, is palpable and real. Whatever the butterfly's "sermon" might be interpreted to signify, Issa appreciates and contemplates—and invites his readers to appreciate and contemplate along with him—its silent eloquence.

In dozens of haiku Issa presents animals in Buddhist temples mingling with human pilgrims and, often, sharing special ceremonial food or drink. The following is a sampling, beginning with a butterfly that accompanies the poet on his after-dinner walk to a temple, an exercise to aid both digestion and karma.

蝶とぶや夕飯過の寺参り (1805; *IZ* 1.166)
chō tobu ya yūmeshi sugi no tera mairi

flitting butterfly –
after dinner, a temple
pilgrimage

Fledgling sparrows attend a morning *kaichō* 開帳, the public display of a sacred image on a festival day.

雀子も朝開帳の間にあひぬ (1813; *IZ* 1.128)
suzumego mo asa kaichō no ma ni ainu

baby sparrows, too
arrive for the Buddha's
morning showing

Pigeons enjoy a special "wisdom gruel" (*chie-gayu* 知恵粥) served at a Tendai temple on the memorial day of the patriarch Chigi.

相伴に鳩も並ぶや大師粥 (1814; *IZ* 1.660)
shōban ni hato mo narabu ya daishi kayu

even pigeons
line up for their share . . .
Patriarch's gruel

And a cat joins the celebration when a sacred image of
the founder of Shingon Buddhism, Kūkai, is brought out
for public viewing.

御影講や泥坊猫も花の陰 (1815; *IZ* 1.103)
mieikō ya dorobō neko mo hana no kage

Founder's image on display –
even the thief cat
in blossom shade

In the last haiku the cat's intention is certainly not to seek
spiritual benefit. Issa describes him as a "thief" (*dorobō* 泥
坊), reminding us of the cat sprawled on the ancestral
altar in a poem that we looked at earlier. The robber cat
on the home altar entered that sacred space to steal food
offerings. Readers can imagine that the cat at the temple
on Kūkai's festival day has a similar agenda: to rob food
from altars or, perhaps, from picnicking pilgrims. Nevertheless, despite its conscious motivation, this cat—like the
butterfly, the baby sparrows, and the pigeons in the other
haiku—has come to a Buddhist temple, taking a step
(even though unaware) toward enlightenment. Like the
old woman in the story following a cow to Zenkōji, all
creatures who arrive at such a place, in Issa's view—a
view reiterated in hundreds of poems—can possibly
receive the blessing of Amida Buddha.

In this next example a butterfly not only visits a
temple; it participates, or *seems* to participate, in a good
luck ritual.

びんづるの御鼻をなでる小蝶哉 (1819; *IZ* 1.172)
binzuru no o-hana wo naderu ko chō kana

        rubbing Binzuru's
        holy nose . . .
        little butterfly

Binzuru is a bodhisattva, one of the Sixteen Enlightened
Ones. Folk custom dictates that if one prayerfully rubs his
statue, he or she will recover from illness.[53] Like human
visitors, the butterfly in the poem also rubs Binzuru,
though humorously on his nose instead of on the top of
his head as most people do. Issa amuses readers while at
the same time inviting them to consider the butterfly's
action as yet another manifestation of unconscious piety.
If Binzuru rewards those who consciously rub his image,
will he not also reward the butterfly? Perhaps, in fact, the
butterfly is even more likely to be rewarded because it has
not asked for reward. Like many other animals in Issa's
haiku that wander into human-defined religious contexts,
the butterfly serves as an exemplum. Issa suggests,
through such images, that people should approach the
sacred as animals do: with innocent spontaneity—a message that might resonate with Christians who recall
Jesus's admonition to, "Let the little children come to me,
and do not hinder them, for the kingdom of heaven
belongs to such as these" (*N.I.V.* Matt. 19:14). Issa's
animals in Shinto and Buddhist settings are not punch
lines in anthropomorphic jokes; they are, often, spiritual
role models.
        The closest parallel to Jesus as a lover and protector
of children in Buddhist tradition is Jizō. In Chinese
Buddhism, Jizō came to be known as one of the eight
Dhyāni-Bodhisattvas, his particular job being that of
guardianship over the earth. A bodhisattva is not a god
but an enlightened being who heroically delays his or her
entry into nirvana on a compassionate mission to lead
other sentient beings to enlightenment. In Chinese
Buddhist myth Jizō became associated with Yama, the

overlord of Hell, most likely because of his (formerly *her*) ancient association with earth's womb. Nevertheless, in folklore he appears as a savior, not a punisher. For example, in one old Chinese tale a son's filial piety moves Jizō to deliver that son's sinful, dead mother out of hell. Similarly, in a later Japanese story, he appears in the form of a beautiful young boy and rescues a righteous man from hell by offering to suffer in the man's place.[54] Of all the bodhisattvas, only Jizō was thought to relieve hell suffering (LaFleur 50). In the Pure Land Buddhism that Issa followed, Jizō gained a reputation as one who could assist sinful mortals in their last moments of life, enabling their rebirth in the Pure Land. This is why, in many Japanese temples, statues of Jizō stand on one side of Amida, while Kannon, the bodhisattva of mercy, stands on the other. Jizō's role in Pure Land Buddhism made him widely popular in medieval Japan, where his move-ment spread far and wide among the masses. Somewhere along the way, he picked up other duties in addition to helping souls reach Amida's Pure Land, such as provid-ing protection for travelers. Even today, stone and wood Jizōs can found all over Japan along remote roads, where they watch over all who journey there. Jizō's kind, generous, and selfless nature led Japanese people to re-vere him, additionally, as a guardian of children.

In Issa's haiku, frogs and plovers appear in Jizō's lap; a horse is tied to him; baby sparrows hide inside his sleeve; a frog squats in his hand; and a beehive dangles from his elbow. All of these images remind us that Jizō's spiritual help extends to all animals, even the nonhuman kind. A close look at this frog poem reveals the core lesson of all of Issa's Jizō haiku.

御地蔵の手に居へ給ふ蛙かな (1815; *IZ* 1.160)
o-jizō no te ni sue tamau kawazu kana

            safe in holy
            Jizō's hand, squats
            a frog

The frog has landed on the hand of a roadside Jizō statue,
a random happenstance charged with religious significance. The bodhisattva appears as the little frog's
protector, mercifully assuring that one day he will be
reborn in Amida's Pure Land where he will attain
enlightenment. The image signals hope for the frog, for
Issa and, by extention, for his readers. There is a benevolent force at work in the universe watching over all animals, including the human kind. Like the frog in the
haiku, we are all safe in the palm of the Protector's hand,
if only we trust—not safe, perhaps, in the physical sense
in a biosphere of necessary violence and a human society
rife with the unnecessary kind, but ultimately and
essentially safe in the Buddha's promise of eventual,
perfect enlightenment . . . or so Issa implies in his haiku.
    As for three-dimensional images of Buddha made of
stone, bronze, or snow, a partial list of animals appearing
with them in Issa's poetry includes mosquitoes lurking
behind a stone Buddha's back; fireflies, a stray cat, a
cocoon, a butterfly, and a snake's discarded skin (the
latter three all symbols of rebirth) resting safely in his lap;
baby sparrows chirping inside a great bronze Buddha's
nose; a dragonfly glaring at a stone Buddha; sparrows
chirping in the lap of a Buddha made of snow; a puppy
befriending a snow Buddha; a butterfly stuck to Amida
Buddha's cheek; fireflies, flies and frogs atop Buddha's
head; a dragonfly on his shoulder; a mosquito clinging to
him; a pheasant hiding in his sleeve; a stink bug (*mushi no
he* 虫の屁) on the tip of Buddha's nose; a laughing
Buddha pointing at a stink bug; and a flea jumping
(luckily!) into a Laughing Buddha's mouth. Images of
animals within or on the way to visit temples are also

legion Issa's haiku; deer, crows, bees, mosquitoes, fleas, horseflies, frogs, ants, spiders, butterflies, sparrows, and fireflies all visit temples. Even bats keep pilgrims company on their way to see Yakushi 薬師, the Buddha of Healing. The present book lacks the space for indepth discussions of all these poetic and religious images, but curious readers are invited to continue their investigation on the *Haiku of Kobayashi Issa* website, searching the keyword "Buddha."

Two huge bronze statues of the Buddha exist in Japan: at Kamakura and at Nara. The one at Nara, in Tōdaiji Temple, is 53½ feet high and made of over 400 tons of bronze. The Kamakura Great Buddha is 37 feet high, weighing more than 90 tons.[55] The following poem by Issa is a wonderful study in contrasts: the vast Buddha and a small bird, stillness and movement.

大仏の鼻から出たる乙鳥哉 (1822; *IZ* 1.141)
daibutsu no hana kara detaru tsubame kana

from the great bronze
Buddha's nose . . .
a swallow![56]

When he wrote this haiku Issa was living in his home province of Shinano, hundreds of kilometers from the Great Buddha statues at Kamakura and Nara, so he must have either remembered the scene, or, what I believe is more likely, invented it. Either way, the haiku is a great one, because it reveals a truth of the universe. The immense, ponderous statue sneezes out a quick, swooping bundle of life in the form of a bird. Issa's visual parable suggests that living things should trust in the Buddha because they (we) come from the Buddha. The enlightenment that awaits all creatures, human and nonhuman, is a return to the Oneness whence we came.

IV. Animals and Karma

In his journal *Oraga haru* Issa writes about the tragic drowning of an eleven year-old child. He attended the boy's cremation and was so moved that he composed a *waka* 和歌, and old verse form of 31 sound units arranged in a 5-7-5-7-7 pattern.

> 思ひきや下萌いそぐわか草を野辺のけぶりになし
> て見んとは (1819; *IZ* 6.137)
> *omoiki ya / shitamoe isogu / waka kusa wo / nobe no*
> *keburi ni / nashite min to wa*

> such is fate, to watch
> sprouts of young grasses
> so quickly
> into the field's fire
> go up in smoke

He compares the boy to newly sprouted grass burned in a fire and turned to smoke too soon. Following this *waka*, the next entry in his journal is the rhetorical question: "Will not even trees and plants one day become Buddhas?" He answers immediately: "They, too; all will acquire Buddha-nature."[57] The next item on the page is the head note for a haiku, the phrase, "Sitting alone." This poem follows.

> おれとして白眼くらする蛙かな[58] (1819; *IZ* 1.162)
> *ore to shite niramikura suru kawazu kana*

locked in a staring contest
me . . .
and a frog

Issa stares at the frog; the frog stares back, and neither blinks. Their standoff is more than the stuff of comedy. The previous entries in the journal—the *waka* about the boy who died so soon, a fresh sprout gone up in smoke, and the comment that even plants will one day become Buddhas—dispose the reader to consider this image of a man and a frog locked in a staring match as a visual statement of the egalitarian premise of reincarnation. Man and frog are peers and equals, for they are on the same path to enlightenment.

Reincarnation and karma are important themes in the Jōdoshinshū Buddhism to which Issa subscribed. The notion that all creatures are possibly en route to the Pure Land certainly contributed much to Issa's open and accepting attitude toward animals.

前の世のおれがいとこか閑古鳥 (1813; *IZ* 1.348)
saki no yo no orega itoko ka kankodori

in a previous
life, my cousin?
mountain cuckoo

過去のやくそくかよ袖に寝小てふ (1825; IZ 1.175)
kako no yakusoku ka yo sode ni neru ko chō

a previous life's bond?
little butterfly
on my sleeve, asleep

We noted in Chapter 1 that Issa considered the Himalayan cuckoo or *kankodori* to be a fellow haiku poet.

In the above first example, he suggests in his question to the bird an even stronger bond of affiliation between them: that, in a previous life, they were cousins. In the second example, he wonders similarly about a past life connection with a butterfly. Though his question in both poems is impossible to answer, by raising the possibility of previous life kinship with a cuckoo and a bond with a butterfly, Issa intimates that they share the same existential condition.

The idea of reincarnation democratizes nature for "Priest Issa." Even a moth larva has lived past lives and has accumulated karma.

養虫の運の強さよ五月雨 (1812; *IZ* 1.260)
minomushi no un no tsuyosa yo satsuki ame

the bagworm
has strong karma . . .
Fifth Month rain

The Fifth Month in the old calendar was roughly equivalent to June in the modern one, a season of daily, saturating rain. The bagworm is a moth larva protected from the elements in its cozy, dry, fibrous case. From this fact it derives its name, literally, the "straw raincoat bug" (*minomushi* 養虫). It must enjoy very good karma from a previous life, Issa muses (jokingly or seriously?), to have such a fine raincoat on a miserable, wet day.

An early haiku alludes to the reincarnation of medieval samurai in the form of crabs.

うたかたや淡の波間の平家蟹 (1792; *IZ* 1.179)
utakata ya awa no namima no heike-gani

sea foam –
in the fleeting wave
a Heike crab

Crabs with special markings resembling faces of twelfth century samurai are thought to be reincarnated heroes who died in a famous naval battle at Dan-no-Ura in 1185. Outnumbered three to one, thousands of heroes of the Heike, also known as the Taira clan, were slaughtered, drowned, or committed suicide in their bloody last stand recounted in the medieval epic poem, *Heike monogatari* 平家物語, *Tale of the Heike*. Ridges and grooves on their back carapaces make these crabs uncannily resemble scowling human faces, a fact that led evolutionary biologist Julian Huxley to hypothesize that over the centuries superstitious fishermen, who threw crabs with such markings back into the sea while eating others, contributed to a process of natural selection that favored the survival of the samurai-resembling crustaceans. Joel W. Martin, however, discounts this theory (30-34). Whatever the scientific explanation for the appearance of Heike crabs may be, Issa's image of catching a fleeting glance of one of them in a wave alludes to a major Buddhist theme of the *Tale of the Heike*: the concept of *mujō* or impermanence, embodied in the precipitous fall of the glorious House of Taira.

Issa revisits this subject several times, but perhaps the most poignant of these haiku appears three years later.

平家蟹昔はここで月見船 (1795; *IZ* 1.179)
heike-gani mukashi wa koko de tsukimi-bune

Heike crabs –
long ago they moon-gazed here
on boats

Issa muses that, in "olden times" (*mukashi* 昔), the crabs were human beings, enjoying moon-gazing parties on boats. Now they are crabs, but the fact that once they were people—like the poet, like his readers—evokes feelings of connection and compassion. Even clams, Issa writes elsewhere, could be people from olden times.

蜆さへ昔男のゆかりにて (1805; *IZ* 1.180)
shijimi sae mukashi otoko no yukari nite

even the clams
are related to the great
men of old

He perceives "connection" or "relationship" (*yukari* ゆかり) between today's clams and the men of bygone days. A belief in reincarnation leads Issa to perceive an interconnectedness among creatures, a fact that goes far to explain his sympathetic vision of animals.

Because he sees animals as fellow travelers to the Pure Land, Issa often depicts them growling, chirping, cooing, or croaking the *nembutsu* prayer.

散桜称名うなる寺の犬 (undated; *IZ* 1.211)
chiru sakura shōmyō unaru tera no inu

in falling cherry blossoms
growling to Amida Buddha . . .
temple dog

雀子も梅に口明く念仏哉 (1804; *IZ* 1.127)
suzumego mo ume ni kuchi aku nebutsu kana

sparrow babies
in plum blossoms
praise Buddha!

露ほろりほろりと鳩の念仏哉 (1810; *IZ* 1.476)
tsuyu horori horori to hato no nebutsu kana

amid weeping dewdrops
pigeons coo
"Praise Buddha!"

なむなむと蛙も石に並びけり (1822; *IZ* 1.163)
namu-namu to kawazu mo ishi ni narabi keri

they praise Buddha too –
frogs on a rock
in a row

In the first haiku *shōmyō* 称名 is another name for the
nembutsu, a prayer of gratitude for Amida Buddha's
"Original Vow" to rescue sentient beings from this world
of suffering by enabling their rebirth in the Pure Land, if
only they faithfully rely upon that vow. Issa fancies that
he hears *Namu Amida Butsu* ("All praise to Amida
Buddha!") in the dog's growling. As the blossoms fall,
reminding us of death and transition, he suggests that
even the temple dog trusts in Amida's promise for a next-
life existence in the Pure Land. He discerns the same
prayer being sung by baby sparrows, pigeons, and frogs
lined up on a rock.

Issa does not exclusively employ Pure Land Buddhist
imagery in his haiku about animal reincarnation. In the
following example he invokes the Shingon belief that
Miroku Bodhisattva will become a Buddha far in the
future to save beings who cannot otherwise achieve
enlightenment.

蛙穴に入て弥勒の御代を頼む哉 (1813; *IZ* 1.536)
kawazu ana ni irite miroku no miyo wo tanomu kana

> the frog enters his hole –
> in the Future Buddha
> he trusts

Issa sees the frog entering his or her hole in autumn as a
movement toward death and spiritual rebirth, not merely
physical hibernation. The frog doesn't need to have conscious knowledge of the Future Buddha for this promise
of spiritual rescue to apply. Issa foresees a bright future
for the frog and, by implication, for himself and his
readers. The important thing is to trust utterly (*tanomu* 頼
む) in a saving Buddha: Miroku or Amida.

Issa imagines a world that teems with fellow creatures
on the road to enlightenment. One of his most explicit
articulations of this vision appears in his early journal
Hanami no ki 花見の紀 (*Blossom-Viewing Record*). He
begins with a prose passage about a Buddhist memorial
service held at Shōrakuin Chōfukujuji, a Tendai temple in
present-day Chiba Prefecture. Throngs of the faithful, he
writes, have gathered to recite Buddhist sutras in honor of
a patriarch's death anniversary. The occasion causes him
to reflect on his own "next life" (*ato no yo* 後の世), but he
concludes that "the Buddha without fail will not forsake
me."[59] This haiku follows.

花桶に蝶も聞かよ一大事 (undated; *IZ* 1.167)
hana oke ni chō mo kiku ka yo ichi daiji

> on the flower pot
> does the butterfly, too
> hear Buddha's promise?

A butterfly alights on one of the flower pots decorating the temple hall. Issa wonders aloud if it, too, is listening to the chant that embodies a promise of eventual enlightenment that applies to it as much as it does to the humans in attendance: the "One Great Thing" (*ichi daiji* 一大事) of Amida Buddha's deliverance, Issa's Pure Land faith in this way coloring the scene in the Tendai temple. In 1808 he slightly revises . . .

あか棚に蝶も聞くかよ一大事 (1808; *IZ* 1.167)
aka tana ni chō mo kiku ka yo ichi daiji

on the offering shelf
does the butterfly also hear
Buddha's promise?

Throughout Issa's haiku, animals indeed hear Buddha's promise, manifesting an attitude that the poet interprets as natural reverence. Out of many examples of this, one of the most poignant involves a dragonfly.

蜻蛉もをがむ手つきや稲の花 (1819; *IZ* 1.578)
tombō mo ogamu te tsuki ya ine no hana

the dragonfly too
folds hands in prayer . . .
rice blossoms

The "too" (も *mo*) implies that a farmer, perhaps Issa, is the other person in the scene offering a prayer of thanksgiving for the rice crop that has gone to blossom and is now ready for harvest. The dragonfly apparently joins in. Its "hands" folding in a prayer-like gesture is coincidental, but this gesture captures Issa's attention and leads him to conclude that the dragonfly sitting in stillness, perhaps on the blooming tip of a rice plant, *is* praying, in its way. If the *nembutsu* is a prayer of gratitude for Amida Buddha's saving power—an experience of trusting in the Beyond while letting go of selfish calculations—then the dragonfly, not worrying about the future, fully attuned to the present moment, might be the pure embodiment of such prayer.

By now the reader should not be surprised to find a small bird in one of Issa's haiku warbling a famous Buddhist sutra—or at least its title.

雀程でもほけ経を鳴にけり (1816; *IZ* 1.135)
suzume hodo demo hokekyō wo naki ni keri

no bigger than a sparrow
yet he warbles
the Lotus Sutra!

The Lotus Sutra is one of Mahayana Buddhism's most popular scriptures. The editors of Issa's complete works identify the sparrow-sized singer as a nightingale: *uguisu* 鶯 (*IZ* 1.135). Shinji Ogawa notes that *hokekyō* ほけ経 (*The Lotus Sutra*) onomatopoetically suggests the sound of a nightingale's song. He adds that the nightingale can warble "big words, which a sparrow cannot." *The Lotus Sutra* contains many of Buddha's teachings in the form of parables. In a related haiku, Issa presents another bird that apparently has knowledge of this sutra and its contents, this time a cuckoo (*hototogisu* 時鳥).

時鳥火宅の人を笑らん (1806; *IZ* 1.337)
hototogisu kataku no hito wo warauran

cuckoo –
laughing at the man
in the burning house?

The poem refers to a parable in *The Lotus Sutra*, Chapter 3. Three children, "addicted to their games," are playing inside a burning house, oblivious to its dangers. The children represent all living beings, helpless to save themselves. Their father (Buddha) coaxes them from the doomed house by offering each one of them a bejeweled carriage: one drawn by deer, one by goats, and one by oxen. The three carriages represent the three main schools ("vehicles") of Buddhism (*Scripture of the Lotus Blossom* 60-67). By having the cuckoo laugh at the man in the burning house—in other words, at himself and at all human beings—Issa implies that the bird has somehow escaped the "house" of worldiness and suffering. Like the little nightingale, this cuckoo seems, in this one sublime moment, filled with Buddhist wisdom.

In the next haiku example, a sparrow sings of Buddha's power to rescue beings from a world of change and suffering.

露ちるや後生大事に鳴雀 (1810; *IZ* 1.475)
tsuyu chiru ya goshō daiji ni naku suzume

dewdrops scatter –
the sparrow sings
of next-life enlightenment

As mentioned earlier, the "Great Thing of the Next Life" (*goshō daiji* 後生大事) is Amida Buddha's vow to enable all who trust in him to be reborn in the Pure Land. As one finds so often in Issa, his language works on multiple levels. The image of a sparrow preaching about the deliverance of Amida, on one level, raises a smile with its sweet, seemingly impossible anthropomorphism. Upon deeper reflection, however, the reader may do a double-take and realize that the sparrow in this poem, like the nightingale and cuckoo in the previous examples, *really is* imparting Buddha's teaching. The image of dewdrops scattering, in Japanese literary tradition, triggers associations with the Buddhist concept of life's transience, *mujō*. The sparrow's lesson is simple: neither it nor Issa— nor any of Issa's readers—can escape the inevitability of change and death. The only answer, from a Pure Land Buddhist perspective, is to live in the present and to sing: letting go of desire and calculation, trusting in Amida's Power. The sparrow doesn't need to realize the religious significance of what it is saying for that significance to exist and be relevant for it and for all creatures, including the human ones who can read Issa's poem.

For people and animals alike, the most fortunate form of reincarnation is to be reborn in the Pure Land. The opposite extreme is to return to life as a sufferer in hell. A naughty cat, Issa suggests playfully, might experience the latter. As we noted in earlier poems about cats, Issa once again echoes the sound of "meow, meow" with the words, *mi yo mi yo* ("look! look!").

浄はりの鏡見よ見よ猫の恋 (1817; *IZ* 1.122)
jōhari no kagami mi yo mi yo neko no koi

into hell's mirror
look! look!
lover cat

According to Buddhist myth, Emma, the king of hell, has a magic mirror that reflects the good or evil deeds performed in the previous lives of new arrivals to his realm. The lover cat, ready to go prowling or returning from a night of amorous adventures, should see his own lust if he were to look in Emma's mirror . . . or so Issa teasingly implies. Even a butterfly, he writes a little later that same year, is not exempt from karma.

蝶の身も業の秤にかかる哉 (1817; *IZ* 1.171)
chō no mi mo gō no hakari ni kakaru kana

the butterfly too
on the scales of karma
is weighed

Butterflies usually appear in Issa's haiku as gentle, harmonious paragons of detachment from worldliness. Yet even such creatures, he writes, will be weighed and judged. Nevertheless, being a butterfly is a clearly more spiritually advanced incarnation than that of other creatures, hence Issa's friendly advice to a snake.

来年は蝶にでもなれ穴の蛇 (1821; *IZ* 1.536)
rainen wa chō ni demo nare ana no hebi

next year
become a butterfly!
snake in your hole

The image of snakes entering holes to begin their hibernation is an autumn seasonal reference in haiku. Issa interprets the event as a movement toward death and rebirth, so he urges the snake to come back as something better, next lifetime: a butterfly.

Being reborn a butterfly is a lucky prospect for Issa, who often associates these gentle, air-light creatures with heavenly grace.

とぶ蝶も三万三千三百かな (1814; *IZ* 1.169)
tobu chō mo san man san-zen san-byaku kana

flitting butterflies –
thirty three thousand
three hundred!

He gives this haiku the head note, "Sanjūsangen-dō": a
Tendai Buddhist temple in the Higashiyama District of
Kyoto. The temple's name translates to, "Hall with
Thirty-Three Spaces between Columns," referring to the
columns in the main building. Inside, there are 1,001
statues of Kannon, the Buddhist goddess of mercy. The
number thirty-three is significant, since according to the
Lotus Sutra, the bodhisattva that the Japanese know as
Kannon can manifest herself in thirty-three different
shapes in her efforts to help suffering beings.[60] Issa, in his
haiku, has fun with the number thirty-three and its
multiples, estimating the number of butterflies to be
33,300. By giving this number associated with Kannon's
myriad forms, he implies that the butterflies might be
living incarnations of the Mercy Goddess.

In the next haiku he offers bees similar reincarnation
advice—this time not telling them what to become but
rather what to *avoid* becoming.

藪の蜂来ん世も我にあやかるな (1807; *IZ* 1.177)
yabu no hachi kon'yo mo ware ni ayakaru na

thicket bees
in the next life don't
be like me

The haiku can be read as self-mocking comedy or,
perhaps, as a sincere reflection on the pain and sorrow of
human existence, particularly a human existence like that
of "Stepchild Issa." After all, the poet's biography from
childhood to old age was grim enough for Ōshiki to title
his book about Issa, *Jinsei no hiai* 人生の悲哀: "The

Sorrow of Life." However one chooses to view the poem—as an expression of comedy, of tragedy, or a bittersweet mixture of the two—Issa acknowledges, once again, that animals—bees, snakes, butterflies, and cats—all will have lives beyond the present one, changing their forms in conformance with karma as they progress toward, or regress from, an ultimate rebirth in Amida's Pure Land. There is no difference between their souls and human souls in this regard.

In Issa's vision of the universe, the final goal for sentient beings (as we have noted, he includes even trees and grasses in this group) is enlightenment. The following three haiku—about a snail, sea slugs, and a toad—provide hints as to how this enlightenment might be realized.

それなりに成仏とげよかたつぶり (1810; *IZ* 1.386)
sore nari ni jōbutsu toge yo katatsuburi

just as you are
become Buddha!
snail

人ならば仏性なるなまこ哉 (1810; *IZ* 1.722)
hito naraba hotokeshō naru namako kana

if they were people
they'd be Buddhas!
sea slugs

福蟇も這出給へ蓮の花 (1806; *IZ* 1.398)
fuku-biki mo haiide tamae hasu no hana

Lucky the Toad
crawl out!
lotus blossom

Issa admires the peaceful, do-nothing snail and sea slugs. They embody the ideal of not striving for rebirth in the Pure Land, which we have seen is a core value of Jōdoshinshū.[61] The lotus blossom from which "Lucky" crawls is traditionally associated with rebirth and Buddhist enlightenment. In this sense, he is lucky indeed. Like the snail and the sea slugs, he shows no sign of self-powered exertion to become a Buddha. Taking his lead from Shinran, Issa poetically divorces enlightenment from all calculation and effort. In this sense, animals like Lucky the Toad are a step closer to the Pure Land than most human beings, since people tend to brood and fret endlessly about what the future might bring, including the future life. Animals, in contrast, usually seem content to live in the present moment which, from Issa's perspective, makes them appear as if they are trusting their fates utterly to Amida—though, it is true, they are not consciously aware of this fact. His admiring attitude toward animals recalls that of American poet Walt Whitman, as expressed in a lovely passage from *Leaves of Grass*:

> I think I could turn and live with animals, they're so
>   placid and self-contain'd,
> I stand and look at them long and long.
> They do not sweat and whine about their condition,
> They do not lie awake in the dark and weep for
>   their sins,
> They do not make me sick discussing their duty to
>   God . . . (47)

Issa never expresses the desire to be reborn as a human being. On the contrary, as we noted in an earlier-discussed haiku that bears repeating, he suggests that returning to this world as an animal, particularly as a butterfly, would represent advancement.

むつまじや生れかはらばのべの蝶 (1811; IZ 1.168)
mutsumaji ya umare kawaraba nobe no chō

such sweet harmony
to be reborn
a meadow butterfly!

Issa is not just a poet who feels compassionately connected to animals, his fellow karma-laden travelers toward the Pure Land and enlightenment. If given the choice, he would *be* an animal of the nonhuman kind.

Chapter 5. ISSA'S BUTTERFLY CHALLENGE

A core tenet of ethical criticism, as old as Plato's *Republic*, is that literature can change the world by changing minds and therefore behavior. Plato wanted children, the future soldiers of his ideal republic, to read only about courageous and correct actions in *The Iliad*, not about Achilles crying or the gods telling lies. Plato stressed the importance of inculcating values through positive role models in poetry, but writers can also instruct readers morally by means of negative exempla: the devils of medieval and early modern drama, or the corrupt men and women ridiculed in satire from ancient times to the present day. Aesop, a Greek more ancient than Plato, presents animal fables to mirror human behavior as a means to moral instruction. In the West, countless writers have done the same, to name just a few: Geoffrey Chaucer's *Nun's Priest's Tale*, Jean de La Fontaine's *Fables*, Jonathan Swift's *Gulliver's Travels* (in which a noble and rational race of horses, the Houyh-nhnms, contrast significantly with the savage humanoids or Yahoos), and George Orwell's political allegory, *Animal Farm*. The use of animals to illustrate good and bad behavior can also be found many places in the Bible (the Lamb of God, sheep versus goats, and Jesus's parable of the sparrows). In Japan, folktales such as one that Issa alludes to, "The Tongue-Cut Sparrow," demonstrate that this tendency in world literature to use animals to critique human actions (the greedy old woman) and to provide role models for human behavior (polite, generous sparrows) certainly reached the Land of the Rising Sun. Japanese folklore also underscores the closeness of people and animals, with tales about human men marrying animal wives: frog-wives and snake-wives, specifically. Though such unions never turn out well, the stories about such inter-species relationships dramatically reduce the imagined distance between human and animal (Kobayashi Fumihiko 235-50). In addition, as in the Bible, Japanese story tellers have featured animals to embody religious lessons, like in the tale of a cow leading a sinful woman to Zenkōji and Amida Buddha. Sometimes animals lead; sometimes (when they reflect or share negative qualities of people) they warn by showing readers what not to do. Issa's haiku portraits of animals sometimes appear as cautionary tales, satirical reflections of the human race exposing what is wrong with it: war, violence, egocentrism, and oppression. More often, however—as we have noted throughout this book—he uses animals to point toward a better way of life: to focus on the present moment and to be natural, spontaneous, and free of guilt, worry, or coveting. In these more typical haiku Issa rearranges the conventional hierarchy of rebirth according to the "Six Ways" reincarnation schema. Normally, human birth is considered a notch above animal birth; in fact, in one haiku Issa describes it as "quite remarkable" (*naka-naka ni* なかなかに).

なかなかに人と生れて秋の暮 (1811; *IZ* 1.441)
naka-naka ni hito to umarete aki no kure

quite remarkable
being born human . . .
autumn dusk

Nevertheless, Issa often implies—as in, for example, his haiku about being reborn a meadow butterfly—that animal existence might be better than human, and that we stand to learn much from animals if we can open our eyes and hearts, and follow their example.

A haiku about a puffed-up frog presents Issa in his satirical mode, indirectly critiquing human behavior.

親分と見えて上座に鳴蛙 (1819; *IZ* 1.162)
oyabun to miete jôza ni naku kawazu

looks like the boss
in the seat of honor . . .
croaking frog

A frog claims the "high seat" (*jōza* 上座) of a log or stone, lording over the other denizens of the pond. Issa describes this self-important frog as *oyabun* 親分, which in his day signified a village headman. Today, *oyabun* is the term for a yakuza crime boss, a godfather. Then and now, the term applies to a man in a position of authority to whom, especially in the strict, hierarchical social structure of Japan, others pledge their loyalty. A boss enjoys his status because he has others of lower status to boss around. Issa pokes fun at the bluster and pomp of people who feel important by subjugating others. Such people, he suggests in this haiku, in the big picture are nothing better than frogs claiming the highest spots on rocks or logs. The headman frog in this haiku is symbolic of a human problem while admittedly reflecting actual frog behavior. The largest and most aggressive frogs, in frog colonies, claim supremacy over their fellows. Issa's comparison of human and amphibian poses a question for us to ponder. Are we any different from frogs in terms of social organization? We have human bosses with human underlings; frogs have frog bosses with frog underlings. Instead of presenting humans as inherently superior to amphibians, Issa's haiku suggests, with a wink, that people and frogs are exactly the same. Both are found lacking.

One of Issa's most popular haiku about animals also takes aim at human injustice and classism.

雀の子そこのけそこのけ御馬が通る (1819; *IZ* 1.130)
suzume no ko soko noke soko noke o-uma ga tōru

baby sparrows
move aside!
Sir Horse passes

Kai Falkman writes of this poem, "To call a dragonfly Mr. Dragonfly and a horse Mr. Horse might seem funny, but it diminishes Issa's haiku . . . Anthropomorphism is alien to haiku" (43). I disagree. By giving the horse a human honorific that can be translated as "Mister" or "Sir," Issa underscores a fact of life for both people and animals. In the semantics of power encoded in languages, certainly Japanese, the strong belong to a different category than the weak. Common, lowly sparrows must move aside when the mighty and powerful horse passes through, or else suffer the consequences. In similar fashion, peasants in Edo period Japan had to clear the road and grovel whenever a daimyo rode past. Issa's sympathy in the haiku clearly goes to the sparrows and, by implication, to the peasants of the world.

The next haiku about birds reflects even more critically on human social structure. It appears in *Kabuban* 株番 ("Stump Guard"), a collection written by Issa with contributions by a fellow poet, Kakurō 鶴老. A long prose introduction sets up the poem.

> On a temple-visit to Tōkaiji in Fuse, chickens followed me inexpediently. At a house in front of the temple gate, I bought just a bit of rice, which I

scattered among the violets and dandelions. Before long though, a fight broke out. Meanwhile, groups of pigeons and sparrows came flying down from the branches, eating with tranquil hearts, but when the chickens returned, back to the trees they quickly fled. The pigeons and sparrows would have liked the kicking-fight to have lasted longer. Samurai, farmers, artisans, and merchants all make their living in this manner.[62]

米蒔くも罪ぞよ鶏がけあふぞよ (1812; *IZ* 1.110)
kome maku mo tsumi zo yo tori ga keau zo yo

even tossing rice
is a sin . . .
sparring chickens

Feeding the birds is a "sin" (*tsumi* 罪), for it has caused a violent kicking match among them. These desperately competing birds at a temple gate serve as a microcosm of human society, summarized in the Japanese expression that Issa employs in his introduction: *shi-nō-kō-shō* 士農工 ("samurai-farmers-artisans-merchants"). The squabbling chickens, pigeons, and sparrows present an image of vicious class struggle.

Indeed, all is not peaceful in the world of animals, a reality that Issa captures in an early haiku.

長閑や雨後の縄ばり庭雀 (1795; *IZ* 1.58)
nodokeshi ya ugo no nawabari niwa suzume

spring peace –
after rain, a gang war
garden sparrows

The poem's season word, *nodokeshi* 長閑 ("spring peace") contrasts ironically with the strife taking place in the garden. The word *nawabari* 縄ばり ("to stretch a rope") means "turf" for mobsters. Showing groups of garden sparrows fighting for territory, Issa provides a miniaturized image of human warfare between clans or countries. Readers, contemplating this image of little birds battling might at first think, "How cute!"—but upon deeper reflection they might lament, with a sigh, "How sad!" Even gentle butterflies, emblems of Buddhist enlightenment in many of Issa's haiku, fight internecine battles.

それぞれや蝶も白組黄色組 (1818; IZ 1.171)
sore-zore ya chō mo shiro-gumi kiiro-gumi

separation
among butterflies too . . .
white gang, yellow gang

黄色組白組蝶の地どりけり (1820; 1.172)
kiiro-gumi shiro-gumi chō no chidori keri

yellow gang, white gang
the butterflies claim
their turf

白黄色蝶も組合したりけり (1820; *IZ* 1.172)
shiro kiiro chō mo kumiai shitari keri

white versus yellow –
the butterflies also
fight

In the second poem *chidori* 地どり is an old word, a form of the verb *chidoru*, which means to measure out a lot on which to build a house (*KD* 1049). The two "gangs" of butterflies, so human-like, lay claim to their respective territories. *Kumiai* 組合 in the third poem means, in modern Japanese, to form an association, but in earlier times it meant to wrestle (*KD* 520). Issa's satirical message is clear: butterflies fighting color-coded enemies behave in a sadly human fashion. However, just as the boss frog claiming his seat of honor is being perfectly froglike, the butterflies in these scenes are acting like butterflies. A superbly observant naturalist, Issa accurately records territorial butterfly skirmishes that may shock readers who think of these insects only as carefree and gentle. Zooligists such as Royce J. Bitzer and Kenneth C. Shaw would not at all be surprised by these haiku. In a study conducted on the campus of Iowa State University, they documented the aggressive behavior of male butterflies patrolling and defending elliptically shaped territories of 12-24 meters long and 4-13 meters wide. Their aerial battles, which lasted from ten to sixty seconds, were fierce. Issa wags his finger, in these poems, at people and insects alike.

In some poems Issa portrays animals of different species interacting in a combative way, as for example the following haiku about a cat and a crow.

若葉して猫と烏と喧嘩哉 (1821; *IZ* 1.417)
wakaba shite neko to karasu to kenka kana

fresh new leaves –
the cat and the crow
quarrel

However, his more typical presentations of interspecies relations among animals are non-satirical. Instead, envisioning animals as positive role models for human behavior, Issa portrays them interacting with harmony, cooperation, mutual respect, curiosity, or tender affection—their actions affirmatively answering Rodney King's famous question amid the Los Angeles riots of 1992, "Can we all get along?"

寝た牛の頭にすはるかはづかな (undated; *IZ* 1.165)
neta ushi no atama ni suwaru kawazu kana

squatting on the head
of a sleeping cow . . .
a frog

大犬の天窓張たる蜻蛉哉 (1815; IZ 1.542)
ōinu no atama haritaru tombo kana

resting
on the big dog's head
dragonfly

雀子や牛にも馬にも踏れずに (1825; *IZ* 1.131)
suzumego ya ushi ni mo uma ni mo fumarezu ni

baby sparrows
by the cow and the horse
untrampled

In the first two examples Issa present the unlikely companions of cow and frog, dog and dragonfly. The images are realistic and symbolic in equal measure. These creatures are, in reality, "getting along"—their peaceful coexistence showing a path that people might follow. The third haiku imparts a decidedly different message from the earlier Sir Horse poem. This time, instead of warning sparrows to move out of the way of the imperious horse that otherwise might trample them—a satirical attack on human authority—Issa shows *this* horse and *this* cow treading delicately, carefully among them.

Though the animals that interact in his haiku often belong to different species, Issa stresses the fact that they share one world.

馬の子も同じ日暮よかたつぶり (1806; *IZ* 1.385)
uma no ko mo onaji higure yo katatsuburi

sharing the sunset
with the pony . . .
a snail

犬と蝶他人むきでもなかりけり (1815; *IZ* 1.170)
inu to chō tanin muki demo nakari keri

the dog and the butterfly
not strangers
at all

丸く寝た犬にべったり小てふ哉 (1813; *IZ* 1.169)
maruku neta inu ni bettari ko chō kana

stuck to the dog
curled asleep . . .
a butterfly

Sunset is the "same" (*onaji*同じ) for a pony and a snail; a dog and a butterfly are not "strangers" (*tannin* 他人) to one another. A skeptic might question the level of awareness that the dog and butterfly bring to their relationship. In one poem the dog is sound asleep; it might as well be a bush that the butterfly has landed on. Each one might be unaware of, or utterly indifferent to, the existence of the other, but Issa nevertheless reveals a deep connection between them in these images of peaceful coexistence. All creatures *are* connected whether they know it or not—or so these haiku might imply.

Issa dwells on harmonius creature-to-creature connections so many times in so many poems, one begins to suspect that his intention is at least partly didactic. In these next three haiku, animals are portrayed realistically and, at the same time, can serve as role models for readers, showing them a better way.

庵崎の犬と仲よいちどり哉 (1811; *IZ* 1.717)
iosaki no inu to nakayoi chidori kana

on friendly terms
with the dog of Iosaki . . .
a plover

蝉鳴や物喰ふ馬の頬べたに (1814; IZ 1.383)
semi naku ya mono kuu uma no hobbeta ni

the cicada chirrs
on the grazing horse's
cheek

亀どのに負さつて鳴蛙哉 (1815; IZ 1.160)
kame dono ni obusatte naku kawazu kana

hitching a ride
on Mr. Turtle . . .
a croaking frog

Iosaki is a coastal city west of Kobe. Issa describes the status of the winter plover and the dog as *nakayoi*仲よい; they are familiar, intimate chums. In the second haiku, a cicada and a horse go about their normal daily business. One chirrs for a mate; the other grazes in a summer meadow. Issa's point seems to be that they do these things *together*. Again, whether or not they are consciously aware of it, the poet perceives them as companions, their mutual tolerance hinting at a way for humans to exist on this planet teeming with life. The third haiku about Mr. Turtle giving a frog a ride is cute enough to delight Issa's youngest readers. However, adults might further appreciate the embedded lesson of Buddhist oneness and compassion.

The turtle and frog appear, quite literally, as fellow travelers in the scene, reminding us of the Pure Land Buddhist concept that all sentient beings are on the same karmic path to enlightenment. Along the way, these particular sentient beings keep each other company and—if we might read the poem as a parable of how humans might "get along"—they help each other. The turtle selflessly carries the frog; the frog entertains the turtle with song. In an earlier chapter we considered Bashō's famous haiku about a solitary crow on a bare branch. While Issa has similar poems of loneliness or *sabi*, this is not the primary message of his myriad poems about animals. Far more typically he depicts them existing in a world of camaraderie and connection: turtles and frogs, horses and cicadas, plovers and dogs. They are not alone. Issa hints, in these portraits, we are not alone either.

In one well-known haiku he wonders aloud if the fleas in his home are lonely, hinting that this is his own emotion in the long autumn night.

蚤どもがさぞ夜永だろ淋しかろ (1813; *IZ* 1.446)
nomi domo ga sazo yonaga daro sabishi karo

for you fleas
the night must be long . . .
and lonely?

Though they might be lonely, his fleas are not alone. Issa is with them, talking to them and concerned about their welfare.

As noted earlier, Issa at times portrays animals killing one another: a crow eating a butterfly, geese and gulls devouring clams, a poor caterpillar writhing in the ants' "hell." More often, however, he presents animals of different species expressing a live-and-let-live attitude. Sparrows accept a wren into their midst.

雀等と仲間入せよみそさざい (1819; *IZ* 1.716)
suzumera to nakama iri seyo misosazai

joining the throng
of sparrows
a little wren

Bees and sparrows coexist like good neighbors.

蜂の巣の隣をかりる雀哉 (1821; *IZ* 1.177)
hachi no su no tonari wo kariru susume kana

renting a spot
next to the beehive . . .
sparrows

And, in an unforgettably hilarious image, a randy cat attempts to woo a chicken.

うかれきて鶏追まくる男猫哉 (1817; *IZ* 1.122)
ukare kite tori oimakuru oneko kana

so love-crazed
he chases a chicken . . .
tomcat

In some poems Issa shows animals seeming to appreciate the beauty or songs of their fellows.

草の蝶牛にも詠られにけり (1806; *IZ* 1.166)
kusa no chō ushi ni mo nagamerare ni keri

meadow butterflies –
the cow also
gazes

さをしかの角傾けて時鳥 (1813; *IZ* 1.340)
saoshika no tsuno katamukete hototogisu

the young buck's
antlers tilting . . .
"cuckoo!"

山猫のあつけとられし雲雀哉 (1822; *IZ* 1.145)
yama neko no akke torareshi hibari kana

the wild cat
looks astonished . . .
a skylark

The cow (like Issa) gazes at butterflies or, perhaps, at a single butterfly; both translations are possible. Issa suggests that the cow appreciates the dainty, colorful insect as much as he does. Of course, as we discussed in Chapter 2, it is hard to prove that nonhuman animals possess an esthetic sense, just as it is equally difficult to prove that they don't. The important thing is that Issa imagines that, on some level, even a cow takes pleasure in the color and movement of her tiny, flitting companion in the meadow. He similarly imagines that a buck tilting his head sideways is listening to, and appreciating, the song of a cuckoo. Even a wild cat, literally a "mountain cat" (*yama neko*山猫), has a poet's heart according to Issa, looking dumbfounded as the song of a lark fills his ears.

In addition to showing animals coexisting peacefully and appreciating one another, Issa portrays them embodying other values that people might do well to embrace. One of these values is to live fully in the present moment, a lesson perfectly expressed in a haiku that we considered in an earlier chapter.

鳴ながら虫の乗行浮木かな (1822; *IZ* 1.538)
naki nagara mushi no noriyuku ukigi kana

still singing the insect
is swept away . . .
floating branch

A flood (we know from the poem's head note) sweeps away branch and insect toward an uncertain future, most likely toward the insect's death; yet he sings. On a deep level, the image is an allegory of life—much like the Zen Buddhist parable of a man chased by a tiger over the side of a cliff, where he dangles from a vine being gnawed upon by mice. Instead of fretting about the future, the man, in different versions of the story, chooses to spend his final moments admiring a flower or the taste of strawberries, honey, or grapes.[63] Issa's insect is similarly attuned to the now. Of course, one might interpret the image differently, perceiving him as a fool to be singing for a mate while flood waters carry him to his doom. Nevertheless, I prefer to read Issa's tone as one of admiration for the insect, not ridicule. The intrepid little singer, like the man hanging from the vine over a precipice, fully realizes the advice of American spiritual teacher Ram Dass: to "be here now."

Another admirable quality of animals in Issa's haiku depictions is their willingness to serve as unswervingly loyal companions to people. Dogs, butterflies, and frogs figure in many such poems, some of which we have examined earlier in this book. Though Issa belonged to a Pure Land sect, this next haiku embodies a Zen parable that is just as resonant with spiritual signification as the one about the man and the tiger.

橋わたる盲の跡の蛙哉 (1812; *IZ* 1.159)
hashi wataru mekura no ato no kawazu kana

crossing the bridge
behind the blind man . . .
a frog

The figure of a blind man crossing a bridge recalls a series of at least eight *zenga* 禅画 (Zen paintings) by Hakuin Ekaku 白隠慧鶴 (1686-1768). In these monochrome paintings of ink on paper, blind men move from right to left across a narrow, precarious bridge. In a verse that accompanies two of these images, Hakuin writes,

Both the health of our bodies
and the fleeting world outside us
are like the blind men's
round log bridge—a mind/heart
that can cross over is the best guide.[64]

The blind men in Hakuin's paintings undertake a dangerous journey to reach the other shore, in other words, enlightenment. In Issa's haiku, the blind man's companion moving toward this enlightenment is a frog. Besides being a reiteration of one of his favorite themes—that all creatures are on the same karmic path to becoming Buddhas—the poem illustrates a feeling of compassion. The blind man, though he might not be aware of this fact, is not alone in the world; the frog faithfully follows behind him.

The innocence of animals in Issa's haiku is also instructive. Earlier, we considered his 1815 poem, "while I'm away/ enjoy your lovemaking . . . / hut's flies." With tongue firmly in cheek Issa implies that the flies' modesty might have prevented them from making love in his presence, but now that he is leaving they will have the hut all to themselves. The haiku is amusing because flies, of course, are not burdened with human ideas about modesty or guilt—and this, Issa implies in another poem about animals having sex, might be a good thing.

のさのさと恋をするかの蛙哉 (1813; *IZ* 1.159)
nosa-nosa to koi wo suru ka no kawazu kana

enjoying your sex
so shamelessly?
frogs

In Chapter 3 we encountered the haiku's key expression, *nosa-nosa*, in a haiku about a big toad at a rice-planting drinking party. While the word can mean several things, in that poem Issa seemed to be conveying an attitude of bold resolve. The same meaning applies in this context. Issa sees the lovemaking of the frogs as bold and shameless: happily unhampered by human modesty. The poet's admonishment of their flagrant, public sex only thinly veils his deeper feelings of admiration and approval. Issa hints at frog superiority over humans in this image of them guiltlessly following their nature.

When lightning strikes (in one of Issa's most striking haiku), only a puppy's face appears free from sinful craving (*muyoku* 無欲).

稲妻や狗ばかり無欲顔 (1820; *IZ* 1.485)
inazuma ya enokoro bakari muyoku kao

> lightning flash –
> only the puppy's face
> is innocent[65]

The word *bakari* ばかり ("only") indicates that other faces appear in the lightning flash, but theirs are marked by the sin of covetousness. These others certainly are people. Only the puppy, innocently enjoying the present moment, shows no sign of sinful greed. If the main goal of Buddhism is to escape the worldly desires that cause suffering, when the lightning flash lays bare the truth about the souls in the scene, only the puppy passes the test. He is the best Buddhist of the lot, showing a way of being that, Issa suggests, people might aspire to emulate.

As noted earlier, Buddhists of Issa's Japan believed in "Six Ways" of future life reincarnation. Returning as a sufferer in hell is the worst possible future (recall that Issa dramatized this future with an image of pond snails screaming in a kettle). The following haiku is third in Issa's "Six Ways" series of six haiku, epitomizing animal existence under the head note, "Beasts" (*chikushō* 畜生).

ちる花に仏とも法ともしらぬ哉 (1812; *IZ* 1.212)
chiru hana ni butsu tomo nori tomo shiranu kana

> in scattering blossoms
> Buddha and Buddhism
> unknown

Rising to the poetic challenge of summarizing what it means to be a nonhuman animal in one breath, Issa conjures this image of falling blossoms coupled with the idea of ignorance, specifically religious ignorance. Animals know nothing about Buddha and Buddha's dharma-law (*nori* 法). An important aspect of this dharma that they don't understand is the notion of impermanence, symbolized by the spring blossoms (probably cherry blossoms) that, after their brief period of glory, fall from branches and scatter to the ground. The most important thing to know about animals, Issa suggests, is that they are ignorant: of how short life is; of the suffering that transience causes; and of Buddha's remedy for the situation, his way to enlightenment. Not knowing there's a problem, they perceive no need for its solution.

How are we to understand this haiku? Is the ignorance of animals tragedy or bliss? Issa might be saying, "Poor beasts! They have no clue about the world of suffering into which they have been born, nor Amida Buddha's vow to rescue them!" Or, he might be saying (as I prefer to read the poem), "Lucky beasts! Not worrying about the law of transience, they live happily in the now!" As noted in the previous chapter, Amida's saving vow seems to apply to animals in Issa's haiku despite their lack of consciousness of this fact. To live contentedly in the here-and-now, receiving Buddha's help without understanding the need for Buddha's help—without even conceiving the existence of Buddha—is a very lucky thing. Ignorant of Buddha and Buddhism, animals, ironically, may be the best Buddhists of all.

In the next examples Issa presents first a toad and then a crow as potential holy men. In Chinese and Japanese folklore, mountain hermits were said to have the ability to ride on mist or clouds.

霧に乗る目付して居る蟇かな (1819; *IZ* 1.355)
kiri ni noru metsuki shite iru hiiki kana

looking like
"I can ride the mist" . . .
a toad

霧に乗る目付して居る烏かな (1819; *IZ* 1.355)
kiri ni noru metsuki shite iru karasu kana

looking like
"I can ride the mist" . . .
a crow

The toad and crow appear as if they can ride the mist, a Japanese expression that can mean, figuratively, that they are "clever looking." On one level, Issa pokes gentle fun at the pretentiousness he perceives in their expressions and attitudes. On a deeper level, the haiku suggests that animals might possess occult knowledge and spiritual power. They are on more intimate terms with the natural mysteries hidden in this world's mist than Issa and most of his readers will ever be; they may know secrets that only the most enlightened mountain arhats ever discover. As we have seen so often in Issa, his poetic jokes hint at deeper truths. Once again, animals in his haiku appear more spiritually advanced than the vast majority of human beings.

At times, in the poetry of Issa, animals bring to the world a feeling of unspeakable rapture.

どち向も万吉とやなく蛙 (1812; *IZ* 1.159)
dochi muku mo yorozu yoshi to ya naku kawazu

in every direction
ten thousand blessings . . .
croaking frogs

The poem describes a pre-electronic age experience of surround sound. From every direction Issa faces, frogs chant "ten thousand blessings" (*yorozu yoshi* 万吉)—a joyous celebration of life and springtime fertility. The myriad frogs croak myriad blessings, making the world a better place for anyone who opens his or her ears and heart to them. Another haiku about frogs is quieter but just as deeply evocative of the blessings that animals bring to the world.

天下泰平と居並ぶ蛙かな (1815; *IZ* 1.160)
tenka taihei to i-narabu kawazu kana

sitting in a row
peace on earth . . .
frogs

No "boss" frog asserts his supremacy here. No frog is fighting, competing for mates, or jockeying for position on a stone or log. For the moment, a perfect peace prevails in all the "world under Heaven" (*tenka* 天下). Issa's image of frogs lined up in a row suggests equality, cooperation, and a sense of common purpose. These "lesser" animals serve as role models in the haiku for human beings who only for such brief interludes, if at all, achieve peace on earth in their time.

In the previous chapter we saw that even a butterfly is weighed on the scales of karma, according to Issa. Nevertheless, this is the animal that most impressively embodies a path to enlightenment in his poetry.

蝶とぶや此世に望みないやうに (1809; *IZ* 1.167)
chō tobu ya kono yo ni nozomi nai yō ni

a butterfly flits
as if wanting nothing
in this world

The phrase, "wanting nothing in this world" can be interpreted in two ways: satisfaction with this world, or a feeling of hopelessness about this world. My Japanese advisor Shinji Ogawa believes that Issa is saying the latter. Indeed, in the context of Pure Land Buddhism, *kono yo*此世, literally "this world," implies the present, corrupt age of *mappō*. The pure and delicate butterfly, in Shinji's view, wants nothing to do with such an imperfect, sinful, and suffering world. I wonder if there might be a third way to read the haiku: that the butterfly is *celebrating* life in this corrupt and hopeless world? With its purity and innocence, it craves nothing in or from such a world; it flits through it but is not *of* it. If this is so, the butterfly is a shining image of hope for Issa and for his readers, Buddhist and non-Buddhist alike. While we might not be able to physically escape the world of suffering, we can all find a better way to live in it: the butterfly's way of gentleness, detachment, and (as noted in other haiku[66]) trust in the Beyond.

***

A haiku is a poem of discovery that requires opening one's mind to the elements of the present moment or, at times, to a remembered or imagined moment. By "one's mind" I mean, initially that of the poet, but later, in the act of reconstructing and reflecting on the moment, the reader's mind. Whether the images and sensations of a haiku enter the poet's consciousness in real time or through memory or imagination, his or her purpose is always to discover, in the act of writing, how disparate elements in the universe connect: a frog and a sunset, buzzing bees and ripening melons, the killing of a chicken and the greenness of a willow tree. Readers join the poet in the act of discovery, coloring it with their own memories, associations, and beliefs. The successful haiku poet never tells readers what to think but, rather, invites them to explore their own hearts and minds, arriving at their own conclusions as images of a moment reveal their intricate connections. The poet does, however, guide this exploration, nudging readers toward this or that revelation. A core assumption of this book has been this: if we wish to make a case for a poet's "argument" through haiku, specifically to grasp what Issa is saying about animals and how we should relate to them, it is necessary to read broadly, judging the meaning and tone of any particular verse in light of others and, when relevant, taking into account literary allusions, historical contexts, and biographical facts.

The resulting picture is complicated, but several strong, clear themes have emerged: animals can serve to satirize human foibles; animals (more often) can function as role models for Issa and his readers; animals and people are fundamentally the same; animals are companions, peers and fellow travelers; and animals can point the way to spiritual enlightenment.

Issa's approach to animals is not one-dimensional. At times he portrays them with stark realism that, depending on the connection in focus, can convey a tone of lament or satirical criticism. For example, his image of birds with their eyes sewn shut juxtaposed with blooming cherry trees is realistic but also implicitly condemns the human beings who would treat animals so cruelly. It may be easy to imagine what he would say about mutilated, mass-produced and warehoused chickens of today, beaks and toes cut off, crammed into cages. Issa's work sensitizes readers to animal reality, inspiring, perhaps, life-changing epiphanies like the one experienced by a sumo wrestler in the following haiku.

角力取が詫して逃す雀かな (1825; *IZ* 1.509)
sumōtori ga wabi shite nogasu suzume kana

the sumo wrestler
apologizing, releases
the sparrow

The wrestler is massive and the bird is tiny, and the difference between them reflects the imbalance of power between human and nonhuman residents of the planet. Issa's point is to recommend tenderness and compassion in this image of setting a caged sparrow free with an apology. Many people in this world may owe apologies to the animals they have directly or by proxy imprisoned and tormented.

More often than functioning as vehicles for satire, Issa's animals—while realistically portrayed—are emblems of a gentler, more tolerant, more enlightened way of interacting with their cousins and second cousins. A frog croaking on a turtle's back is a perfectly believable image that, at the same time, suggests creaturely camaraderie. One of Issa's most important discoveries throughout his poems of discovery is that animals are his (and our) peers. He talks to them because he recognizes that they are like him. He listens to them because he acknowledges that they have a legitimate perspective. He warns the katydid that he is turning over in bed because the katydid's life has value. He reminds us countless times that the blessings of Shinto and the awakening promised by Buddhist sects—Pure Land, Zen, Shingon, and others—pertain to animals as much as they do to people. Karmically, people might even be a step behind. A puppy may be ignorant of Buddha or of the contents of holy sutras, and yet, in Issa's view, it is closer to enlightenment than most people.

けさ秋としらぬ狗が仏哉 (1820; *IZ* 1.430)
kesa aki to shiranu enoko ga hotoke kana

not knowing that
autumn's begun, puppy
Buddha!

The puppy in this haiku stands for all animals. All the mammals, birds, amphibians, crustaceans, insects, arachnids, reptiles, fish, and other creatures that inhabit Issa's poetry might not be aware that autumn has begun or of the symbolic implications of this season—the notions of aging and inevitable death—but they are Buddhas in the making, nonetheless. This book has also shown that Issa likes to nestle profound truths inside word play and jokes. The above poem is typical. *Shiranu ga hotoke* 知らぬが仏 ("Know-nothing Buddha") is a Japanese expression for "Ignorance is bliss." On one level, Issa is merely saying, "How lucky the ignorant puppy is, not knowing that autumn has begun!" Looking deeper though, readers might conclude that the puppy—living in the present moment, not calculating, not dreading the cold weather, its own death, or whatever awaits it in the next life—*is* a Buddha and, therefore, a role model.

In the Introduction, we noted that feminist ethicists have emphasized that intellectual argument alone is not the most effective way to convince people to adopt a more compassionate approach to animals. What is needed, these philosophers say, is to awaken feelings of empathy for nonhuman creatures.[67] In this book we have seen Issa evoke such empathy through his poetry, underscoring connections and similarities that link all animal life: nonhuman animals can be poets, musicians, and dancers; like people, they make love, and they build families which they defend with their lives. Animals work like people, play like people, and participate in seasonal celebrations from New Year's Day to end-of-year drinking parties—as portrayed in the haiku of Issa. Their ignorance of the meaning that humans place on such rituals does not negate the fact that they are physically and consciously *present*. Issa discovers in his haiku—and readers discover alongside him—that human space and animal space overlap such that these categories become meaningless. Planet Earth is, indeed, a shared space for all animals, including the human kind. Although Issa never asserts that animals have "rights" or that people have specific "obligations" toward them, he coaxes his readers toward an insight about animals that is sorely needed in our time: they are like us in important ways and thus deserve our care and compassion. Reading and considering deeply the haiku of Kobayashi Issa can benefit farmers, food producers, consumers, scientists, teachers, students, politicians, and voters. Recognizing animals, as Issa does, as relatives and fellow travelers in a shared world is a first step toward their ethical treatment.

NOTES

1. While some readers believe that the "monstrous thesis" that animals feel no pain is implicit in the argument that Descartes puts forth in his *Meditations*, John Cottingham disagrees. Descartes' assertion that animals do not think, according to Cottingham, "need not commit him to denying any feeling or sensation to animals" (230). Whatever Descartes' true thought on this point, his philosophy has been used to justify all manner of cruelty to animals, including vivisection.

2. Regan and Singer 12. My colleague at Xavier University of Louisiana, Jason Berntsen, believes that "The Kantian position in particular is arguably the most plausible version of the view that animals and humans are essentially different kinds of beings. Moreover, many contemporary philosophers accept modified versions of Kant's view, and it continues to loom large in philosophical discussions about the moral status of animals. What sets us apart from other species, according to Kant, is the fact that we can reflect on our instincts and desires and ask ourselves whether we *ought* to act on these instincts and desires. We are moral agents in a way other species of animals are not. This capacity, Kant thought, is what marks the difference between persons and non-persons and is the source of moral rights and duties. Kant's view may be mistaken, of course, but note that one can accept Kant's idea that our autonomy puts us in a morally different category from other animals without accepting his view that we do not have moral duties to animals or that we can treat them however we please."

3. Many sources continue to list Issa's death year as 1827. He died on the 19th day of Eleventh Month in the old Japanese calendar year that corresponds to 1827, but the equivalent date on the Western calendar was January 5, 1828.

4. Kobayashi Issa, *Issa zenshū* (Nagano: Shinano Mainichi Shimbunsha, 1979) 1.627; this haiku is undated. All texts from Issa are from the nine-volume *Issa zenshū* (hereafter *IZ*). For the *hiragana* transcriptions I use the old system that Issa used for the most part (for example, だまって instead of だまってand いうぜんinstead of ゆうぜん). Here and henceforth, English translations of Japanese are my own unless otherwise designated.

5. The extent to which a snail feels pain is one that will perhaps, one day, be answered by scientific research. A study by R. W. Elwood of Queens University Belfast (2013) suggests that shore crabs respond to mild electric shock in a way that is consistent with a pain response. Until the day that science ultimately settles the question of snails feeling pain, I choose to share Issa's compassionate assumption that they do.

6. I am indebted to Laurence Stacey who connected Issa's approach to animals with the deep ecology movement in his talk, "Issa and the African American Perspective in Haiku," at the South-East Regional Haiku Society of America conference in Atlanta, 26 October 2013.

7. Qtd. from "Between the West and the East," a presentation at the World Haiku Association Conference in Tenri, Japan, 4 Oct. 2003. Balabanova's insightful talk was later published in *World Haiku 2005*.

8. When I speak of Issa in this book, I mean the individual portrayed or implicit in his writing, not (perhaps) the real Kobayashi Issa, whose true thoughts and feelings may or may not be accurately embodied by his literary self-imagining. Personally, I choose to believe that the warm-hearted Issa whom we meet in his pages is an accurate reflection of the flesh-and-blood man, but whether or not this is true is impossible to tell.

9. Issa's home province of Shinano is now called Nagano Prefecture, the site of the 1998 Winter Olympics. In his poetry, he often describes himself as a Buddhist priest, for example:

一茶坊に過たるものや炭一俵 (1813; *IZ* 1.704)
issa-bō ni sugitaru mono ya sumi ippyō

more than enough
for Priest Issa . . .
one bag of coal

His "temple" is the Temple of Haikai, *haikai* being the name for the type of short poetry that he wrote. The word "haiku" was coined much later by Masaoka Shiki (1867-1901). In this book, I use the more familiar term "haiku" to describe what Issa would have called *haikai*. Adopting his priestly identity was like a rebirth or reinvention of himself: the death of Yatarō and the birth of Priest Issa.

春立や弥太郎改め一茶坊 (1818; *IZ* 1.31)
haru tatsu ya yatarō aratame issa-bō

new spring
Yatarō dies, Priest Issa
is born

春立や弥太郎改めはいかい寺 (1819; *IZ* 1.31)
haru tatsu ya yatarō aratame haikai-ji

new spring
Yatarō is reborn . . .
into Haiku Temple

10. In this book I follow the traditional Japanese way of counting age, according to which a child is one at birth and gains a year with each New Year's Day. Issa was born on the fifth day of Fifth Month, 1763: June 15 on the Western calendar. That next New Year's Day, he turned two—though Western parents would have described him as only eight months old. This is why, though he was officially three years old when his mother died in 1765, by Western reckoning he would have been just over two and a half.

11. Much of this discussion of "The Tongue-Cut Sparrow" first appeared in my essay, "Stories Behind the Haiku: Cultural Memory in Issa."

12. Nakada Norio, ed. *Kogo daijiten* (Tokyo: Shogakukan 1983) 622. Hereafter *KD*.

13. Over the course of several years, Shinji Ogawa visited *The Haiku of Kobayashi Issa* website frequently, generously offering comments and insights on hundreds of the translations. A man of mystery, Shinji never revealed his literary or educational background, but his knowledge of Japanese literature, art, philosophy, and religion clearly ran deep. All that he would ever say about himself is that he was an expatriate who left Japan decades ago to live somewhere in the Western hemisphere.

14. The Japanese text reads as follows.

西にうろたへ東にさすらひ、一所不住の狂人有。且に
は上総に喰ひ、夕には武蔵にやどりて、白波のよるべ
をしらず、たつ淡のきえやすき物から、名を一茶坊と
いふ. *IZ* 5.15.

15. *IZ* 3.472; 6.152. The Japanese texts read as follows.

老翁岩に腰かけて一軸をさづける画.

老翁岩に腰かけて、一軸をさづける図に.

16. See M. Seiler, C. Schwitzer, M Gamba, and M. W.
Holderied, "Interspecific Semantic Alarm Call Recog-
nition in the Solitary Sahamalaza Sportive Lemur,
Lepilemur Sahamalazensis; H. Takatsu, K. Tainaka, J.
Yoshimura, and M. Minami, "Spontaneous Flash
Communication of Females in an Asian Firefly"; R.
Sacchi, D. Pellitteri-Rosa, M. Marchesi, P. Galeotti, and
M. Fasola, "A Comparison among Sexual Signals in
Courtship of European Tortoises; and C. Masco,
"Neighbor-Stranger Discrimination on the Basis of a
Threat Vocalization in the Great Black-Backed Gull."

17. In *A History of Haiku* R. H. Blyth identifies the verb in
the middle phrase as *uwasu* ("gossip"), 1.369-70. However, the editors of *Issa zenshū* render it, *hanashi* ("talk");
IZ 1.84.

18. Ueda (103) writes that the poem was written in
January 1816 by the Western calendar. This date seems to
be off. The haiku appears in Issa's poetic journal
Shichiban nikki in Twelfth Month 1816; *IZ* 3.457. This

means, in the Western calendar, the date of composition would have been early 1817, not 1816.

19. The Japanese text reads as follows.

鎮西八郎為朝、人礫うつ所に. *IZ* 6.152.

20. The editors of *IZ* identify "Heaven" (*ken* 乾) as the top sign but incorrectly describe "southeast" (*tatsumi* 巽) as the bottom one; *IZ* 2.148, note 4. See Blofeld 172-73.

21. The following analysis of this haiku first appeared in my essay, "Stories Behind the Haiku: Cultural Memory in Issa."

22. Lewis Mackenzie believes that this haiku was written when Issa's wife, Kiku, "lay ill of the sickness from which shortly afterwards she was to die." Harold G. Henderson makes the same claim. However, the poem was composed in Seventh Month, 1822. Kiku didn't fall into her "last illness" until the following year, on the 19th day of Second Month, 1823—according to Kobayashi Keiichirō. See Mackenzie *The Autumn Wind: A Selection from the Poems of Issa* (London: John Murray, 1957; rpt. Tokyo: Kodansha International, 1984), 67; Henderson *An Introduction to Haiku* (New York: Doubleday, 1958), 133; and Kobayashi, *Kobayashi Issa* 小林一茶 (Tokyo: Kissen Kōbunkan, 1961) 263.

23. In a later haiku of 1824 we find Issa still playing with this scene of river-separated cats:

恋猫や答へる声は川むかう (1824; *IZ* 1.124)
koi neko ya kotaeru koe wa kawa mukau

the lover cat's
call is answered . . .
facing the river

24. This is *waka* number 337 from *Man'yōshū* 万葉集:
"And now Okura really must be departing. My children
must be crying, and their mother too must await my
return." Trans. Jeremy Robinson in Shirane 100. Issa
changes the endings of the two verbs from *-mu* むto *-n* ん.

25. The haiku in question, written in Fifth Month 1810, is
the following.

古郷やよるも障るも茨の花 (*IZ* 1.424)
furusato ya yoru mo sawaru mo bara no hana

the closer I get
to my village, the more pain . . .
wild roses

In a head note to this haiku Issa reports that he entered
his home village on the morning of Fifth Month, 19th
day, 1810. First, he paid his respects at his father's
gravesite, and then he met with the village headman.
While the content of their meeting is not revealed, it
plainly had to do with the matter of the poet's inheritance
that his stepmother and half-brother had withheld from
him for years. He goes on to write, tersely, "After seeing
the village elder, entered my house. As I expected they
offered me not even a cup of tea, so I left there soon." In
another text dated that same year, he recopies this "wild
roses" haiku and signs it, *mamako issa* まま子一茶: "Issa
the Stepchild"; *IZ* 3.61; 1.424.

26. Because Issa seems to be reliving his own past in this and similar poems, I prefer to imagine a male pony, even though its gender is not specified in the Japanese texts.

27. Matsuo Bashō, *Matsuo Bashō shū* 1.70. Basho wrote this haiku in 1680.

28. Issa used the two spellings of snail, *katatsuburi* and *katatsumuri*, interchangeably.

29. For example, she prefaces the first chapter of her book with this haiku that was cited earlier in this book, using and crediting my translation.

足元へいつ来りしよかたつぶり (1801; *IZ* 1.385)
ashi moto e itsu kitarishi yo katatsuburi

at my feet
when did you get here?
snail

30. See, for example, Bekoff and Byers, eds., *Animal Play: Evolutionary, Comparative, and Ecological Perspectives*.

31. According to Shokan Tadashi Kondo, who advised me on this haiku, *gebana* 夏花 ("summer flowers") in this context is another word for *geango* 夏安居 : a "summer retreat" decorated with flowers.

32. According to Moller, bilateral symmetry is a signal of quality genes and therefore important in mate selection for barn swallows. However, Zaidel and Cohen found that, for human beings, "very beautiful faces can be functionally asymmetrical" (1165). Whether our concept of beauty and attractiveness in human faces is sym-

metrical or slightly asymmetrical, these perceptions seem to be as hard-wired for people as they are for swallows.

33. The Japanese text reads as follows.

乞食袋首にかけて、小風呂敷せなかに負たれば、影法師はさながら西行らしく見へて殊勝なるに、心は雪と墨染の袖と、思へば . . . (*IZ* 6.140).

34. *IZ* 1.143. For a fuller discussion of this work, see Berenbaum 325.

35. This poem was written in Second Month, 1818. Later that month Issa revised it, changing the location and making "dance" a command.

> まへや蝶三弦流布のあさじ原 (1818; *IZ* 1.172)
> *mae ya chō samisen rufu no asaji-bara*
>
> dance, butterfly!
> someone plays samisen
> in Asaji Field

36. Many readers are familiar with the Robert Hass translation of this haiku: "Don't worry, spiders,/ I keep house/ casually" (153)—a wonderful version that suffers only from its omission of the specific seasonal reference of winter soot-sweeping.

37. Issa loved this image of animals passing nonchalantly through sitting rooms. Here is one more example.

> 鶏の座敷を歩く日永哉 (1823; *IZ* 1.62)
> *niwatori no zashiki wo aruku hi naga kana*

a chicken strolls
through the sitting room...
a long day

In his clever translation that zooms in to focus on a detail
that Japanese readers would take for granted, Makoto
Ueda has the chicken walking on "the tatami floor" (150).

38. This undated haiku seems to be a rewrite of one that
Issa composed in 1813. The original version begins with
the phrase, "weak tea" (*cha no awa* 茶の淡); *IZ* 1.168.

39. See *IZ* 1.236 and 1.197.

40. *Nosa-nosa* can denote performing an action with com-
posure (*heizen* 平然), with lighthearted nonchalance (*nonki*
暢気), lacking dread (*habakaru tokoro no nai* 憚ところのな
い), or shamelessly (*ōchaku* 横着); *KD* 1292. In other
haiku, Issa uses *nosa-nosa* to describe frogs making love
(1813), a village dog guiding him across a low-tide beach
(1816), lice on a straw mat (1822), lice in his blossom-
viewing robe (1822), and a big toad at a rice-planting
drinking party (1822). The images of frogs and lice
suggest a sense of shamelessness; the images of the dog
and toad suggest fearless, bold resolve.

41. *Tsumuri* つむり is an old word for "head"; *KD* 1106.

42. Charity fundraisers understand this aspect of human
psychology quite well; people are more likely to care
about and give money for a single starving child, pictured
and individualized, than to contribute to a general fund
that will help thousands of nameless, un-pictured children
who suffer the same hunger.

43. The Japanese text reads as follows.

されば生とし活るもの、蚤・虱にいたる迄、命をしき
は人に同じからん。ましてつるみたるを殺すは、罪深
きわざなるべし. *IZ* 6.145.

44. For a fuller discussion of Issa and Pure Land
Buddhism see my essay, "The Haiku Mind: Pure Land
Buddhism and Issa" and my book, *Pure Land Haiku: The
Art of Priest Issa.*

45. The Japanese text reads as follows.

弥陀たのむすべもしらで、うかうか月日を費やすこそ、
二ッ子の手前もはづかしけれと思ふも、其坐を退けば、
はや地獄の種を蒔て、膝にむらがる蠅をにくみ、膳を
巡る蚊をそしりつつ、剰仏のいましめし酒を呑む.*IZ*
6.148.

In their translations, Sam Hamill and Nobuyuki Yuasa
render "Amida" generically as "Buddha," losing the
specific Pure Land Buddhist flavor of the passage; see
Hamill 54 and Yuasa 94.

46. The Japanese text reads as follows.

しかる時は、あながち作り声して念仏申に不及、ねが
はずとも仏はも守り給ふべし。是則当流の安心とは申
也. *IZ* 6.157.

47. In *Pure Land Haiku: The Art of Priest Issa* I added the
phrase, "in the Western Paradise," to qualify "heavenly
being" (103). I now believe that this qualification was
incorrect. The fortunate ones reborn in the Western
Paradise are not gods or, as of yet, Buddhas. They enjoy

an existence removed from the corruption of the present world that makes their ultimate enlightenment, Buddha-hood, attainable.

48. "Blossoms" (*hana* 花) can signify cherry blossoms in the shorthand of haiku, hence my translation.

49. Two versions of this series exist. One appears in Issa's haiku collection *Kabuban* 株版 (1812), while the other was published posthumously by Issa's students in *Issa hokku shū* 一茶発句集 in 1829. The present haiku appears only in the later, 1829 version; see *IZ* 6.48 and *IZ Supplementary Volume* (*Betsuken* 別巻) 223; 256.

50. Issa spells *fugu* 河豚 ("pufferfish") here using the Japanese character for *awabi* 鰒 ("abalone").

51. *Kufū* 工夫is an old word that has the modern equivalent, *shian* 思案: a thought or a plan; *Kogo dai jiten* 518.

52. The Japanese text reads as follows.

さん俵法師といふを作りて、笹湯浴せる真似かたして、神は送り出したれど、益す益すよはりて. *IZ* 6.150.

53. Maruyama Kazuhiko 丸山一彦, ed. *Issa haiku shū* 一茶俳句集 (Tokyo: Iwanami Shoten, 1990; rpt. 1993) 223, note 1169.

54. For more on Jizō see my essay, "Not Your Ordinary Saint: Jizō in the Haiku of Issa"; and Dykstra.

55. Two huge bronze statues of the Buddha exist in Japan: at Kamakura and at Nara. The one at Nara, in Tōdaiji Temple, dates back to the Eighth Century (its

dedication ceremony was in 752). It is 14.98 meters tall, according to the temple's website (*Tōdaiji* 東大寺), though Kobayashi Takeshi puts it at 16.19 meters (40).

56. In his translation of this haiku, as Bob Jones envisions the moment, several swallows "pour forth" (49). I prefer to imagine only a single swallow, following the same principle of parsimony that guided my translation of the crow snacking on the butterfly.

57. The Japanese text reads as follows.

草木国土悉皆成仏とかや。かれらも仏生得たるものに
なん。*IZ* 6.137.

58. This haiku appears in two poetic diaries: *Hachiban nikki* in an 1819 entry, and *Oraga haru*, also from the year 1819. *IZ* 4.236; 6.137.

59. The Japanese text reads as follows.

御仏必見捨給ふなよ。*IZ* 2.467.

60. Buddha lists the thirty-three different bodies that the bodhisattva Avalokiteśvara can occupy in his efforts to help suffering beings; *Scripture of the Lotus Blossom* 289-90. Avalokiteśvara, his sex changing to female, became Guanyin in China and Kannon in Japan.

61. For more discussion of sea slugs in the haiku of Issa and others, see Gill.

62. The Japanese text reads as follows.

布施東海寺に詣けるに、鶏どもの跡をしたひぬること
の不便さに、門前の家によりて、米一合ばかり買ひて、
菫蒲公のほとりにちらしけるを、やがて仲間喧嘩をい
く所にも始たり。其うち木末より鳩雀ばちばちとび来
たりて、心しづかにくらひつつ、鶏の来る時、小ばや
くもとの梢へ逃さりぬ。鳩雀は蹴合の長かれかしとや
思ふらん。士農工商其外さまざまの稼ひ、みなかくの
通り。*IZ* 6.52.

63. See, for example, Reps and Senzaki, 39.

64. For an analysis of these *zenga* see Seo and Addiss,
139-41.

65. In *Pure Land Haiku: The Art of Priest Issa*, I translate
enokoro in this haiku as "dog" (47) but I have since
discovered that this word more likely indicates a puppy,
making it all the more innocent.

66. For example, we have considered the highly suggestive images of a butterfly on a flowerpot and on an
offering shelf listening to Amida's Buddha promise.

> 花桶に蝶も聞かよ一大事 (undated; *IZ* 1.167)
> *hana oke ni chō mo kiku ka yo ichi daiji*

> on the flower pot
> does the butterfly, too
> hear Buddha's promise?

> あか棚に蝶も聞くかよ一大事 (1808; *IZ* 1.167)
> *aka tana ni chō mo kiku ka yo ichi daiji*

on the offering shelf
does the butterfly also hear
Buddha's promise?

67. The feminist position is akin to the neo-Aristotelian virtue ethics approach that asserts that morality emerges from concrete relationships and facts, not abstract reasoning. Because Issa seeks to see the world through the eyes of animals that he encounters in real life as members of his community, he elicits identification with and sympathy for those animals. See "The Moral Status of Animals," *Stanford Encyclopedia of Philosophy*.

WORKS CITED

Ashliman, D. L. *The Tongue-Cut Sparrow: A Fairy Tale from Japan.* n.p. Web. 5 Sept. 2011.

Bailey, Elizabeth Tova. *The Sound of a Wild Snail Eating.* Chapel Hill: Algonquin Books of Chapel Hill, 2010. Print.

Balabanova, Ludmila. "Between the West and the East." Ban'ya Natsuishi, ed. *World Haiku 2005.* Tokyo: World Haiku Association, Nishida-shoten, 2005. 95-104. Print.

Barnhill, David Landis and Roger S. Gottlieb. American Academy of Religion. *Deep Ecology and World Religions: New Essays on Sacred Grounds.* Albany: State University of New York Press, 2001. Print.

Bekoff, Marc and John Alexander Byers, eds. *Animal Play: Evolutionary, Comparative, and Ecological Perspectives.* Cambridge: Cambridge University Press, 1998. Print.

Berenbaum, May R. *Bugs in the System: Insects and Their Impact on Human Affairs.* Reading, Mass.: Addison-Wesley Publishing Group, 1995. Print.

Bitzer, R.J. and K. C. Shaw. "Territorial Behavior of the Red Admiral, *Vanessa atalanta* (L.) (Lepidoptera: Nymphalidae)." *Journal of Research on the Lepidoptera* 18 (1979): 36-49. Print.

Blyth, R. H. *Haiku.* Reset paperback ed. 4 vols. Tokyo: Hokuseido, 1981-1982. Print.

---. *A History of Haiku.* 2 vols. Tokyo: Hokuseido, 1964; rpt. 1969. Print.

Bodart-Baily, Beatrice M. *The Dog Shogun: The Personality and Politics of Tokugawa Tsunayoshi*. Honolulu: Univ. of Hawai'i Press 2006. Print.

Bolitho, Harold. *Bereavement and Consolation: Testimonies from Tokugawa Japan*. New Haven and London: Yale Univ. Press, 2003. Print.

Borgen, Robert. *Sugawara no Michizane and the Early Heian Court*. Honolulu: Univ. of Hawai'i Press, 1994. Print.

Buber, Martin. *I and Thou*. New York: Charles Scribner's Sons, 1937. Print.

Cavallaro, Dani,. *The Fairy Tale and Anime: Traditional Themes, Images and Symbols at Play on Screen*. Jefferson, N.C.: McFarland & Co., 2011. Print.

Cholley, Jean. *En village de miséreux: Choix de poèmes de Kobayashi Issa*. Paris: Gallimard, 1996. Print.

Chuang-tzu [Zhuangzi]. *The Way of Chuang Tzu*. Trans. Thomas Merton. New York: New Directions Books, 1969. Print.

Cottingham, John. "Descartes' Treatment of Animals" in John Cottingham, ed., *Descartes: Oxford Readings in Philosophy*. Oxford: Oxford University Press, 1998; rpt. 2005. Print.

Cunningham, Don. *Taiho-Jutsu: Law and Order in the Age of the Samurai*. Boston, Rutland Vermont and Tokyo: Tuttle Publishing, 2004. Print.

Devall, Bill. *Simple in Means, Rich in Ends: Practicing Deep Ecology*. Salt Lake City: Peregrine Smith Books, 1988. Print.

Devall, Bill and George Sessions. *Deep Ecology : Living as if Nature Mattered*. Salt Lake City: Peregrine Smith Books, 1985. Print.

Dykstra, Yoshiko Kurata. "Jizō, the Most Merciful. Tales from *Jizō Bosatsu Reigenki*." *Monumenta Nipponica* 33, 2 (1978): 179-200. Print.

Elwood, R. W., and B. Magee. "Shock Avoidance by Discrimination Learning in the Shore Crab (*Carcinus*

Maenas) is consistent with a Key Criterion for Pain." *Journal of Experimental Biology* 216 (2013): 353-58. Print.

Falkman, Kai. *Understanding Haiku: A Pyramid of Meaning*. Winchester, VA: Red Moon Press, 2002. Print.

Fujimoto Jitsuya 藤本實也. *Issa no kenkyū* 一茶の研究. Tokyo: Meiwa Insatsu, 1949. Print.

Garner, Robert. *Animals, Politics, and Morality*. Manchester: Manchester University Press, 2004. Print.

Gill, Robin D. Gill, *Rise, Ye Sea Slugs*. Key Biscayne, Florida: Paraverse Press, 2003. Print.

Griffis, William Elliot. *Japanese Fairy World. Stories from the Wonder-Lore of Japan*. Schenectady, N.Y.: J.H. Barhyte, 1880. Print.

Hakuin Ekaku. "The End of the Bridge." Trans. unknown. *108zenbooks*. Web. 6 June 2012.

Hamill, Sam. *The Spring of My Life and Selected Haiku by Kobayashi Issa*. Boston: Shambhala 1997. Print.

Hass, Robert. *The Essential Haiku: Versions of Bashō, Buson, & Issa*. Hopewell, N.J.: The Ecco Press, 1994. Print.

Hearn, Lafcadio. *In Ghostly Japan*. Boston: Little, Brown, 1899. Print.

Henderson, Harold G. *An Introduction to Haiku*. New York: Doubleday, 1958. Print.

Highwater, Jamake. *Dance: Rituals of Experience*. 3rd Edition. Pennington, New Jersey: Princeton Book Company, 1992. Print.

Huey, Robert N. "Journal of My Father's Last Days: Issa's *Chichi no Shūen Nikki*." *Monumenta Nipponica* 39:1 (1984): 25-54. Print.

I Ching: The Book of Changes. Trans. John Blofeld. New York: Penguin Arkana, 1991. Print.

Jones, Bob. "Seasonality." *Modern Haiku* 27.3 (1996): 47-50. Print.

Jordan, Michael. *Dictionary of Gods and Goddesses*. New York: Infobase Publishing, 2004. Print.

Kaplan, Gisela and Lesley J. Rogers. "Elephants That Paint, Birds That Make Music: Do Animals Have an Aesthetic Sense?" 1 Oct. 2006. *The Dana Foundation.* Web. 20 May 2012.

Kasulis, Thomas P. *Shinto: The Way Home: Dimensions of Asian Spirituality.* Honolulu: Univ. of Hawai'i Press, 2004. Print.

Kenkō Yoshida 兼好吉田. *Essays in Idleness.* 徒然草. Trans. Donald Keene. New York: Columbia Univ. Press, 1983. Print.

Kobayashi Issa 小林一茶. *Issa zenshū* 一茶全集 (*IZ*). Ed. Kobayashi Keiichirō 小林計一郎. 9 vols. Nagano: Shinano Mainichi Shimbunsha, 1976-79. Print.

Kobayashi Fumihiko. "Is the Animal Woman a Meek or an Ambitious Figure in Japanese Folktales?" *Fabula: Journal of Folktale Studies.* 51.3-4 (2010): 235-50. Print.

Kobayashi Keiichirō 小林計一郎. *Kobayashi Issa* 小林一茶. Tokyo: Kissen Kōbunkan, 1961. Print.

Kobayashi Takeshi. *Nara Buddhist Art: Todai-ji.* Tran. Richard L. Gage. New York & Tokyo: Weatherhill & Heibonsha, 1975. Print.

Kojiki. Trans. Donald L. Philippi. Princeton & Tokyo: Princeton Univ. Press & Univ. of Tokyo Press, 1968. Print.

LaFleur, William R. *The Karma of Words: Buddhism and the Literary Arts in Medieval Japan.* Berkeley: Univ. of California Press, 1983. Print.

Lanoue, David G. "Animals and Shinto in the Haiku of Issa." *Simply Haiku* (Autumn 2012/ Winter 2013). Web.

---. "Beauty-Loving Animals in the Haiku of Issa." *Kadō: Calea Poeziei* 1.1 (April 2012): 164-74. Print.

---. *The Distant Mountain: The Life and Haiku of Kobayashi Issa.* Hindi trans. by Angelee Deodhar. Chandigarh: Azad Hind, 2009. Print.

---. "The Haiku Mind: Pure Land Buddhism and Issa" in *Eastern Buddhist* 39.2 (2008): 159-76. Print.

---. *The Haiku of Kobayashi Issa.* <http://haikuguy.com/issa/>. Web. 2000-present.

---. "Issa's Frogs and Toads: Mirrors of Humanity." Keynote speech for the Haiku International Association conference, Tokyo, Nov. 27, 2011.

---. "Not Your Ordinary Saint: Jizō in the Haiku of Issa." *World Haiku Review* 3.2 (December 2003). Web. 6 June 2012.

---. *Pure Land Haiku: The Art of Priest Issa.* Reno, Nevada and Fukagawa-shi, Hokkaido: Buddhist Books International, 2004. Print.

---. "Stories Behind the Haiku: Cultural Memory in Issa." *Modern Haiku* 44.3 (Fall 2013): 21-33. Print.

Laurence, Stacey. "Issa and the African American Perspective in Haiku." South-East Regional Haiku Society of America. Atlanta. 26 October 2013.

Legge, James Trans. *Shijing.* Trans. *Chinese Text Initiative.* Web. 16 Feb. 2011.

Louv, Richard. *Last Child in the Woods: Saving our Children from Nature-Deficit Disorder.* Chapel Hill, N.C.: Algonquin Books of Chapel Hill, 2008. Print.

Mackenzie, Lewis. *The Autumn Wind: A Selection from the Poems of Issa.* London: John Murray, 1957; rpt. Tokyo: Kodansha International, 1984. Print.

Martin, Joel W. "The Samurai Crab." *Terra* 31.4 (Summer 1993): 30-34. Print.

Maruyama Kazuhiko 丸山一彦, ed. *Issa haiku shū* 一茶俳句集. Tokyo: Iwanami Shoten, 1990; rpt. 1993. Print.

Masco, C. "Neighbor-Stranger Discrimination on the Basis of a Threat Vocalization in the Great Black-Backed Gull." *Wilson Journal of Ornithology* 125.2 (2013): 342-7. Print.

Mason, Jim and Peter Singer. *Animal Factories.* New York: Crown Publishers, 1980. Print.

Matuso Bashō 松尾芭蕉. Ed. Imoto Nōichi 井本農一. *Matsuo Bashō shū* 松尾芭蕉集. Vol. 1. Tokyo: Shogakukan, 1995. Print.

McCallum, Donald F. *Zenkōji and Its Icon: A Study in Medieval Japanese Religious Art.* Princeton: Princeton Univ. Press, 1994. Print.

McCullough, Helen Craig. *Brocade by Night: "Kokin Wakashū" and the Court Style in Japanese Classical Poetry.* Palo Alto: Stanford Univ. Press, 1985. Print.

Miner, Earl et al. *The Princeton Companion to Classical Japanese Literature.* Princeton: Princeton Univ. Press, 1984. Print.

Moller, A. P. *Sexual Selection and the Barn Swallow.* Oxford: Oxford University Press, 1994. Print.

"The Moral Status of Animals." *Stanford Encyclopedia of Philosophy.* Web. 5 August 2014.

Murasaki Shikibu 紫式部, *The Tale of Genji.* Trans. Edward G. Seidensticker. New York: Alfred A. Knopf, 1987. Print.

Næss, Arne and David Rothenberg. *Ecology, Community, and Lifestyle: Outline of an Ecosophy.* Cambridge; New York: Cambridge University Press, 1989. Print.

Nakada Norio 中田祝夫, ed. *Kogo dai jiten* 古語大辞典 (*KD*). Tokyo: Shogakukan 1983. Print.

Oliveira, Ana Flora Sarti, et al. "Play Behaviour in Nonhuman Animals and the Animal Welfare Issue." *Journal of Ethology* (January 2010, Vol. 28, Issue 1): 1-5. Print.

Ōshiki Zuike 黄色瑞華. *Jinsei no hiai: Kobayashi Issa* 人生の悲哀小林一茶. Tokyo: Shintensha, 1984. Print.

Ozaki, Yei Theodor. *The Japanese Fairy Book.* Edinburgh: Archibald Constable & Co., 1903. Print.

Plato. *The Republic.* Trans. Robin Waterfield. New York: Oxford University Press USA, 2008. Print.

Regan, Tom and Peter Singer. *Animal Rights and Human Obligations*. Englewood Cliffs, N.J.: Prentice-Hall, 1976. Print.

Regan, Tom. *The Case for Animal Rights*. Berkeley: University of California Press, 1983. Print.

Reps, Paul and Nyogen Senzaki. *Zen Flesh Zen Bones: A Collection of Zen and Pre-Zen Writings*. Tokyo: Tuttle, 1998. Print.

Sacchi R., et. al. "A Comparison among Sexual Signals in Courtship of European Tortoises." *Journal of Herpetology* 47.2 (2013): 215-21. Print.

Sachs, Curt. *World History of the Dance*. New York: W. W. Norton, 1963. Print.

Scripture of the Lotus Blossom of the Fine Dharma [The Lotus Sutra]. Trans. Leon Hurvitz. New York: Columbia University Press, 2009. Print.

Seiler M. et. al. "Interspecific Semantic Alarm Call Recognition in the Solitary Sahamalaza Sportive Lemur, Lepilemur Sahamalazensis." *PloS one* 8.6 (2013). Print.

Seo Audrey Yoshiko and Stephan Addiss, *The Sound of One Hand: Paintings and Calligraphy by Zen Master Hakuin*. Boston: Shambhala 2010. Print.

Shijing. Trans. James Legge. *Chinese Text Initiative*. n.p. Web. 16 Feb. 2011.

Shinran 親鸞. *The* Kyōgyōshinshō: *The Collection of Passages Expounding the True Teaching, Living, Faith, and Realizing of the Pure Land*. 教行信証. Trans. D. T. Suzuki. Kyoto: Shinshu Otaniha, 1973. Print.

Shirane Haruo. *Traditional Japanese Literature: An Anthology, Beginnings to 1600*. New York: Columbia University Press, 2008. Print.

Singer, Peter. *Animal Liberation*. New York: Random House, 1990. Print.

Swift, Jonathan. *Gulliver's Travels*. Ed. Albert J. Rivero. Norton Critical Editions. New York: W. W. Norton & Co., 2001. Print.

Takatsu H. et. al. "Spontaneous Flash Communication of Females in an Asian Firefly." *Journal of Ethology* 30.3 (2012): 355-60. Print.

Tao Qian. *T'ao the Hermit, Sixty Poems by T'ao Chi'en (365-427)*. Trans. William Acker. London & New York: Thames and Hudson, 1952. Print.

Taylor, Angus. *Animals and Ethics: An Overview of the Philosophical Debate*. Peterborough, Ontario: Broadview, 2009. Print.

Taylor, Bron Raymond. *Dark Green Religion: Nature Spirituality and the Planetary Future*. Berkeley: University of California Press, 2010. Print.

Tōdaiji 東大寺. n.p. Web. 6 June 2012.

Tsukasa Tamaki 司玉城. *Issa kushū* 一茶句集. Tokyo: Kadokawa Gakugei, 2014. E-book.

Tucker, Mary Evelyn and Duncan Ryūken Williams. *Buddhism and Ecology: The Interconnection of Dharma and Deeds*. Cambridge, Mass.: Harvard University Press, 1997. Print.

Ueda, Makoto. *Dew on the Grass: The Life and Poetry of Kobayashi Issa*. Leiden/Boston: Brill, 2004. Print.

Whitman, Walt. *Complete Poetry and Selected Prose*. Ed. James E. Miller. Boston: Houghton Mifflin, 1959. Print.

Yeats, William Butler. Ed. M. L. Rosenthal. *Selected Poems and Two Plays of William Butler Yeats*. New York: Collier Books, 1966; rpt. 1970. Print.

Yuasa Nobuyuki. *The Year of My Life: A Translation of Issa's* Oraga Haru. 2nd ed. Berkeley: Univ. of California Press, 1972. Print.

Zaidel, D. W. and J. A. Cohen. "The Face, Beauty and Symmetry: Perceiving Asymmetry in Beautiful

Faces." *International Journal of Neuroscience* 115 (2005): 1165-73. Print.

ABOUT THE AUTHOR

David G. Lanoue is a professor of English at Xavier University of Louisiana. He is a cofounder of the New Orleans Haiku Society, an associate member of the Haiku Foundation, and President of the Haiku Society of America. His books include translations (*Cup-of-Tea Poems; Selected Haiku of Kobayashi Issa* and *The Distant Mountain: The Life and Haiku of Kobayashi Issa*), criticism (*Pure Land Haiku: The Art of Priest Issa*), and a series of "haiku novels," including *Haiku Guy*, *Laughing Buddha*, *Haiku Wars, Frog Poet* and *Dewdrop World*. Some of his books have appeared in French, German, Spanish, Bulgarian, Serbian, and Japanese editions. He maintains *The Haiku of Kobayashi Issa* website, for which he translated 10,000 of Issa's haiku.

Made in the USA
San Bernardino, CA
30 September 2014